By The Editors of
crafts Magazine

A Treasury of Christmas Ornaments

An extraordinary collection of designer Christmas ornaments to add a touch of handmade beauty to generations of holiday celebrations.

PJS Publications Inc.

Contents

SENSATIONAL SANTAS 4

Cross Stitch Santa..5
Plastic Canvas Jumping Santa.....................5
Mr. and Mrs. Santa..6
Spool Santa..7
Knitted Wee Folks 7
Victorian Wax Santa 8
Beaded Mr. and Mrs. Santa 9
Patterns..10

CHARMING COUNTRY 12

Straw Angel 13
Scallop Layered Wreath..............................13
Straw Ribbon and Wheat Ornaments 14
Mini Tea-Dyed Stockings.............................15
Felt Nativity..16
Crochet Snowflakes 17
Cinnamon Dough Couple.............................18
Mr. & Mrs. Snowman Mistletoe 18
Little Dolly Darlings 19
Stenciled Angel Hearts 20
Machine Embroidery....................................21
Potpourri Bag Angels...................................22
Plastic Canvas Trio 23
Patterns..24

GARLANDS GALORE 29

Lace Hearts 30
Plastic Canvas Angels..................................30
Candy Canes...31
Country Clothesline 32
Fabric Chain With Bows..............................32
Gingerbread Kids..33
Patterns..34

QUICK & EASY 36

Lace Cornucopias..37
Felt Teddy Bears 37
Igloo Trio...38
Feather Angel...39
Braided Ribbon Candy Cane......................39
Ribbon Loops 40
Ribbon Angels 41
Victorian Doily 41
Ribbon and Lace 41
Lace Angel 42
Patterns..42

CROSS STITCH HEIRLOOMS ... 44

Family Stockings 45
Red Frame Ornaments 46
Stars 46
Metallic Thread Ornaments 47
Poinsettia 47
Snowflakes 48
Patterns..49

ESPECIALLY FOR KIDS............. 53

Paper Punch 54
Sun Catcher 54
Pom Pom Cookie Cutters 55
Doily Angel...56
Simmering Spice Bag....................................56
Glue Ornaments...57
Pinwheels..58
Marbleized Wooden Cutouts......................58
Christmas Angels...58
Rudolph and Rhoda Reindeer Clip-Ons 60
Chenille Candy Canes..................................61
Patterns..61

FANCIFUL VICTORIANA 65

Battenberg Lace Snowflakes 66
Perforated Paper 66
Elegant Wreath 67
Lace Hat 67
Potpourri Ball 68
Lace Tree 68
Parasol 69
Nosegay 69
Lace Fan 70
Iridescent Ball 70
Frosted Ball 71
Crochet Covered Glass Balls 71
Stiffened Spider Web 72
Stiffened Diamonds and Squares 73
Quilled Poinsettias 74
Crochet Balls 75
Little Stitches 76
Painted Folk Art Balls 77
Patterns 78

DECORATOR TREES 83

Paper Lace 84
Perforated Paper Tree 86
Victorian Pink and Mauve Tree 87
Victorian Garland and Ornaments 90
Satin and Lace Tree 91
Country Calico Tree 92
Ribbon Rose Instructions 93
Patterns 94

GENERAL INSTRUCTIONS 95

Cross Stitch Chart 95
Battenberg Lace Stitch Chart 95
Plastic Canvas Stitch Chart 96
Crochet Stitch Chart 96

EDITORIAL/ART STAFF

Editor: Judith Brossart
Art Director: Laurie Rath Hahn
Book Editor: Carol R. Zentgraf
Copy Editor: Pat Rickey
Graphic Design: Pudik Art Studios, Inc.
    Washington, Illinois
Layout Artist: Teri Ehrenhardt

BUSINESS STAFF

Publisher/President: Jerry R. Constantino
Vice President/Creative Woman's
    Group Publisher: Del Rusher
Vice President Circulation: Harry Sailer
Executive Art Director: Wayne Mathison
Chief Financial Officer: Dennis Dietrich

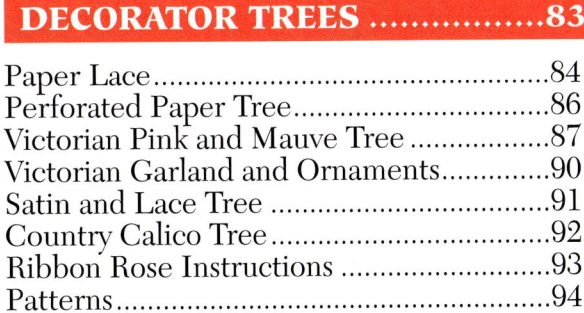

© 1991 by PJS Publication, Inc.
Crafts Magazine
P.O. Box 1790,
Peoria, Illinois 61656

All rights reserved. No part of this book may be reproduced without written permission from the publisher.
  Due to differing climatic conditions and variations in materials, PJS Publications disclaims any liability for untoward results in doing the projects presented.

Library of Congress Catalog Card Number: 91-90516
Manufactured in the United States of America
First Printing

Cover photography: Clarence Lynxwiler and
    Sutter's Art & Photography

Sensational Santas

Santa Claus, that jolly old fellow from the North Pole, has been known and loved by generations of children and adults. His generous and jolly nature has won him a loyal following and a high profile on our Christmas trees.

As varied as the looks of our robust, toy-packing friend are the ornament projects presented here. For a nostalgic look, we offer the **Cross Stitch** and **Victorian Wax Santas**, which depict the hero of olden days. Our **Plastic Canvas Jumping Santa** is designed to entertain—pull the string and he'll dance for joy.

Behind every successful man, they say, there's a successful woman, and our **Mr. and Mrs. Santa** pairs are designed for successful decorating. Lace-trimmed or beaded, these duos will win hearts.

Our tiny **Spool Santa** is fun to make, while the **Knitted Wee Folks** will add a whimsical touch to any tree.

CROSS STITCH SANTA

By Nancy Hoerner

MATERIALS: CROSS STITCH SANTA

14-count ecru Aida cloth, 6x8 inches

Embroidery floss: red (DMC 498, Anchor 20); blush (DMC 353, Anchor 8); flesh (DMC 754, Anchor 778); green (DMC 937, Anchor 268); off-white (DMC 739, Anchor 885); light brown (DMC 611, Anchor 898); brown (DMC 610, Anchor 889); gray (DMC 413, Anchor 401); black (DMC 310, Anchor 403); dark brown (DMC 844, Anchor 401)

Medicis * white wool thread, one skein

White felt, 6 x 3¾ inches

Lightweight posterboard, 6 x 3¾ inches

Fleece, two 6 x 3¾-inch pieces

Red and gold cord, 26 inches

Shrink plastic *, one sheet

White craft glue

Colored pencils or permanent markers

Miscellaneous items: black felt-tip pen; paper punch; cuticle scissors; white sewing thread; iron; terrycloth towel; foil-lined cookie sheet; spatula; oven

Note: A Stitch Graph and Color Key and Toy Patterns are given on page 11.

* DMC Medicis Wool and Aleene's Shrink Art plastic were used in the sample project.

1. Refer to the Stitch Graph and Color Key on page 11 and the General Cross Stitch Instructions on page 95 to begin stitching. Use two strands of floss to cross stitch design.

2. Backstitch using one strand of red floss for shoelaces and one strand of gray for remainder of project. Backstitch around the beard before filling in.

3. Make French knots with one strand of floss wrapped three times around the needle for eyes and nose. Stitch three-wrap French knots for beard and hair using one strand of Medicis wool thread. *Note:* Two strands of white floss may be substituted. Make one French knot in each square of the fabric.

4. When stitching is completed, press with a warm iron.

5. Using the toy outlines on the pattern on page 11, trace each toy onto the sheet of shrink plastic using a black felt-tip pen. Color each with colored pencils. Cut out with sharp scissors. Make two holes in each toy with the paper punch. The train does not need holes.

6. Following manufacturer's directions, place toys into the oven and shrink.

7. Sew each toy to Santa's bag with matching floss. Attach the train by stitching over the car connectors.

8. Glue a piece of fleece to each side of the posterboard. Center design and stretch stitched piece around the padded board, sewing opposite sides together. Place felt over the back and slipstitch around ornament, attaching Aida front to felt back.

9. Glue cording around ornament edge, forming a loop at the center top for hanging.

PLASTIC CANVAS JUMPING SANTA

By Darla J. Fanton

MATERIALS: PLASTIC CANVAS JUMPING SANTA

7-mesh clear plastic canvas, one sheet

No. 16 tapestry needles, two

Hot glue gun

Monofilament line

4-ply worsted knitting yarn: red, 8 yards; white, 4 yards; flesh, 2 yards; black, 3 yards; gold, 1 yard; pink, 1 yard

6mm blue plastic eyes with washers, two

Faceted beads, one each: 4mm red; 8mm white

Red seed beads, three

¾-inch green leaf sequins, two

½-inch white pom pom

Fine gold cord, 4 yards

Miscellaneous items: scissors; wirecutters; clear nail polish

Note: Cutting and Stitch Graphs and a Color Key are given on page 10.

1. Refer to the Cutting and Stitch Graphs on page 10 and the General Plastic Canvas Instructions on page 96 to cut and stitch designs. Work pieces with continental and slanting gobelin stitches.

2. Cut out Santa body, head, two legs, two arms, and buckle.

Stitch pieces, reversing one leg and one arm. Use slanting gobelin stitches for beard, all fur trim, and cheeks; work remaining areas in the continental stitch. Backstitch red mouth and white mustache after all other stitching is completed. For mustache work each stitch twice. Backstitch buckle with gold and overcast edges with same strand of yarn.

Overcast all remaining edges with corresponding colors.

3. Insert eyes where indicated. Attach washers to back and cut shanks with wirecutters close to washer. With monofilament line, attach 4mm bead for nose and sequins and seed beads where indicated. With black yarn, attach buckle to center of belt by stitching over center bar. Glue pom pom to end of hat.

4. To assemble, place arms and legs behind body, matching Xs. Insert tapestry needle between canvas pieces then stitch together with monofilament line. This will insure proper ease so arms and legs will move freely. Tie off securely. Remove needle.

5. Cut four 10-inch pieces of gold cord. Tie one end of one cord to top inner edge of each arm and leg. Dot each knot with nail polish to keep knot from working loose. With arms and legs hanging straight down, bring cords together and tie in a knot below body. Insert cord ends into 8mm bead and tie a knot below bead. Trim ends. When bead is pulled down, arms and legs should move.

6. Glue head to body, tilting at a slight angle if desired. Thread an 8-inch piece of cord through center top of head and tie for hanging loop.

MR. AND MRS. SANTA

By Chere Brodsky

1. *To make each ornament*, cover two self-adhesive padded ovals following manufacturer's instructions. Use red calico for Santa and pink cotton for Mrs. Santa.

2. *To make the Santa*, trace the face pattern and cut two faces from light pink felt. Reversing one, glue a face to the center of each calico-covered oval.

For eyes, glue two blue beads close together, near the top of the face that slants downward to the right. Use the fine-tip black marker to draw sleeping eyes on the other face as shown on the face pattern.

For the cheeks, cut two ½-inch hot-pink circles and glue to face, ¼-inch apart, below eyes.

Cut a 2¼-inch piece of eyelet for the mustache. Place a drop of glue in the center and pinch to form curve. Glue to face, covering lower half of cheeks; glue pom pom nose on top.

Trace the mouth patterns and cut one each from red felt. Glue the smiling mouth onto the awake face and the snoring mouth onto the sleeping face.

3. Cut one 7-inch, two 6-inch, and two 5-inch pieces of eyelet. Glue the bound edge of the 7-inch piece along the back edge of the awake Santa oval, between the Xs shown in the Step 3 illustration. Fold the ribbon in half and glue backs of the ovals together with the ribbon ends between them at the top.

MATERIALS: MR. AND MRS. SANTA
For Both Projects

Self-adhesive padded ovals mounting board, 3x4-inch, two per project

¾-inch plastic holly leaves with berries, three small sprigs

White craft glue or hot glue gun

For Santa

Red cotton Christmas calico fabric, 4½ x 6-inch piece

Felt: light pink, 5-inch square; hot pink and red, one small piece each

¼-inch red satin ribbon, 7 inches

White craft fur, ½ x 7-inch piece

½-inch gathered white eyelet, 1 yard

½-inch red pom poms, two

1-inch red pom pom, one

5mm blue beads, two

⅜-inch gold jingle bell

Fine-tip black marker

For Mrs. Santa

Cotton fabric: 6-inch white circle; 10-inch light-pink square

Iron-on interfacing, 6-inch circle

Red felt, small piece

Gathered white eyelet: ½-inch, ⅝ yard; ¾-inch, ⅛ yard

⅛-inch red with white dots satin ribbon, 1 yard

1/16-inch white satin ribbon, 7 inches

4-ply red worsted weight knitting yarn, 5 inches

Gray doll hair fiber, small amount

5mm black beads, four

¼-inch pink pom poms, two

Gold wire: medium-gauge, 4½ inches; fine-gauge, 2 inches

Miscellaneous items: scissors; tape measure; iron; tracing paper; pencil

Note: Full-size patterns are given on page 11.

Step 3
Glue lace to back edge of oval between Xs.

Glue a 5-inch piece of eyelet around the sides and bottom of each felt face. Trim the ends on a slant to align with the top of the face. Glue the 6-inch piece of eyelet around each face with the bound edge under the ruffle of the 5-inch piece. Trim ends to align with top of face. *Note:* If desired add a third piece of eyelet for a fuller beard.

4. Glue craft fur strip around the top edges of face and eyelet, surrounding the ornament. Glue small holly sprig above fur trim on awake-Santa side. Glue 1-inch pom pom below fur trim on lower side; glue jingle bell to center of pom pom.

5. *To make the Mrs. Santa*, glue the bound edge of the ¾-inch eyelet along the lower back edge of one fabric-covered oval. Fold the white ribbon in half and glue backs of ovals together with ribbon ends between them at the top.

6. For the hat, iron interfacing to the wrong side of the cotton circle; sew ½-inch eyelet around edge of circle on the right side. Gather circle close to the lace, adjusting hat to fit top of head. Cut a small slit in hat top, pull ribbon through, and glue hat to head at sides.

Apply a thin layer of glue around the head, under the hat ruffle, and arrange hair fiber in the glue. Cut the red ribbon and fine-gauge wire in half. Make two multi-looped bows and secure the centers with twisted wire; trim wire ends. Glue a bow to the left side of the hat on each side and glue a sprig of holly in each bow center.

7. On front and on back of ornament, make Mrs. Santa's face by gluing two beads close together near hairline for eyes and a pom pom below beads for nose. Trace the cheek pattern and cut our from red felt. Cut the yarn in half and glue the ends of each piece to the back of a heart point. Position and glue hearts with yarn on face, creating a smiling mouth with the yarn. Glue the yarn at the bottom of the mouth.

8. Cut gold wire in half. Bend ends of each piece around a pencil to make glasses. Glue glasses to nose on front and back.

SPOOL SANTA

By Roni Cassista

MATERIALS: SPOOL SANTA

2-inch spool

Felt: beige, 2 x 5½ inches; red, 4 x 5 inches

White jumbo bump Chenille, two-bump length

White jumbo curly Chenille, 5 inches

¾-inch white pom pom

5mm red pom pom

7mm wiggle eyes, two

9mm red bead

Gold snowflake sequin

Monofilament line, 16 inches

White craft glue *

Miscellaneous items: tracing paper; pencil; scissors

Note: A full-size hat pattern is given on page 10.

* Aleene's Thick Designers Tacky Glue was used in the sample project.

1. Trace the hat pattern and cut from red felt. Glue beige felt around spool, overlapping ends at back.

2. Fold monofilament line in half and insert ends through hole of spool. Add bead to monofilament at bottom of spool and knot securely.

Use scissors blade to nick top side of spool at hole. Pull monofilament taut and glue in nick.

3. Glue curly chenille around bottom of spool for beard, butting ends in back.

4. Overlap and glue straight edges of hat; let dry. Trim bottom edge of hat to make round and even.

Pull monofilament through hat top and glue hat on top of spool. Glue bump chenille around bottom edge of hat, twisting ends in back. Glue white pom pom to top of hat in front of monofilament.

5. Glue wiggle eyes and pom pom nose in place. Glue snowflake sequin to center front of hat brim. Bend hat forward in center; pinch and glue one side to hold. Let dry.

KNITTED WEE FOLKS

By Val Love

MATERIALS: KNITTED WEE FOLKS

Baby yarn: black, red, white, beige

Embroidery floss: light blue, red

Size 1 knitting needles

Polyester fiberfill

Miscellaneous items: tapestry needle; scissors; ruler

1. *To make each ornament*, cast on 32 sts and work in St st (K 1 row, P 1 row) throughout unless otherwise indicated. Refer to the Knitting Chart on page 8. *Note*: When changing yarn colors, leave 6-inch tails and always twist new color around color in use to prevent holes.

2. *To knit Santa*, work 6 rows black, 4 rows red, 2 rows white, and 12 rows red for the body. To make the head, work 8 rows of beige.

3. To make the hat, use white to K 2 rows, P 1 row, then starting with a P row, work 5 rows with red.

Shape the hat as follows:

Row 1: (K6, K2 tog) 4 times. (28)

Rows 2-4: Work in St st.

Row 5: (K5, K2 tog) 4 times. (24)

Rows 6-8: Work in St st.

Row 9: (K4, K2 tog) 4 times. (20)

Rows 10-12: Work in St st.

Row 13: (K3, K2 tog) 4 times. (16)

Rows 14-16: Work in St st.

Row 17: (K2, K2 tog) 4 times. (12)

Rows 18-20: Work in St st.

Row 21: (K1, K2 tog) 4 times. (8)

Rows 22-24: Work in St st.

Row 25: K2 tog 4 times. (4)

Rows 26-28: Work in St st.

Row 29: K2 tog twice.

Row 30: P2, K last 2 sts tog.

End off, leaving a 12-inch tail.

4. To make the hat tassel, cut ten 1½-inch pieces of white yarn. Tie center of bundle to tip of hat with red yarn. Fold tassel ends down and tie matching yarn around strands near top.

Fold top of hat over and tack to side of head near brim. Sew a hanging loop to top back of head with two 5-inch strands of matching yarn.

5. *To knit Mrs. Santa*, work 6 rows black, 2 rows red, 8 rows white. Work the following in the next 6 rows: 13 red sts, 6 white, 13 red. Work 2 rows red.

To make the head, work 8 rows of beige. Follow steps 3 and 4 to make hat.

6. *To finish each ornament*, use tapestry needle to thread matching yarn through each loop of cast-on edge. *Note:* Do not gather.

To form neck, without gathering, pick up one-half of each knitted st of first beige row with matching yarn.

Knitting Stitch Chart

Abbreviations

K . . . . Knit
lp(s) . . . . Loops
P . . . . Purl
st(s) . . . . Stitch(es)
St st . . . . Stockinette Stitch
tog . . . . Together

Beginning Slip Knot

Wrap yarn over needle from front to back, over the working yarn, and through loop; pull taut.

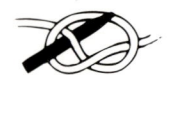

Cast On

(1) With needle in right hand, wrap tail over left thumb and working yarn over index finger. (2) Insert needle up through thumb lp, then draw a lp from working yarn through lp. (3) Release thumb lp; tighten lp on needle by pulling tail forward.

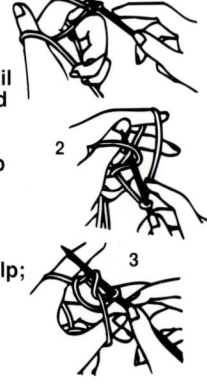

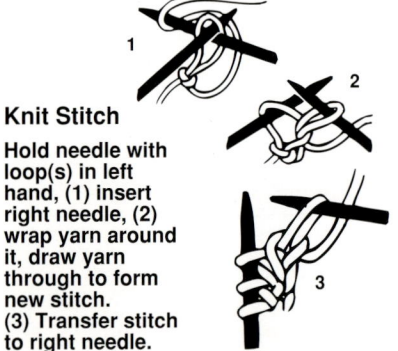

Knit Stitch

Hold needle with loop(s) in left hand, (1) insert right needle, (2) wrap yarn around it, draw yarn through to form new stitch. (3) Transfer stitch to right needle.

Purl

With yarn in front of work, (1) insert right needle into front of stitch, wrap yarn over, and (2) draw new loop through.

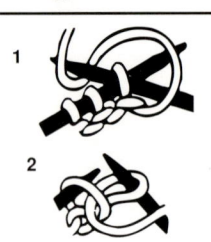

With wrong side out and matching yarn, sew the two edges together from head to toe with small running sts, one st in from each edge. Take one stitch per knitted st. *Note*: Avoid picking up threaded yarn. Turn right side out and stuff loosely, leaving shaped portion of hat empty. Gather yarn at cast-on edge and close opening.

Gather yarn at neck and tie securely.

7. To form legs, use matching yarn to sew small,tight running stitches all the way through body from base upward for about eight rows.

To form arms, sew through body ⅜-inch in from sides, beginning eight rows up from base, for about 10 rows.

Weave all loose ends into stuffing or seam.

8. Using all six strands of floss, cross stitch light-blue eyes. Make two red straight stitches, one on top of the other, for mouth.

9. *To finish Santa*, add white moustache by taking a short stitch, a long stitch, and another short stitch, leaving two short tails on top. Fray tails. See the Step 9 illustration.

Step 9
Take three stitches above mouth, leaving ends on top.

Make white beard by sewing progressively larger loops in a curve from the right of mouth to under the center of mouth. From center of mouth to left side, make progressively smaller loops. Make approximately 25 loops.

10. *To finish Mrs. Santa*, thread needle with white yarn and run it through top of apron bib, making shoulder straps at corners. Take each end over shoulder, cross them in back, and sew to center back of apron. Tie ends in a bow.

Make white hair by sewing vertical loops from right side of face under rim of hat to about two rows above neckline. Making progressively longer loops, continue around back of head, then to left side of face, making loops shorter in front.

VICTORIAN WAX SANTA

By Barbara Guyette

MATERIALS: VICTORIAN WAX SANTA

Beeswax, ½ pound

Hard candle wax, ½ pound (will make several ornaments)

Santa figure candy mold *

Enamel paints: white; flesh; red; green; black; gold metallic

Paintbrushes: No. 4 flat; No. 1 liner

Gold metallic thread, 3 inches

Miscellaneous items: craft knife; candy thermometer; large needle; coffee can; pan; old, large spoon; aluminum foil; cookie sheet; scissors; ruler; candle

* Wilton Enterprises candy mold was used for the sample project.

1. Place the candy mold on a foil-covered cookie sheet.

Break up equal amounts of beeswax and candle wax into a coffee can. Set the can in a pan of hot water over medium heat. *Note:* The water should cover half of the can. Heat wax to 190°, then spoon it into the candy mold. Keep wax at 190° for each pouring. Let mold cool completely.

2. Slightly twist the mold and the ornament will pop out. Trim excess wax from the edges with the craft knife.

3. Stir paints well and refer to the photo to paint. *Note:* Apply the gold metallic last. Traditionally, only the raised design area is painted. If desired, dry brush a bit of gold over the painted details.

4. To hang the ornament, heat the point of a needle over a candle flame, then insert it into the top back of the ornament. Push the gold thread ends into the hole. Let cool. If the thread is not securely anchored, dab melted wax over the ends on the back of the ornament.

BEADED MR. AND MRS. SANTA

By Carol Krob

MATERIALS: BEADED MR. AND MRS. SANTA

14-count ivory perforated paper, 2½ x 3½-inch pieces, four

Glass seed beads * 1 tube each: jet (81T); cream (123T); Christmas red (165T); emerald (332); and coral (275)

No. 10 crewel needle

Ivory sewing thread

Miscellaneous items: scissors; pencil; ruler

Note: A Stitch Graph and Color Key are given on page 10.

* Mill Hill glass seed beads were used in the sample project.

1. Count in 17 holes from each side and 23 holes from top and bottom to find the center of each piece of perforated paper. Mark center on back, rougher side. Find the center of the Stitch Graph on page 10 by following the arrows. Count up and over to the left or right and begin stitching at this point. *Note:* Leave two rows of empty holes on all sides.

2. Refer to the General Cross Stitch Instructions on page 95 to attach beads with a half cross stitch. Using unknotted, doubled sewing thread, work the beading left to right or right to left from the top down. Make sure all stitches go in the same direction for the beads to lay properly. Do not jump more than three or four stitches without securing the floss on the back or the last bead will be looser than the others.

Clip loose thread ends. Cut around designs as close to the stitching as possible.

3. *To make Santa's beard,* thread needle, weave ends through stitching on wrong side of front and bring needle up through the first hole on the bottom left, as marked by a triangle on the graph. String 12 cream beads and insert needle through hole to the right, as marked by a triangle. Pull to form a loop.

Bring needle up again through the first hole and down through the second to secure. Repeat across bottom to make 10 more loops with the following number of cream beads in each loop: 16, 16, 20, 20, 24, 20, 20, 16, 16, 12. Repeat to attach 11 loops to the back piece.

4. *To make Mrs. Santa's collar,* follow Step 3 to make 11 loops on front with the following beads: *Loops 1 through 5:* three emerald, one cream, one red, one cream, and three emerald. *Loop 6 (center):* three cream, three red, one cream, one emerald, one cream, five red, one cream, one emerald, one cream, five red, one cream, one emerald, one cream, three red, and three cream. *Loops 7 through 11:* Repeat Loops 1 through 5. Make 13 loops the same as the small loops on the back piece.

5. Place the front and back pieces of each ornament together. Leaving a 3- or 4-inch tail at each end, stitch pieces together through the outer row of holes, beginning and ending at top center. Knot thread ends together and close to the design to make a hanging loop.

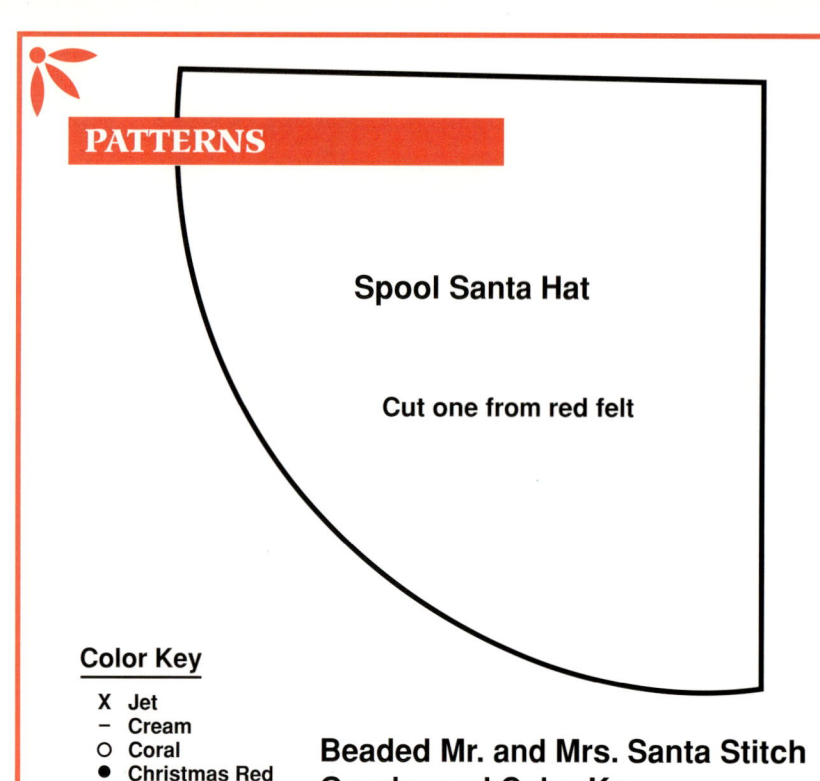

PATTERNS

Spool Santa Hat

Cut one from red felt

Color Key
- X Jet
- − Cream
- ○ Coral
- ● Christmas Red
- V Emerald

Plastic Canvas Jumping Jack Cutting and Stitch Graphs and Color Key

Color Key
- ○ Red
- ⌀ White
- ╱ Brown
- ● Black
- ⌀ Pink
- ☐ Flesh Background
- — Backstitching

Jumping Santa Body
Cut one.

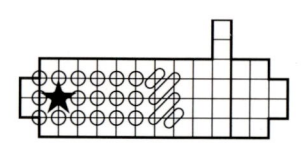

Jumping Santa Arm
Cut two (reverse one to stitch).

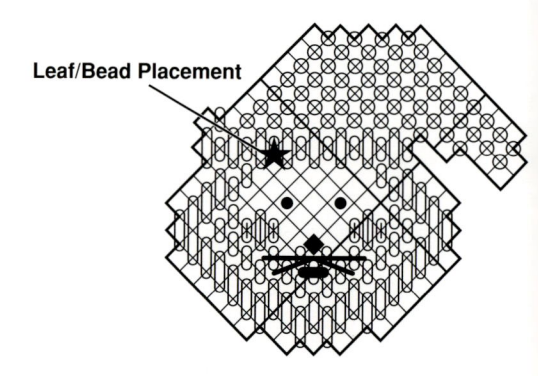

Jumping Santa Head
Cut one.

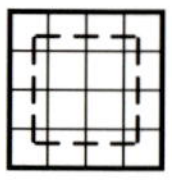

Jumping Santa Buckle
Cut one.

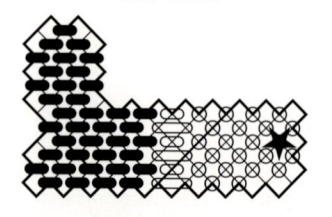

Jumping Santa Leg
Cut two (reverse one to stitch).

Beaded Mr. and Mrs. Santa Stitch Graphs and Color Key

Santa Front | Santa Back

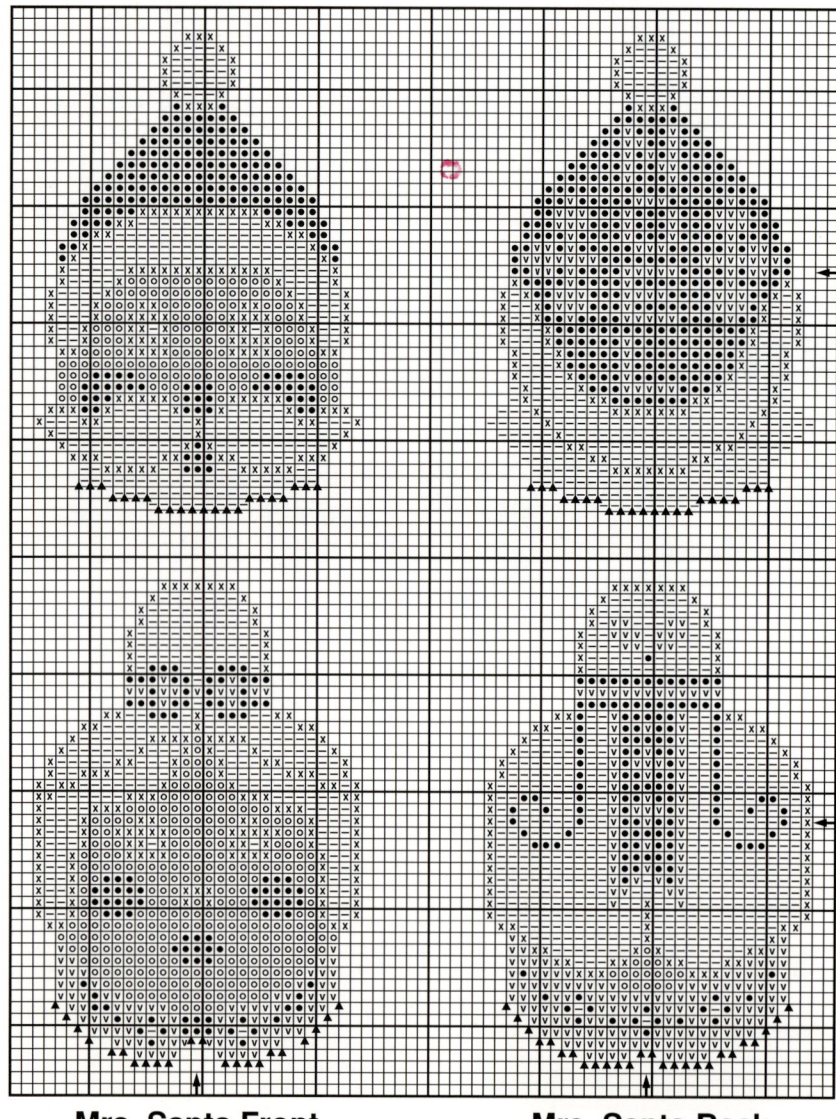

Mrs. Santa Front | Mrs. Santa Back

Cross Stitch Santa Stitch Graph, Color Key and Toy Patterns

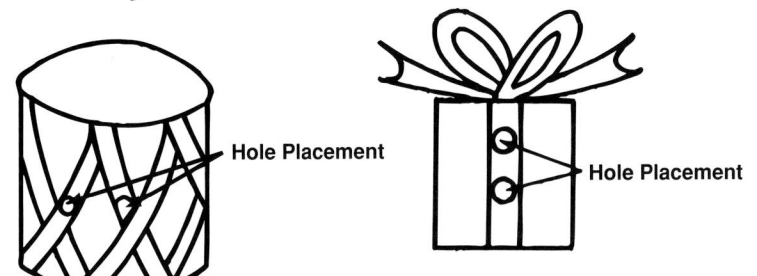

Color Key

- S Black
- X Red
- ● Off-White
- ▲ Green
- • Flesh
- C Blush
- + Brown
- I Light Brown
- B Dark Brown
- — Backstitching

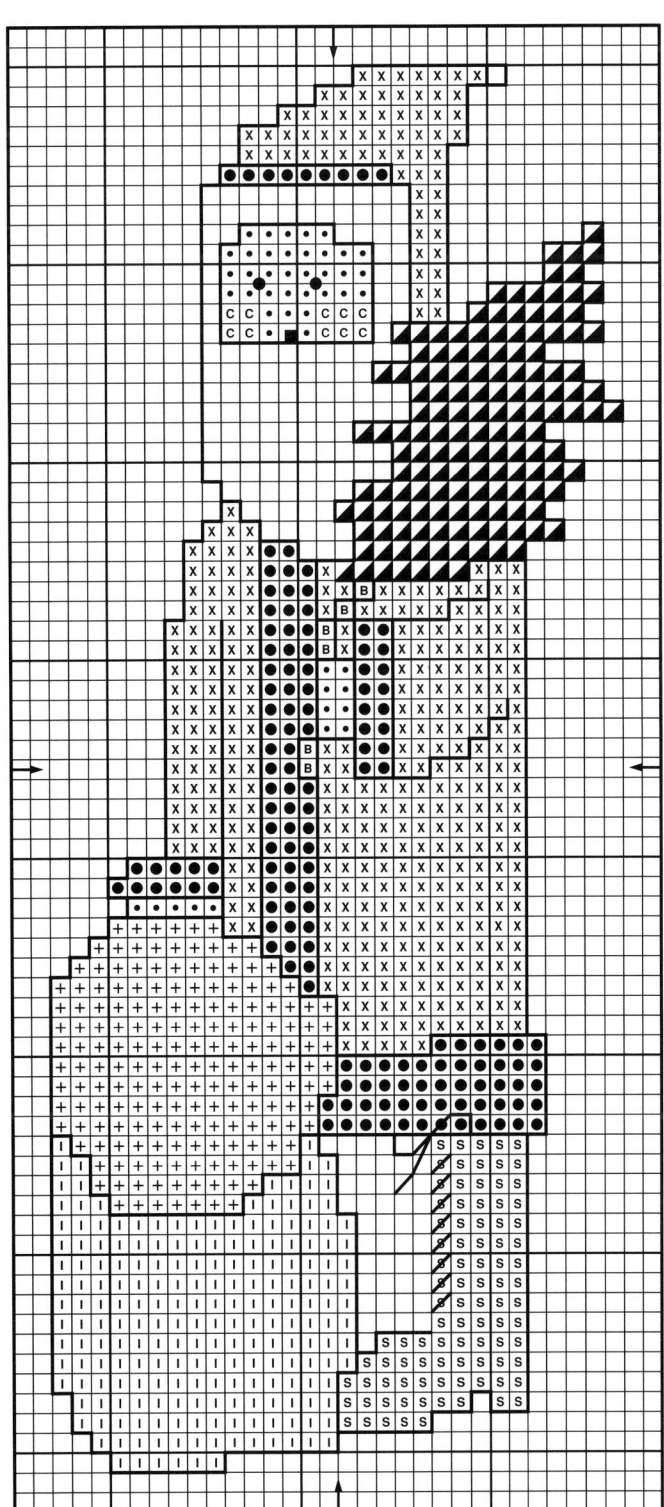

Toy Drum — Hole Placement

Hole Placement

Toy Doll — Hole Placement

Toy Bear — Hole Placement

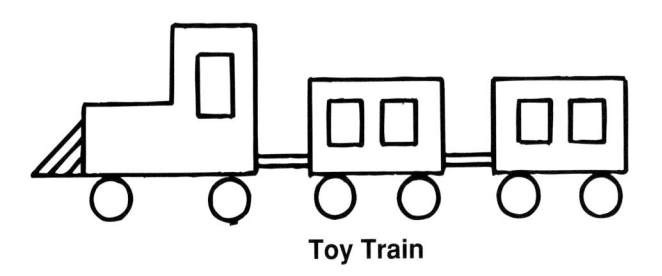

Toy Train

Mr. and Mrs. Santa Ornaments Patterns

Awake Mouth

Santa Face

Mrs. Santa Cheek

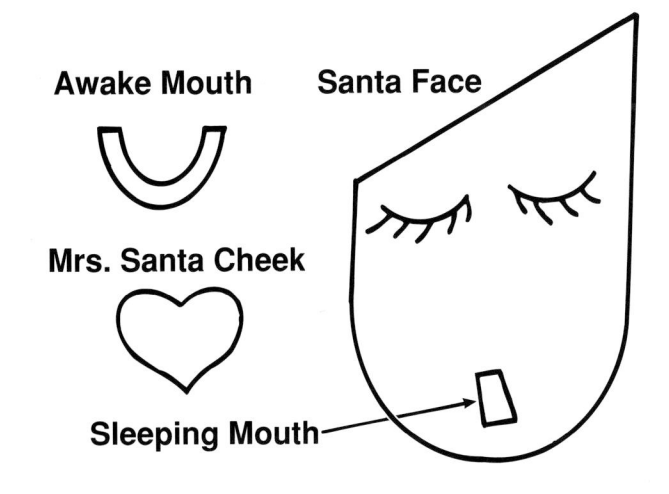

Sleeping Mouth

11

Charming Country

Country crafts are so warm, cozy, and inviting that they go hand in hand with the spirit of the holiday season.

"Charming Country" highlights 46 ornaments. There are several oh-so-appealing, straight-from-the-fields wheat and straw projects, an adorable hand-crafted **Cinnamon Dough Couple**, and a set of **Mini Tea-Dyed Stockings** that are reminiscent of Grandma's tree. The uniqueness of a felt ornament collection doubling as a nativity will charm all who see it.

Complete the homeyness of a country Christmas for your holiday tree with **Little Dolly Darlings**, with their many and varied looks, and sweet-smelling from-the-garden **Potpourri Bag Angels**.

STRAW ANGEL

By Doxie Keller

3. Gather 40 straws without heads with large ends together; tie 4 inches from large ends to create waistline. Trim the large ends into a slight curve for the dress bottom.

4. Insert and center arms in straw. Tie straw 1 inch above waist to create the neck. Tie ¾ inch above neck for the top of the head.

5. To make the hair, fold the straw over a scissors blade to the back and tie loosely at the neck. Do not trim ends. Cover the neck ties with raffia and knot in back. Make a loop for hanging with the raffia ends and knot to secure.

6. Fan the dress and ends from hair out at the bottom. Glue scalloped straw ribbon 1 inch from the lower edge, overlapping ends in the back.

7. To make the halo, tie 10 straws with heads together at the base of the heads and trim ½ inch from tie. Glue to back of angel at neck tie.

8. Tie hands together in front. Tie three wheat heads together at base and glue to hands for a bouquet.

MATERIALS: STRAW ANGEL

Wheat: 12-inch or longer straws without heads, 49; straws with heads, 13; 13 to 15mm scalloped ribbon, 10 inches

Natural raffia, 10 inches

Beige button and carpet thread

White craft glue or hot glue gun

Miscellaneous items: shallow pan; sharp pointed scissors; straight pins; terrycloth towel; ruler; wooden board (optional)

1. To prepare the wheat, cut the straw above the first joint and remove leaf sheath. Soak in a pan of warm water for 15 to 30 minutes. Dry slightly on a towel.

2. To make the arms, cut a 12-inch piece of thread and secure the ends of nine straws without heads with a clove hitch knot. See the Step 2 illustration. Tie an overhand knot to finish the clove hitch. Pin knotted end to wooden surface to create tension and braid straws for 4 inches; secure end with knot.

Step 2

Loop thread around wheat from front to back, over tail, around wheat from back to front and through loop.

SCALLOP LAYERED WREATH

By Doxie Keller

MATERIALS: SCALLOP LAYERED WREATH

Scalloped straw ribbon, 1 ½ yards

Wheat heads with straw, 12

⅝-inch straw roses, three

Natural gypsophila, small bunch

5-inch cardboard ring with 3-inch opening

⅛-inch ivory satin ribbon, 8 inches

Hot glue gun

Miscellaneous items: beige button and carpet thread; sharp pointed scissors; shallow pan; terrycloth towel; ruler; pins; heavy corrugated cardboard

1. Hot glue the straw ribbon, right side up, around the inner edge of the cardboard wreath. Glue a second ribbon row, wrong side up, overlapping the first. Glue a third row, right side up, overlapping the second.

2. Soak wheat in warm water for 15 to 20 minutes. Wrap in a damp towel.

3. Divide wheat straws in half and glue to each side of wreath, crossing them at the top. Glue gypsophila and straw roses on top of intersecting heads.

4. Glue ends of satin ribbon to center back of wreath for a hanging loop.

STRAW RIBBON AND WHEAT ORNAMENTS

By Doxie Keller

MATERIALS: STRAW RIBBON AND WHEAT ORNAMENTS

For Each Project

Beige button and carpet thread

Natural gypsophila, small bunch

Hot glue gun

For the Painted Heart

Natural scalloped straw ribbon, 1 yard

3-inch tin heart with embossed rope design

Acrylic paints: white; red; black; green; metallic gold

Paintbrushes: small flat; No. 1 liner

Disposable palette

Tracing paper

Graphite paper

1/8-inch dark green satin ribbon, 8 inches

5/8-inch straw rose

For the Scalloped Mini Wreath

Natural scalloped straw ribbon, 10 inches

Wheat, three heads with straws

5/8-inch straw roses, two

For the Braided Heart

Wheat, 12 heads with straws

5/8-inch straw rose

1/8-inch dark green satin ribbon, 1 yard

For the Circle Eight

10mm braided wheat straw: red, 1 1/2 yards; green, natural, 12 inches each

Wheat, three heads

1/4-inch red satin ribbon, 1/2 yard

1-inch silk leaf

3/8-inch red plastic berries, three

Miscellaneous items: sharp pointed scissors; shallow pan; terrycloth towel; ruler; pins; heavy corrugated cardboard

Note: Full-size painting patterns are given on page 24.

1. *To make the painted heart ornament,* soak straw ribbon in cold water for three minutes. Cut one piece of straw ribbon 2 inches larger than outline of the tin heart. Bend into heart shape and tie with thread.

Cut another piece of straw ribbon 4 inches larger than the first piece and bend into a slightly larger heart. Refer to the photo to tie both hearts together at center top.

2. To paint the tin heart, basecoat border with red and center of heart with green. Paint the rope gold.

Trace the painting patterns on page 24 onto tracing paper. Use graphite paper to transfer Santa to center of tin heart and holly to upper left of heart.

Mix small amount of white and red to paint Santa's face flesh. Paint hair and moustache white. Use thick white paint to dab on beard and fur and tassel on the hat. Paint hat, nose, and mouth red.

Paint holly leaves green and berries red. Highlight leaves with gold; use liner to paint gold veins.

Use liner brush and thinned black to outline Santa's face and holly. Paint black dot on each berry and paint Santa's eyes black with white highlights on lower sides of each eye. Paint eyebrows white.

3. Tie satin ribbon through hole in heart for a hanger. Hot glue ribbon so painted heart hangs in center of straw hearts. Glue small cluster of gypsophila and a straw rose to top of hearts.

4. *To make the scalloped mini wreath,* soak straw ribbon in cold water for three minutes. Form a circle and tie with a clove hitch knot. This will be the center bottom. Flatten and pin to cardboard to dry.

5. To clean the wheat straws, cut the straw above the first joint. Slide the sheath off the straw. See the Step 5 illustration.

Soak straws in warm water for 15 to 20 minutes. Wrap in a damp towel.

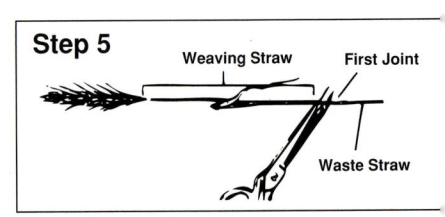

Step 5

Cut straw at first joint and slide off sheath.

6. Cut heads from straws. Carefully split the straws open with scissors. Flatten by running inside of the straw over scissors blade and cut several thin strips. Make several loops, tie together, and glue to wreath at left of center bottom.

Glue wheat heads, then gypsophila and roses to bottom of wreath.

7. *To make the braided heart,* prepare the wheat following Step 5.

Tie 12 10-inch straws below the heads using the clove hitch knot. Braid the straws in three groups of four straws each. Braid right over center, then left over center; tie ends together. Refer to the photo to bend into heart shape over the wheat heads and tie with clove hitch knot. Pin to cardboard and let dry.

Tie satin ribbon around wheat heads in a double-loop bow. Tie a ribbon loop for a hanger. Glue gypsophila, hanging down, and straw rose to bow center.

8. *To make the circle-eight ornament,* cut one 38-inch and one 7½-inch piece of red straw ribbon. Soak all straw ribbon in cold water for two minutes. Tie one end of long red and the natural pieces together. Form a 3-inch red circle with a slightly larger natural-color circle around it; tie together. Tie one end of the green ribbon at top and let hang down. Continue to form a larger red circle on outside of natural circle; tie together at top. Tie a 2-inch red circle centered above large circle. Tie all circles together. With green straw ribbon, form two spiral loops and glue end to outer red circle.

Refer to photo to glue wheat heads, gypsophila, and silk leaf to top of large red circle. Tie satin ribbon into a two-loop bow and glue it and berries in center.

MINI TEA-DYED STOCKINGS

By Martie Sandell

MATERIALS: MINI TEA-DYED STOCKINGS
For Each Stocking
Printed cotton or lightweight wool fabric, 5½ x 8 inches
Muslin, 8 x 9 inches
Acrylic stencil paint: red, green, yellow
⅜-inch stencil brush
Stencil plastic, one sheet
Red or green No. 8 pearl cotton or embroidery floss
Black fine-point permanent marker
Miscellaneous items: two tea bags; masking and transparent tape; craft knife; glass pane; sewing machine; sewing and large-eyed needles; thread to match fabrics; paper towels; iron; straight pins; tracing paper; pencil
Note: Full-size patterns are given on page 24.

1. Trace the stocking patterns on page 24 onto tracing paper and cut from appropriate fabric at indicated cutting lines. *Note:* Muslin pieces must be cut on the straight of the grain to fringe correctly.

2. To tea dye muslin, brew a cup of tea using both tea bags. Let the tea steep 10 minutes; squeeze tea bags and remove. Add muslin pieces to tea and let set 10 minutes. Squeeze excess tea from fabric and let dry; press.

3. Using the marker, trace the desired stencil patterns onto stencil plastic. To cut each stencil, place plastic over glass and cut openings with the craft knife. Holding the knife like a pencil, cut on the traced lines, turning the sheet, not the knife. Move slowly, always cutting toward yourself. To correct a knife slip, tape both sides of cut with transparent tape and recut.

4. To stencil, place desired stencil over muslin square. *Note:* If stenciling a two-color motif, cover second-color opening with masking tape. Dip brush lightly in paint and work it in a clockwise-counterclockwise motion on several layers of paper towels. With a nearly dry brush, paint in opening using the same brush motion and concentrating paint more at outer edges.

If using a two-color motif, remove tape from opening and repeat with second color.

5. For apple motif, add a stem with the black marker.

For tree/star and heart stockings, also stencil three stars or three small hearts across top of a muslin stocking, ⅜ inch from edge with bottom of stencil facing top edge.

Using a dry iron, heat set stenciling two to three minutes.

6. To fringe muslin pieces, pull threads for ¼ inch along straight edges, including top edges of stocking pieces.

7. Using the stocking pattern as a guide, position heel, toe, and stenciled square muslin pieces on right side of front stocking piece. Using pearl cotton or two to three strands of embroidery floss, hand stitch each piece in place along straight edges with a small running stitch. If desired, tie ends in a bow at bottom corner of square applique.

8. To sew the stocking, place printed fabric pieces right sides together. Place both muslin pieces together on top of them and pin. *Note:* If muslin stocking cuff is stenciled, place stenciled side facing out. Sew around edges, using a ¼-inch seam allowance and leaving top open. Clip curves and turn printed fabric layers to outside.

Turn muslin cuff down over top of stocking. Using the same pearl cotton used to stitch other muslin pieces, sew a short running stitch around cuff just above fringed edge. *Note:* Be careful not to catch other side of stocking in stitches.

9. Cut a 5½-inch piece of pearl cotton or of six strands embroidery floss, fold in half, and knot 1 inch from ends. Thread ends onto large-eyed needle and stitch through top left side of stocking, from inside of stocking to outside, ⅛ inch from top edge; knot the two ends together close to stocking and trim even.

FELT NATIVITY

By Cindy Groom Harry

MATERIALS: FELT NATIVITY

For All Figures
White baby rickrack
White craft glue *

For Mary
Felt: light blue, 4x6 inches; peach, 2x3 inches; dark blue, 4½-inch square; brown, 3-inch square; pink ¾x1½ inches; red, small piece

For Joseph
Felt: gray, 4x5 inches; dark blue, 4½-inch square; peach, 2¼x3½ inches; brown, 1x2 inches; pink, 1½x2 inches; red, small piece

For Baby Jesus
Felt: light blue, 1½x3½ inches; brown, 3x3½ inches; peach, 2-inch square; yellow, 1x2½ inches; pink, ¾x1½ inches; red, small piece

For the Shepherd
Felt: brown, 5-inch square; camel, 4-inch square; peach, 2¼x3½ inches; pink, ¾x1½ inches; red, small piece
Camel color chenille stem, 8½ inches

For the Lamb
Felt: white, 4-inch square; brown, pink, small piece of each
White loopy chenille, 1 inch

For the White King
Felt: purple, 4x7 inches; lavender, 4½-inch square; peach, 2¼x3½ inches; pink, ¾x1½ inches; brown, 2½-inch square; gold, 1x1¾ inches; yellow, red, small piece of each

For the Black King
Felt: yellow, 4x7 inches; gold, 4½-inch square; brown, 2¼x3½ inches; white, 1x1½ inches; black, red, small piece of each
Black baby rickrack, 9 inches

For the Oriental King
Felt: black, 4x5 inches; gold, 2¼-inch square; yellow/cream, 2¼x3½ inches; red, 1x2 inches; pink, white, small piece of each

Miscellaneous items: straight pins; small craft or manicure scissors; tracing paper; pencil; ruler

Note: Full-size patterns are given on pages 27-28.

* Aleene's Tacky Glue was used in the sample projects.

1. Trace the patterns on pages 27-28 onto tracing paper and cut out; label the traced patterns. Cut pieces from the following felt colors, cutting through two layers of felt when two identical shapes are needed:

For Mary, cut one body from light blue; two sleeves from dark blue; one hair piece and two eyes from brown; one mouth from red; and two hands from peach. Also cut one 1⅝-inch peach circle for head and two ½-inch pink circles for cheeks.

For Joseph, cut one body from gray; two sleeves from dark blue; one hair piece and two eyes from brown; one mouth from red; and two hands from peach. Also cut one 2-inch peach circle for head; two ¾-inch pink circles for cheeks; and one ¼-inch pink circle for nose.

For Baby Jesus, cut one blanket from light blue; one manger from brown; one halo from yellow, one hair piece and two eyes from brown; and one mouth from red. Also cut one 1⅝-inch peach circle for head and two ½-inch pink circles for cheeks.

For shepherd, cut one body, one hair piece, and two eyes from brown; two sleeves from camel; one mouth from red; and two hands from peach. Also cut one 2-inch peach circle for head; one ¼-inch pink circle for nose; and two ½-inch pink circles for cheeks.

For lamb, cut one body front, one body rear, and three ear/tail pieces from white; one mouth from pink; and two eyes from brown. Also cut one 1½-inch white circle for head.

For white king, cut one body and one collar from purple; two sleeves and one crown from lavender; hair/beard and two eyes from brown; one mouth from red; two hands from peach; one gift from gold; and one gift top from yellow. Also cut one 2-inch peach circle for head; one ¼-inch pink circle for nose; and two ½-inch pink circles for cheeks.

For black king, cut one body and one collar from yellow; two sleeves and one crown from gold; two hands from brown; one mouth from red; and two eyes from black. Also cut one 2-inch brown circle for head and one 1⅜x¾-inch white rectangle and one each of 1⅜x⅛- and ¾x⅛-inch gold strips for gift box.

For Oriental king, cut one body, one hair piece, and two eyes from black; one belt, one mouth, and three crown gems from red; one crown from gold; two cheeks from pink; and two hands from yellow/cream. Also cut one 2-inch yellow/cream circle for head and one 1⅜x¾-inch gold rectangle and one each of ¾x⅛- and 1⅜x⅛-inch white strips for gift box.

2. *To make Mary,* arrange all pieces before gluing. Refer to color photo. Place sleeves on top of body, then position head, hair, cheeks, eyes, and mouth. Tuck wrists of hands under sleeves.

3. Cut 4 inches of rickrack and glue across bottom of body. Glue ends of a 6-inch rickrack piece to back of head for a hanging loop.

4. *To make Joseph,* repeat Steps 2 and 3, gluing mouth on top of cheeks and nose above mouth.

5. *To make Baby Jesus,* arrange all pieces before gluing. Place blanket on top of manger. Cut head in half and glue straight edge of one half to back of blanket top. Glue open end of halo to back of head top. Cut 6 inches of rickrack and glue ends to back of head for a hanging loop. Glue other head half to cover ends of loop and halo, lining its straight edge with straight edge of attached head. Glue eyes, hair, and mouth to face. Tuck half of cheeks under blanket top.

Cut two 3-inch pieces of rickrack and, crossing them, glue both pieces to front of manger.

6. *To make the shepherd,* repeat Step 4. Curve top 2½ inches of chenille stem in the shape of a candy cane. Bend tip upward to form a slight S shape. Glue center of staff under both hands.

7. *To make the lamb,* position all pieces before gluing. Place the one curved edge of the body rear to the

16

back, right side of the body front. Place the head over the top of the body front, overlapping rear. Place straight edge of ears and tail behind head and rear. Place eyes and mouth on lower half of face.

Bend 1-inch loopy chenille in a circle and glue to top of head between ears. Trim and fluff loops. Cut a 6-inch piece of rickrack and glue ends to back of head to form hanging loop.

8. *To make the white king*, position all pieces before gluing. Place sleeves on body, then collar at top of body, overlapping sleeves. Place head on top of collar, beard/hair piece over head, and crown and mouth over beard/hair piece. Tuck bottoms of cheeks in beard, then position eyes and nose.

Place gift over collar in center of body and the gift top across neck of gift. Overlap and place hands over bottom of gift and tuck wrists in sleeves.

Cut 1½ inches of rickrack and glue across crown. Repeat Step 3 to finish.

9. *To make the black king*, follow Step 8 to assemble body, sleeves, collar, head, mouth, and eyes. Cut pieces of black rickrack and glue to top of head for hair. Glue crown to top of head. Overlap and tuck wrists in sleeves. Glue gift box strips vertically and horizontally on center of king, overlapping sleeves and collar and tucked into top hand.

Cut 1½ inches of rickrack and glue across crown. Repeat Step 3 to finish.

10. *To make the Oriental king*, position all pieces before gluing. Place bottom half of head over body. Position hair, crown, and the three crown gems. Keeping features low, position eyes, cheeks, then mouth. Glue gift box strips vertically and horizontally to gift box and position box vertically at center bottom of body. Glue on belt, then hands, overlapping gift.

Glue ends of rickrack to back of head to form the hanging loop.

CROCHET SNOWFLAKES

By Verna S. Fuller

MATERIALS: CROCHET SNOWFLAKES

Size 20 white crochet thread *
Size 10 steel crochet hook
Fabric stiffener *
Spray starch
Sponge brush
Monofilament line
Miscellaneous items: rust-proof straight pins; wax paper; corrugated cardboard; paper towels; scissors

* DMC Cebelia crochet thread and Aleene's fabric stiffener were used in the sample projects.

1. To crochet each snowflake, refer to the Crochet Stitch Chart on page 96.

2. *To crochet the daisy snowflake*, ch 7, join with a sl st to form a ring.

Rnd 1: Ch 1, °3 sc in ring, ch 6, dc in 3rd ch from hook, ch 3, sl st in same sp as dc, ch 14, sl st in 10th ch from hook. Let work dangle from lp on hook and twirl so you can work from right to left in ring just made. In this ring work: Ch 1, sc [ch 2, hdc in 2nd ch from hook, ch 2, sl st in same sp as hdc (picot made), sc] 9 times, ch 1 , sl st in same lp. Sl st in next 4 ch; ch 3, dc in 3rd ch from hook, ch 3, sl st in same sp as dc, sl st in base of opposite dc; sl st in next 3 ch. Repeat from ° five more times; end with sl st in beg sc.

Fasten off and weave in ends.

3. *To crochet the fan snowflake*, ch 7, join with a sl st to form a ring.

Rnd 1: Ch 3, 2 dc in ring, ch 3, (3 dc, ch 3) five times, join with sl st in top of beg ch 3.

Rnd 2: Ch 1, °sc in next 3 dc; in ch-3 sp work: (2 sc, ch 7, sl st in 5th ch from hook. Let work dangle from lp on hook and twirl so you can work from right to left in ring just made. In this ring work: Ch 1, 11 sc, ch 1, sl st in same lp. Sl st in next 2 ch; 2 sc). Repeat from ° 5 more times; join rnd with sl st in beg sc; fasten off.

Rnd 3: Join thread in 3rd sc of ch-11 lp with sl st; ch 5, tr in next sc, (ch 1, tr in next sc) 5 times, ch 4. °Tr in 3rd sc in next 11-sc lp, (ch 1, tr in next sc) 6 times, ch 4. Repeat from ° 4 more times; join rnd with sl st in 4th ch of beg ch-5.

Rnd 4: (Sl st in next ch-1 sp, ch 3, dc, ch 3, sl st, all in same ch-1 sp) 6 times; 4 sc in next ch-4 sp. Repeat from ° five more times; end with sl st in beg ch-1 sp.

Fasten off and weave in ends.

4. *To block both snowflakes*, place two or three layers of paper towels on top of cardboard. Pin snowflakes to board as follows: Pin tip of each cluster, then spread and pin the other detail picots. Spray with starch and let dry.

Place snowflakes on wax paper and, using the sponge brush, press fabric stiffener into them. Pick up each snowflake and place on a new piece of wax paper and let dry.

5. Make a hanging loop with monofilament line on each snowflake.

CINNAMON DOUGH COUPLE

By Chere Brodsky

1. To make cinnamon dough, empty cinnamon into plastic bag. Drop ½ teaspoon of applesauce into bag and work into cinnamon mixture to moisten. Continue to add applesauce, small amounts at a time, working it into cinnamon until a doughlike consistency is formed.

Keep extra dough in plastic bag or remoisten with applesauce as needed.

2. Trace the pattern in the pattern section onto tracing paper and cut from lightweight cardboard.

MATERIALS: CINNAMON DOUGH COUPLE
For One Couple

- Powdered cinnamon, 1-ounce tin
- Regular consistency applesauce, small jar
- White rattail cording, 1 yard
- 3 ½ mm black half-round beads, seven
- Red self-adhesive felt, small piece
- Six-strand red embroidery floss, 2 inches
- 1-inch white gathered lace, 2 ½ inches
- ⅛-inch satin ribbon, ⅓ yard each: red with white pindots, green with white pindots
- Child's wooden rolling pin, 4 ½ inches long
- ¼-inch gold press-on letters to spell "Noel"
- Lightweight cardboard, 4 x 5 inches
- Thick white craft glue or hot glue gun
- Miscellaneous items: small plastic bag; ½ teaspoon measuring spoon; wax paper; plastic cutting board; rolling pin; ruler; sharp knife; spatula; toothpick; emery board; black ballpoint pen; scissors; tracing paper; pencil

Note: A full-size pattern is given on page 25.

Place dough on cutting board, cover it with wax paper, and roll it out to a ¼-inch thickness. Remove wax paper, place cardboard template on dough and cut out, using the sharp knife. Use the toothpick to make a hole ¼ inch from top of head.

Remove cutout from cutting board with spatula and place on a flat surface to dry.

Repeat for second cutout.

Keep cutouts away from direct heat and turn them often. Pieces will become progressively lighter in color as they dry. Let dry 24 hours then smooth rough edges with emery board or your finger.

3. Glue cording around front of each cutout ⅛ inch from edges with ends butting.

4. To make each face, glue two black beads close together for eyes just under hanging hole.

Cut embroidery floss into two 1-inch lengths and glue in U shape for each mouth. Trace the heart pattern in the Step 4 illustration and cut four from red felt. Peel backing from hearts and press one over each floss end for cheeks.

Step 4 — Trace heart onto tracing paper. Cut four from red felt.

5. *To finish the cinnamon dough girl,* draw eyelashes using the ballpoint pen. Fold under ¼ inch at each short end of lace and glue across waistline for apron. Thread red ribbon through hole, knot close to head, and tie an end to each end of child's rolling pin for hanger. Following the manufacturer's instructions, press letters in place as desired across front of rolling pin.

6. *To finish the cinnamon dough boy,* glue three beads down center front for buttons. Thread green ribbon through hole and tie ends in a bow for hanger.

MR. & MRS. SNOWMAN MISTLETOE

By Barbara Bennett

MATERIALS: MR. & MRS. SNOWMAN MISTLETOE

- Oven-baked clay *: white; red; green; black; brown
- Glaze *
- Acrylic paints: black; white; red; green
- Paintbrushes: medium flat; liner
- Palette knife
- ⅛-inch red satin ribbon, 2 yards
- ⅜-inch silver jingle bells, six
- Mistletoe sprig with 4-inch stem
- Red ball head straight pins, two
- White craft glue
- Green floral tape
- Miscellaneous items: scissors; baking sheet; aluminum foil; paper clips; toothpicks; garlic press; wirecutters; oven

* Sculpey III and Glaze by Polyform Products Co. were used in the sample project.

1. Line baking sheet with foil and form ornament on it.

2. To form the bodies, roll and flatten two white oval ½-inch balls of clay. Refer to the Assembly And Painting Guide on page 19 to shape and attach each piece.

Roll and flatten two slightly smaller round white balls for the heads and roll a 1-inch L-shaped log for an arm on each body. *Note:* Do not attach Mr. Snowman's arm.

3. *To make Mrs. Snowman,* shape a 1-inch red log and wrap around neck. Cut a ½-inch triangle for the scarf's streamer, and use the palette knife to cut a fringed edge on the streamer.

To make the hat, flatten a ¼-inch piece of green clay and press to top of head. Use palette knife to shape and trim off excess. Roll tiny green ball for top of hat and a thin snake roll for hat brim. Make vertical indentations in brim with palette knife.

To make the apron, flatten a ¾-inch green oval and attach to right side below scarf. Attach three tiny green balls under scarf over top end of

18

Assembly and Painting Guide

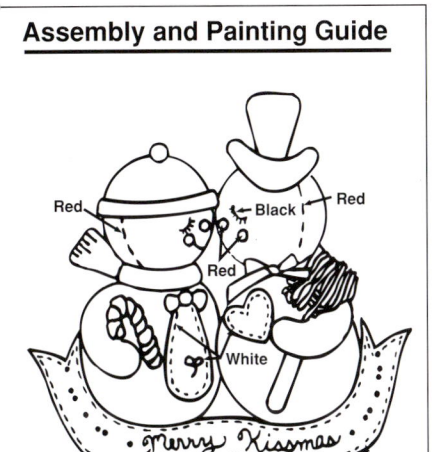

Use this guide for Steps 2 through 5 and Step 8.

apron and indent centers with a toothpick.

To make candy cane, twist very thin roll of white and red clay together.

4. *To make Mr. Snowman*, roll a thin brown 1½-inch snake roll for the broom handle. Load a garlic press with white clay and press out ¾-inch strands for mop; attach to handle. Attach arm over handle.

Shape a ½-inch red heart and attach to chest.

To make the hat, flatten black clay to ¼ inch and make a 1-inch triangle. Roll a 1-inch black roll and curve ends upward for hat brim.

5. To make the banner, roll a 5½-inch white log. Wrap along bottom of couple and up sides. Flatten in place. Cut a V with palette knife on each end.

6. For both figures, use wirecutters to cut pins leaving ¼ inch to insert for noses, barely touching.

Using wirecutters, cut paper clip in half. Insert one U-shaped half between hats and other half to center bottom of banner.

7. Bake ornament in oven at 225° for 30 minutes. *Note:* Ornament may feel soft when removed from oven, but will harden as it cools.

8. Using the liner brush, paint details following the Assembly and Painting Guide. Use black for eyes, eyelashes, and lettering; red for mouths, dots or hearts if desired on banner, and dash lines on heads; green for dash lines on banner; and white for dash lines on apron and heart.

9. Using the flat brush, apply two or three coats of glaze to all sides of ornament. Let dry.

10. To finish ornament, bend stem of mistletoe in half and slip through top hanger loop. Floral tape stem leaving a hook on end of wire for a hanger.

Glue small ribbon bow to neck of Mr. Snowman. Cut remainder of ribbon into three assorted lengths. Thread and tie each ribbon length at center through bottom hook and tie a bell to each end.

LITTLE DOLLY DARLINGS

By Laurel Nixholm Tessmer

MATERIALS: LITTLE DOLLY DARLINGS

For Each Doll

Felt, 4-inch squares: flesh, choice of color for dress

Crewel yarn *, choice of color for hair, 1 yard

Embroidery floss, choice of color for mouth and eyes

Needles: embroidery and sewing

Choice of trims: ribbons; laces; appliques; tiny buttons; seed beads

Polyester fiberfill, small amount

Miscellaneous items: scissors; ruler; tracing paper; pencil; straight pins; sewing threads to match fabrics and trims; toothpick; sewing machine

Note: Full-size patterns are given on page 25.

* Paternayan yarn was used in the sample projects.

1. Trace the patterns on page 25 onto tracing paper.

2. To make the doll, cut doll from one piece of flesh felt. Fold felt doll shape horizontally at waist. Clip a vertical slit at center of fold to make a ¾-inch opening for stuffing. See the Step 2 illustration.

Place doll shape centered on another piece of felt; pin to hold.

Step 2
Fold at waist; cut a vertical slit at waist center.

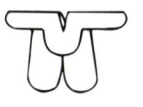

Set machine at 12 stitches per inch. Begin at top of head and stitch 1/16 inch from edge around entire doll shape.

19

Cut doll from bottom piece of felt, using the doll shape as a cutting guide.

3. Stitch each arm from shoulder to underarm, back tacking at beginning and end of each seam. Also stitch the legs in a wide-angled V-shape from one hip to the crotch, then to opposite hip. See the Step 3 illustration.

Step 3
Follow dotted lines to stitch across arms and legs.

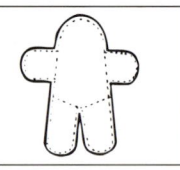

4. Use a toothpick and pea-sized fiberfill to stuff the body. Slipstitch back opening.

5. Refer to the pattern for stitching facial features with one strand of embroidery floss. Follow the Step 5a illustration to outline the mouth and the Step 5b illustration to make French knots for the eyes.

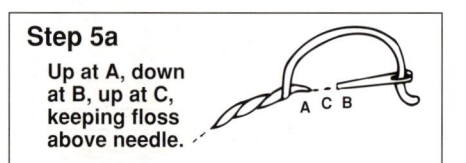

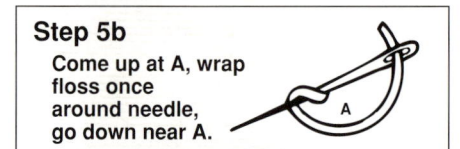

Step 5a
Up at A, down at B, up at C, keeping floss above needle.

Step 5b
Come up at A, wrap floss once around needle, go down near A.

6. To make the hair, cut seven 5-inch pieces of yarn. Separate each piece into three strands. Knot one end of matching thread in needle and insert at back center seam, coming up at front center of forehead.

See the Step 6 illustration to backstitch two or three strands of yarn at a time three-fourths of way down center back of head; do not cut thread.

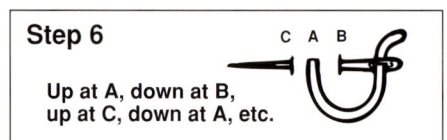

Step 6
Up at A, down at B, up at C, down at A, etc.

7. To make the ponytails, insert needle at base of hairline at back center and come up at either of the side seams just above where ears would be.

Gather the yarn neatly to make a ponytail, hold close to head, and wrap thread around it tightly two or three times. Tack to head at this point. Insert needle and come out on opposite side of head. Repeat to make second ponytail; trim ponytails.

8. To make the dress, cut pattern from desired color of felt. Center the dress on doll's front and fold the two long outer tabs under the arms and around the back of the doll. Cross tabs in back, fold over each shoulder, and tack corners under dress bodice at shoulders. See the Step 8 illustration.

Step 8
Cross dress tabs in back, fold tabs over shoulders to front.
Dress Back

9. Refer to the photo to trim dress as desired. Lace can be stitched to sleeves, neck or around bottom of dress. Tie a tiny bow and tack to neckline. To make a bodice, stitch a wide piece of embroidered ribbon across front. Stitch an applique to the skirt, or sew or string beads together.

STENCILED ANGEL HEARTS

By Frances Hartsky

MATERIALS: STENCILED ANGEL HEARTS

⅜-inch wooden heart cutouts, 3 x 2½ inches: plain *for standing angel;* with center top hole *for flying and teddy angels*

Stencil plastic *, one sheet

Acrylic paints *: slate blue; nutmeg; medium flesh; burgundy rose; roseberry; off white; golden harvest; wicker

Paintbrushes: 10/0 liner; 1-inch sponge

Black fine-tip permanent marker

⅛-inch ecru satin ribbon, ½ yard *per ornament*

Clear paste varnish

Thick white craft glue *

Fine grain kitchen sponges

Disposable palette

Miscellaneous items: craft knife; spray glass cleaner; paper towels; masking and transparent tape; pane of glass; wiping cloths; container of water; scissors

Note: Full-size patterns are given on page 27.

* Mylar® stencil sheets; Plaid Folk Art, Delta Ceramcoat, and Illnois Bronze Country Colors paints; and Aleene's Thick Designer glue were used for the sample projects.

1. To make the stencil for each ornament, place a 4 x 3½-inch piece of Mylar® over the pattern on page 27. Use the marker to trace heart outline and the No. 1 shape and mark that stencil No. 1. Continue, tracing solid lines and labeling a different stencil for each numbered shape(s), including additional ones in the Step 1 illustration.

Place each stencil over glass and use knife to cut along traced lines. Cut slowly, toward yourself, feeding Mylar® into blade to cut around corners.

Step 1
Draw and cut out hair and heart stencils.
No. 3   No. 5

2. To color each area, follow these general instructions.

Cut sponge into 1-inch pieces, rounding off corners. Put puddles of paint on palette.

Dip sponge into puddle, dab it on folded paper towels to remove excess paint, and use a light up-and-down motion to fill the area. *Note:* Avoid too much paint; add a second coat.

Use stencils in numerical order, letting each color dry before proceeding. Clean the stencil with glass cleaner and dry before using a different color on it. Cut off and discard sponge end when finished with each color.

3. *To paint the standing angel,* use sponge brush to basecoat heart with slate blue.

Position No. 1 (dress) stencil over heart and sponge on roseberry. Clean and replace stencil. Use a fresh-cut end of sponge to lightly add off white over the roseberry to create a speckled look.

Using the No. 2 (head, hands, feet) stencil, sponge on two coats of medium flesh. Using No. 3 (hair) stencil, sponge in nutmeg. Using No. 4 (wings) stencil, sponge in off white.

Place No. 5 (heart) stencil over dress and right hand and sponge on two coats of burgundy rose.

4. Use the liner brush to freehand the remaining details, referring to the color photo and pattern as needed.

Paint hair strands with a mix of nutmeg and golden harvest and linework on wings and dress with slate blue. Paint cuffs, collar, hem edge, bodice heart, and hearts around hem with off white. Make off white four-dot flowers on sleeves and around crown for a wreath. Do border work with off white dots.

Paint eyes slate blue and highlight beneath them with off white. Paint nose and mouth burgundy rose and eyebrows nutmeg.

5. To finish, follow manufacturer's instructions to varnish heart.

6. Tie a knot in center of ribbon and glue knot to center top of heart. Tie ends in a bow for hanging.

7. *To make the flying angel,* follow Steps 1 through 5, using the Step 7 illustration to make the No. 3 stencil for the hair; add the No. 5 heart stencil between hands.

Lightly sponge a hint of burgundy rose of the cheeks and chin. Add four-dot flowers to the dress in an all-over

Step 7
Use this full size pattern to cut hair stencil.
No. 3

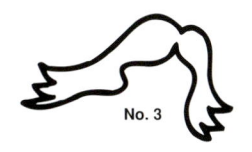

pattern. Using burgundy rose, add lines to the wings and paint a bow next to the heart, highlighting it with off white.

8. Cut ribbon ends at an angle. Insert ribbon through hole, tie a knot, then tie ends together in a bow for hanging.

9. *To make the teddy angel,* follow Steps 1 through 5 with the following color changes. Trace the heart in the Step 1 illustration for stencil No. 4 and stencil in between hands.

Sponge dress in burgundy rose. Paint body nutmeg and speckle with wicker. Use marker to draw facial details and nails on paws. Paint tongue burgundy rose.

Follow Step 7 to paint the dress, heart, and wings. Paint alternating dots and comma strokes with burgundy rose for the border.

Follow Step 8 to finish.

MACHINE EMBROIDERY

By Tedi Pickering

1. Trace the patterns on page 26 onto the tracing paper. Using dressmaker's carbon, transfer each design onto the wrong side of a square of satin fabric.

2. To stitch each ornament, place the satin fabric, design side down, in the embroidery hoop; turn the hoop over and stitch from this side.

To set your machine for embroidery, remove the presser foot and lower the feed dogs. Loosen the tension and insert a size 11 needle; lower the presser bar. Set the stitch for zigzag, varying the width as needed and fill in the design.

3. Cut out each design ¼ inch beyond stitching. Center the embroidery, right side up, on the red fabric square and, using green or gold thread, stitch in place using a wide satin stitch.

4. With right sides together and using a ¼-inch seam allowance, stitch the front of the ornament to the print backing, leaving an opening for turning.

MATERIALS: MACHINE EMBROIDERY
For Each Ornament

Fabric: Christmas print, solid red cotton: 4-inch squares of each; white satin, 3-inch square

Metallic rayon machine-embroidery thread: red, pink, medium green, blue, gold, black

4mm gold beads, four

⅛-inch satin ribbon, 15 inches

Polyester fiberfill

Miscellaneous items: sewing machine with zigzag stitch; size 11 sewing machine needle; embroidery hoop; tracing paper; dressmaker's carbon; scissors; pencil; sewing needle; thread to match fabrics

Note: Full-size patterns and a Color Key are given on page 26.

Turn right side out and stuff firmly with polyester fiberfill. Slipstitch opening.

5. Tack a gold bead to each corner of the ornament. Cut 8 inches of ribbon and tack a loop to the top of design so ends extend on right side. Tie remaining ribbon in a bow and tack over loop ends.

POTPOURRI BAG ANGELS

By Mary E. Seigfried

MATERIALS: POTPOURRI BAG ANGELS
For All Five Angels

Assorted potpourri scents

48mm wood beads with 12mm hole, five

Acrylic paints *: red, green, flesh, black, brown, white

Detail paintbrush

Stencil brushes, four small

Osnaburg fabric, three 9½x11-inch pieces

Muslin, two 9½x11-inch pieces

2⅝-inch ribbon, 18 inches each: osnaburg; muslin

⅛-inch satin ribbon: bright green, rust, forest green, 12 inches of each; red, 24 inches

Curly chenille: yellow, brown, 1 yard of each; gold, ½ yard

4½-inch-diameter ecru doilies, two

Ecru lace: 2½-inch flat lace, 9 inches; ½-inch gathered lace, 24 inches

Knotted fringe, 4 inches

Polyester fiberfill

Mylar®, 8½x11-inch sheet

Embroidery floss: red, green, light green, white

Miscellaneous items: scissors; tape measure; masking tape; craft knife; tracing paper; pencil; dressmaker's carbon; white thread; needle; paper towels; jar of water; sewing machine (optional)

Note: Full-size patterns are given on page 24.

* Delta Ceramcoat acrylic paints were used for the sample projects.

1. Trace the wing pattern on page 24 onto tracing paper and cut three sets from osnaburg ribbon and two sets from muslin ribbon.

2. *To make angel No. 1*, stitch right side of ½-inch gathered lace along wrong side of one 9½-inch edge of muslin fabric, with raw edges even. Press lace outward and topstitch in place. See the Step 2 illustration. Fold the fabric in half lengthwise with right sides together and stitch along the 11-inch sides, using a ¼-inch seam allowance. Turn right side out.

Center the seam at the back of the tube. Pin ½-inch lace along the bottom front with right sides together and raw edges even. Turn the tube to wrong side and sew across bottom. Turn bag right side out.

3. Trace the holly and bow patterns on page 24 onto tracing paper. Using dressmaker's carbon, transfer the bow to the center front of the bag. Transfer the large holly design around the bottom edge on the right side and the small holly design around the top edge on the wrong side of the fabric.

Paint the bow and berries red. Mix a small amount of white with green to get a light green. Paint the leaves light and dark green. Let dry.

4. Fill the bag one-fourth to one-half full of potpourri, then add a small amount of fiberfill. Thread the open end through the wood bead so 5 inches of the bag is below the bead. Bring the fabric down over the bead, so the holly design shows on the collar, and tie 12 inches of red satin ribbon around the neck.

5. Following the Step 5 illustration, paint the eyes black, the mouth red, and the cheeks and nose flesh.

Step 5 Paint facial features on fabric-covered bead.

Tack the center of a pair of matching wings to the back of the head.

6. Coil and glue the yellow curly chenille to the top of the head. Sew on a looped thread hanger to top of head.

7. *To make angel No. 2*, transfer the wreath pattern in the pattern section to the center, right side of a piece of osnaburg fabric. Using all six strands of embroidery floss, make a French knot at each circle. See the Step 7 illustration. Make the top, outside knots white and randomly make the wreath knots white, red, light green, and dark green.

Step 7 Up at A, wrap floss twice; down near A.

8. Omitting the lace, follow Step 2 to make the fabric into a bag. Turn right side out and tack fringe along the bottom edge.

9. Follow Steps 4 and 5, tying off neck with forest green ribbon. To finish bag, paint face, and attach wings. Using six strands of red embroidery floss, blanket stitch around edge of collar. See the Step 9 illustration.

Step 9 Come up at A, down at B, up at C. Repeat.

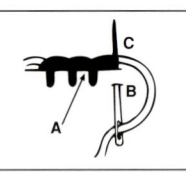

10. Tack long coils of gold curly chenille to top of head and sew on a looped thread hanger.

Step 2 Stitch lace to wrong side of fabric. Press out; topstitch.

11. *To make angel No. 3,* sew a doily to the center right side of a piece of osnaburg fabric, using red and green embroidery floss to tack it in place. Using four strands of floss, make red French knots at center of flowers or circle designs.

12. Omitting the lace, follow Step 2 to make fabric into a bag. Follow Steps 4 and 5 to attach head, tying off neck with 12 inches of red ribbon, and to paint face and sew on wings.

13. Glue four rows of brown curly chenille across the top of the head. Add small coils at the ears. Add a looped thread hanger.

14. *To make angel No. 4,* tack the 2½-inch flat lace across the right side of one 9½-inch end of osnaburg fabric, using red and green embroidery floss. Using six strands of red embroidery floss, add French knots to accent lace design.

15. Omitting the lace, follow Step 2 to make the fabric into a bag. Follow Steps 4 and 5 to attach head, tying off neck with 12 inches of bright green ribbon, and to paint face and attach wings. Using six strands of red embroidery floss, blanket stitch around edge of collar.

16. Tack short coils of yellow curly chenille to top of head and sew on a looped thread hanger.

17. *To make angel No. 5,* trace the stenciling pattern in the pattern section onto the Mylar®, using the black marker. To cut the stencil, hold the craft knife like a pencil and cut along traced lines, moving the knife slowly toward yourself. Feed the stencil into the blade and avoid lifting it until the entire outline is cut. To correct a mistake, tape both sides and recut.

Center the stencil on the right side of the muslin fabric and tape in place. Tape off all areas except No. 1 and stencil red. To stencil, pour a small amount of paint into a disposable container. Dip only the tip of the brush into the paint. On a stack of paper towels, work brush in a circular motion to remove excess paint. Hold the brush upright over area to be stenciled, and apply the color with quick up-and-down motions. Work paint well into fabric, making sure stenciled area is evenly covered. Use a clean brush for each color.

Repeat to stencil No. 2 areas light green, No. 3 dark green, and No. 4 brown.

18. Cut a doily in half and follow Step 2 to make bag, attaching half doily to bottom edge and ½-inch lace around top edge.

19. Follow Steps 4 and 5 to finish bag, tying off neck with 12 inches of rust ribbon, and to paint face and attach wings.

20. Tack large loops of brown curly chenille to top of head and add a looped thread hanger.

PLASTIC CANVAS TRIO

By Barbara Hicks Robinson

1. *To stitch each design,* refer to the Stitch Graph and Color Key on page 25 and the General Plastic Canvas Instructions on page 96.

Work the design in a continental stitch.

2. *To finish the candle design,* use 2 plies of red yarn to work one-wrap French knots over continental stitches.

Making sure all corners are well covered, overcast around edges with green yarn.

3. Cut 6 inches of red yarn. Dab glue on the ends and attach ends to each top back corner of design. Let dry.

4. Fold under edges of felt to fit back of ornament and slipstitch in place on three sides. Stuff ornament with yarn scraps or polyester fiberfill and slipstitch fourth side.

5. *To finish the Noel design,* cut off six holes from each corner, following the stitch graph.

Use 1 ply of green yarn to work long stitches along border.

Making sure all points are well covered, overcast edges with red yarn.

6. Cut 6 inches of green yarn. Dab glue on the ends and attach to back of upper two corners.

7. Repeat Step 4 to finish.

8. *To finish the bell design,* repeat Step 5 to shape canvas. Repeat Steps 2 through 4 to stitch and finish ornament, using 6 inches of green yarn for the hanger.

MATERIALS: PLASTIC CANVAS TRIO

For All Three Ornaments

Needles: No. 20 tapestry, sewing

Polyester fiberfill or yarn scraps

White craft glue

Scissors

For the Candle Design

10-mesh plastic canvas, 27 x 29-hole piece

4-ply acrylic yarn: Christmas red, dark green, light green, 4 yards each; yellow, 1 yard; white, 10 yards

Green felt, 4-inch square

Green sewing thread

For the Noel Design

10-mesh plastic canvas, 18 x 32-hole piece

4-ply acrylic yarn: Christmas red, 4 yards; dark green, 3 yards; white, 12 yards

Red felt, 3½ x 4 inches

Red sewing thread

For The Bell Design

10-mesh plastic canvas, 24 x 30-hole piece

4-ply acrylic yarn: Christmas red, 5 yards; dark green, 3 yards; white, 12 yards

Red felt, 3¾ x 4½ inches

Red sewing thread

Note: A Stitch Graph and Color Key are given on page 25.

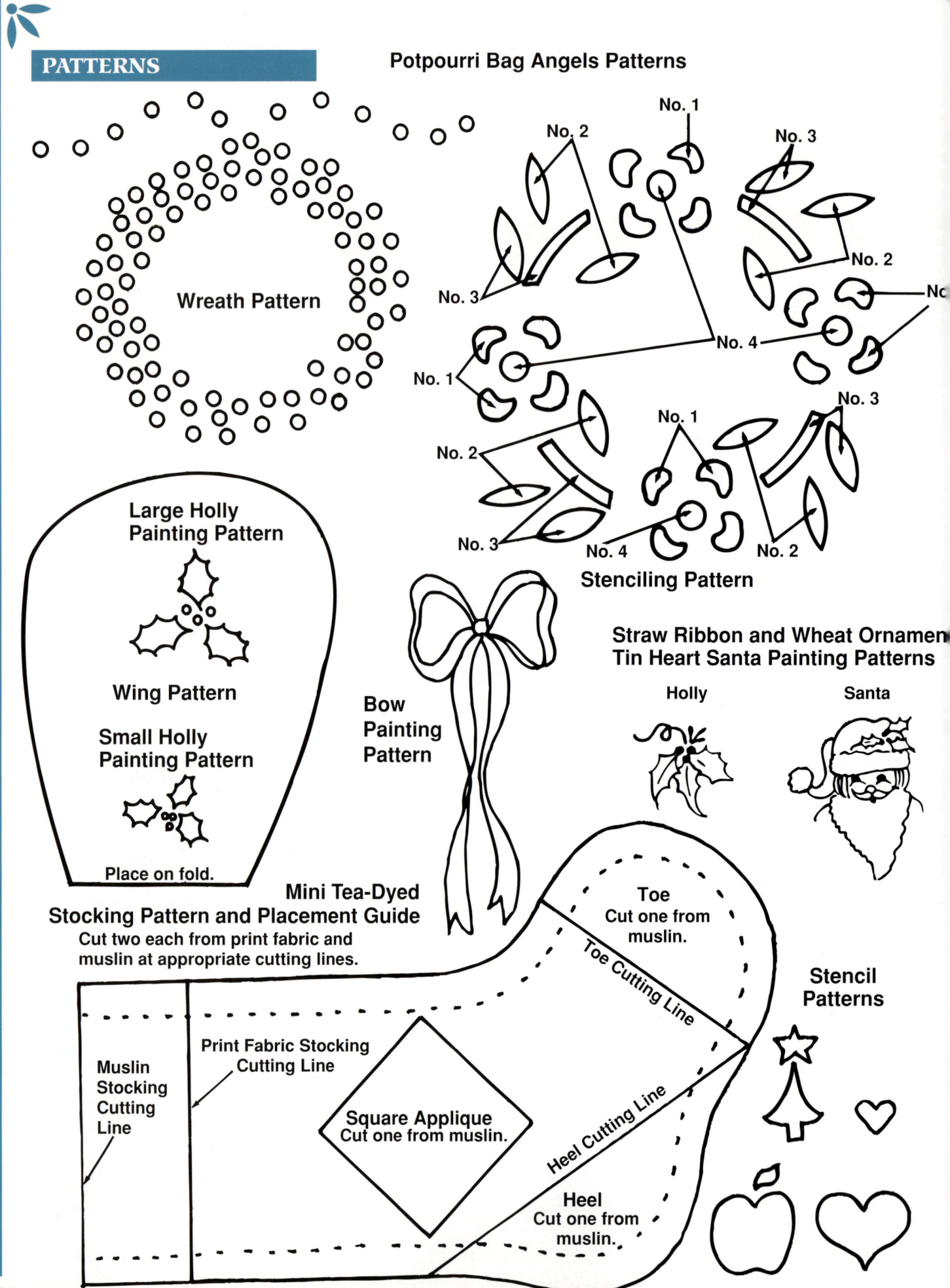

PATTERNS

Potpourri Bag Angels Patterns

Wreath Pattern

Stenciling Pattern

No. 1, No. 2, No. 3, No. 4

Large Holly Painting Pattern

Wing Pattern

Small Holly Painting Pattern

Place on fold.

Bow Painting Pattern

Straw Ribbon and Wheat Ornament Tin Heart Santa Painting Patterns

Holly

Santa

Mini Tea-Dyed Stocking Pattern and Placement Guide
Cut two each from print fabric and muslin at appropriate cutting lines.

Muslin Stocking Cutting Line

Print Fabric Stocking Cutting Line

Square Applique
Cut one from muslin.

Toe
Cut one from muslin.

Toe Cutting Line

Heel Cutting Line

Heel
Cut one from muslin.

Stencil Patterns

Cinnamon Dough Couple Pattern

Boy and Girl Cutout

Plastic Canvas Stitch Graphs and Color Key

Bell Design

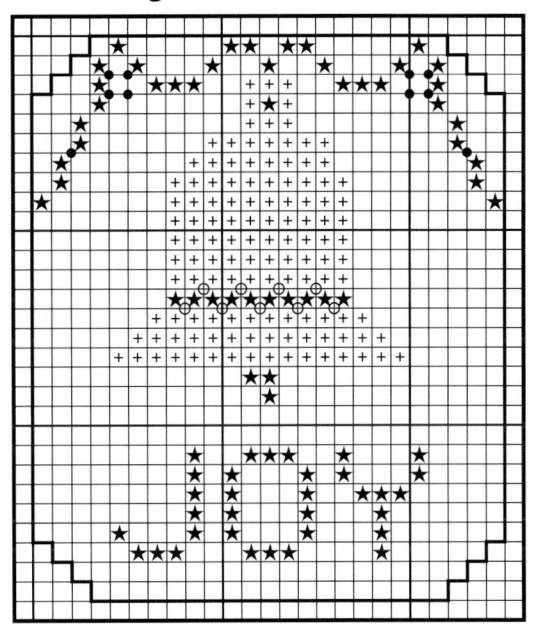

Candle Design

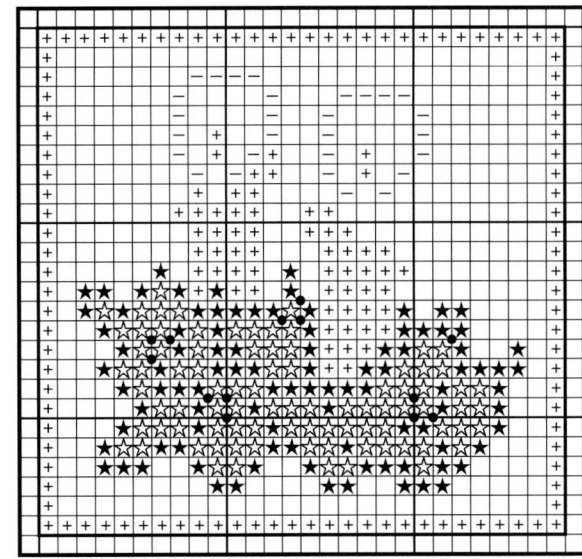

el Design

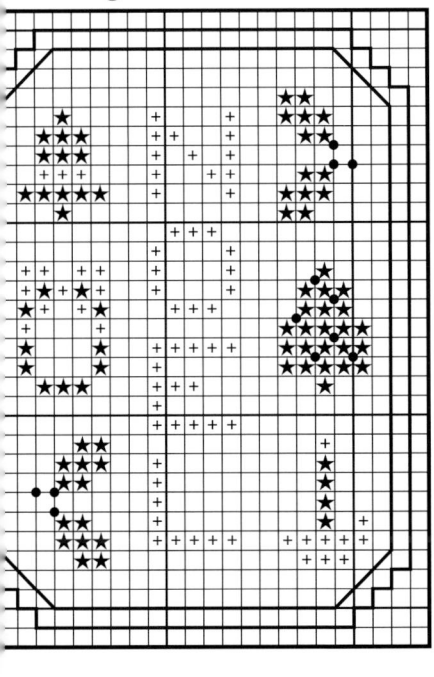

Color Key

- + Red
- ★ Dark Green
- ☆ Light Green
- — Bright Yellow
- □ White
- ● Red French Knot
- ○ Dark Green French Knot
- — Longstitching

Little Dolly Darlings
Doll and Dress Patterns

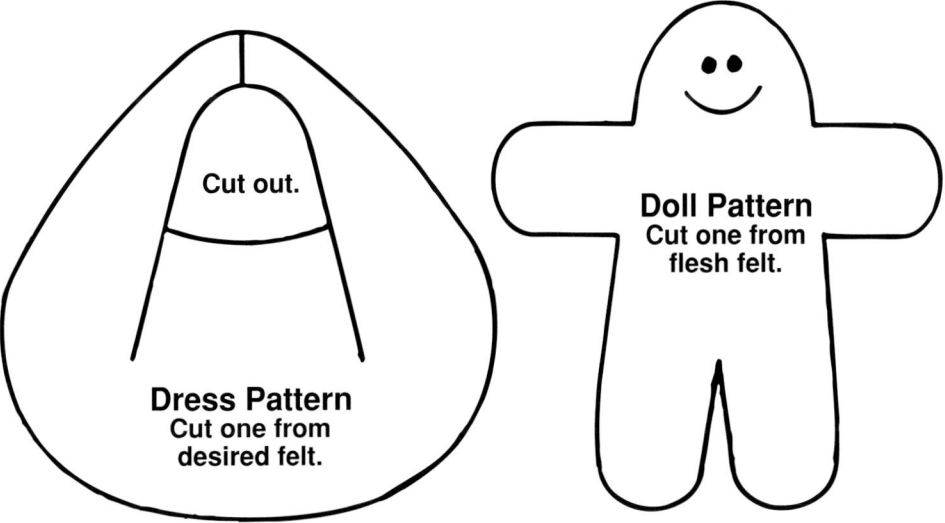

Dress Pattern
Cut one from desired felt.

Cut out.

Doll Pattern
Cut one from flesh felt.

Machine Embroidery Patterns

Pattern No.1

Pattern No. 2

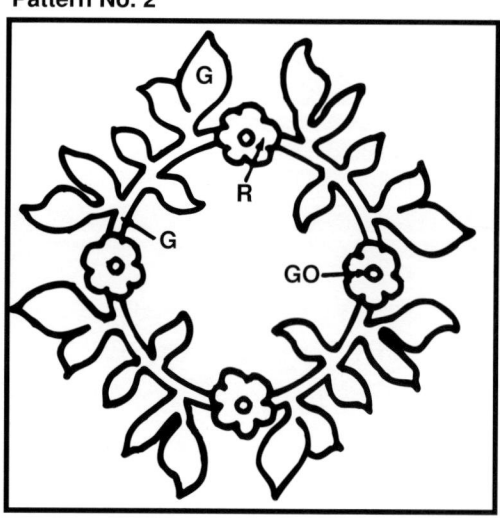

Color Key
- R Red
- G Green
- GO Gold
- P Pink
- B Blue
- BK Black

Pattern No. 4

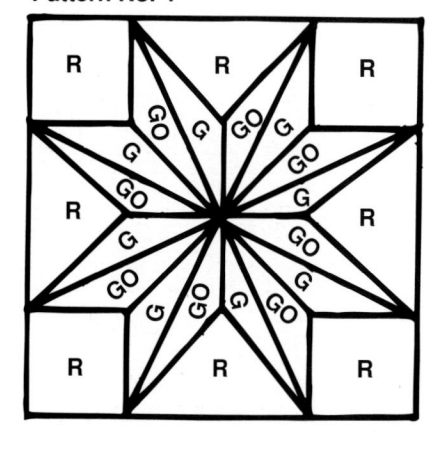

Pattern No. 5

Pattern No. 7

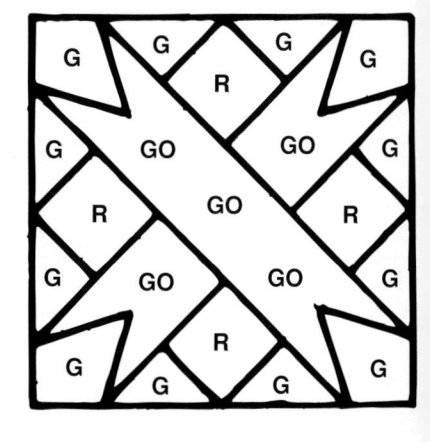

Pattern No. 3

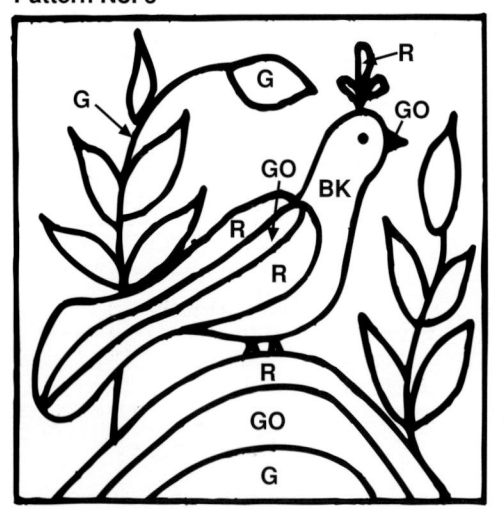

Pattern No. 6

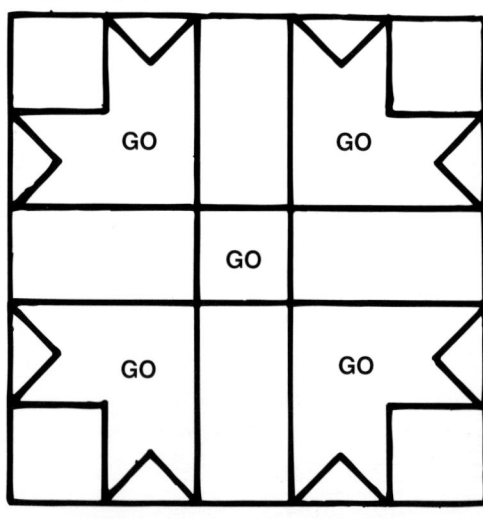

Pattern No. 8

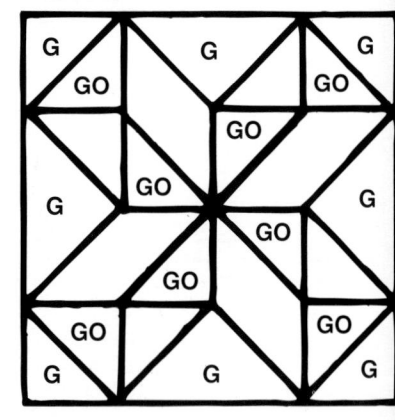

26

Stenciled Angel Heart Patterns

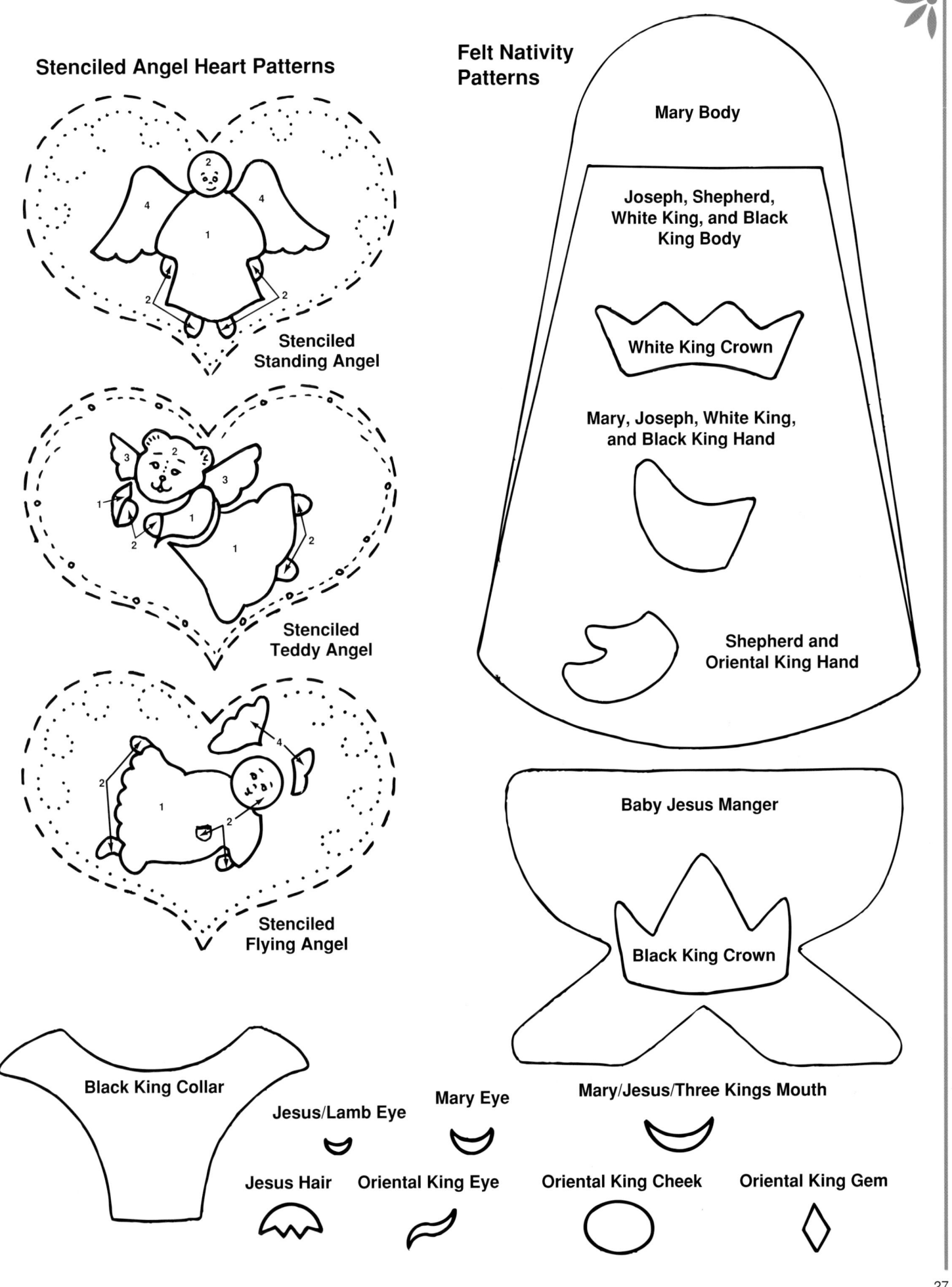

Felt Nativity Patterns

Mary Body

Joseph, Shepherd, White King, and Black King Body

White King Crown

Stenciled Standing Angel

Mary, Joseph, White King, and Black King Hand

Shepherd and Oriental King Hand

Stenciled Teddy Angel

Baby Jesus Manger

Black King Crown

Stenciled Flying Angel

Black King Collar

Jesus/Lamb Eye

Mary Eye

Mary/Jesus/Three Kings Mouth

Jesus Hair

Oriental King Eye

Oriental King Cheek

Oriental King Gem

27

Felt Nativity Patterns

- Joseph Hair
- Oriental King Crown
- Mary Hair
- Lamb Mouth
- Lamb Body Rear
- Shepherd Hair
- Oriental King Hair
- White King Gift Top
- Joseph/Sheperd Mouth
- White King Hair/Beard
- Oriental King Belt
- Joseph/Sheperd/White King/Black King Eye
- White King Collar
- Jesus Halo
- Baby Jesus Blanket
- Oriental King Body
- White King and Black King Sleeve
- Joseph and Shepherd Sleeve
- Lamb Ears/Tail
- White King Gift
- Mary Sleeve
- Lamb Body Front

Garlands Galore

Here's a gala collection of garlands designed for holiday "decking." From the sweetly scented lace and beaded heart chain to the delightfully **Country Clotheslines**, these garlands will satisfy a variety of decorating fancies. Especially appealing are the **Candy Canes** and **Gingerbread Kids**, which, like the other seven garlands, can be hung on the Christmas tree or used to highlight a mantel or doorway.

LACE HEARTS

By Betty J. Cook

Stuff with fiberfill, and sew opening closed. Beginning at top of heart, sew lace around outside edge on front.

3. Using the flat brush, apply fabric stiffener to the back of the heart and the front of the lace edging. Blot with a paper towel to remove excess stiffener and let dry completely. Check occasionally to make sure edges remain flat while drying.

4. Cut a 1-inch piece of green ribbon and fold in half to form a pointed loop for the leaf. Glue ends together. Cut a 5-inch piece of blue ribbon and tie in a bow. Trim stems on ribbon rose to ½ inch.

At the top front center of the heart, glue the leaf and rose to the lace. Glue the bow on top of the stem, just below the blossom.

On the front of each heart, place a tiny dot of scented oil near the bottom point of the heart. Do not allow oil to touch bow, as it will cause the glue to release.

5. To make the hanging loop, cut a 6-inch piece of quilting thread and insert through a picot loop at the top of the heart. Thread both strands through the beading needle, and string a gold oval bead, a 4mm pearl, and another gold oval bead. Do not cut thread.

Repeat for all hearts.

6. To make each icicle, cut a 12-inch piece of quilting thread, and using the beading needle, string a gold seed bead to the center of the thread. Fold thread at the bead to form a double strand, then string two small pearls and a gold oval bead three times. String a large pearl, a gold oval bead, and a seed bead. Do not cut threads.

Repeat to make 17 icicles.

7. To assemble the garland, use ends of thread to alternately tie the hearts and icicles along the length of the garland, spacing them evenly. Do not cut thread.

Tie ends of all threads together to form hanging loops. Use these loops to attach ornament hooks for securing the garland to tree or greens.

MATERIALS: LACE HEARTS

45-inch white or ivory lace fabric, ⅛ yard

½-inch white or ivory picot-edge flat lace, 5 yards

Satin ribbon: ¹⁄₁₆-inch light blue, 2½ yards; ⅛-inch moss green, ½ yard

9mm light blue ribbon roses, 16

Polyester fiberfill, small amount

Beads, one package each: 4mm and 2mm pearls; gold seed and small oval

Gold bead garland, 6 to 8 feet

Scented oil, fragrance of your choice

Fabric stiffener

No. 5 flat paintbrush

Beading needle

Wire ornament hooks

Hot glue gun

Miscellaneous items: typing paper; quilting thread; scissors; container of water; ruler; pencil

Note: A full-size pattern is given on page 34.

---

1. Lay a piece of typing paper over the heart pattern on page 34, trace the design, and cut out. Cut 32 hearts from lace fabric.

2. To make each heart, sew two hearts together, using a ⅛-inch seam allowance and leaving a small opening for stuffing. Do not turn.

PLASTIC CANVAS ANGELS

By Carole Rodgers

MATERIALS: PLASTIC CANVAS ANGELS

7-mesh plastic canvas: red, one sheet; white, two sheets

Acrylic yarn: yellow, 14 yards; gold, 3 yards; red, 18 yards; white, green, 12 yards each; pink, 6 yards; blue, 1 yard

Tapestry needle

Scissors

Note: Cutting and Stitch Graphs are given on page 34.

* These materials will make a 5- to 6-foot long garland. If you want a longer or shorter garland, adjust your materials accordingly.

---

1. Using the graphs on page 34 and referring to the General Plastic Canvas Instructions on page 96, cut seven angels and 12 hearts from white plastic canvas.

Cut 12 hearts from red plastic canvas.

2. Following the heart graph and using white yarn on white canvas and red yarn on red canvas, long stitch each heart. Do not overcast the edges.

3. Following the graph, overcast the edges of the angels, using the appropriate yarn for each section.

4. Following the graph and using the continental stitch, stitch each angel's face, hair, and one row of yellow above the hair. Stitch eyes blue and mouth red. Also stitch dress sleeves and bodice trim.

Stitch the rest of each angel using the long stitch.

5. To make the garland, thread the needle with green yarn.

Working from left to right, go down in the upper right corner on the side of a red heart. Come up in the upper left corner of a white heart. Tie the yarn in a small bow and cut ends.

In the same manner attach a red heart to the right of the white heart. Attach the red heart to the angel's left (facing you) hand.

Repeat with the angel's right hand with a white/red/white heart sequence.

Continue attaching angels and three hearts until garland is completed.

CANDY CANES

by Lynn Hallett

MATERIALS *: CANDY CANES

Opaque shrink plastic **, 8½ x 11-inch sheets, four

Fine black felt-tip marker **

Acrylic paints: white, bright red

Sable paintbrushes: No. 8 flat; No. 2 or No. 4 liner

Disposable palette

¼-inch red satin ribbon, 17 yards

Miscellaneous items: ¼-inch paper punch; water container; paper towels; tracing paper; pencil; toothpicks; oven; cookie sheet; spatula; sharp scissors

Note: A full-size pattern is given on page 34.

* These materials will make a 5-foot long garland. If you want a longer or shorter garland, adjust your materials accordingly.

** Shrink Art Plastic from Artis Aleene and a Sharpie marker were used in the sample project.

1. Trace the pattern on page 34 onto tracing paper.

2. Position the candy cane pattern under the upper left corner of a sheet of shrink plastic and trace around it with the marker. Move the pattern to the right and trace four more canes across the sheet. *Note:* Trace only the outline of the cane at this time.

Turn the pattern upside down and trace five more canes across another row. See the Step 2 illustration.

Repeat, tracing two more rows of canes on the bottom half of the shrink plastic.

Step 2

Position canes "heel to toe" across the sheet.

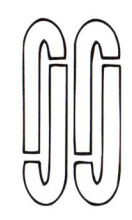

Repeat with the other three sheets using the first sheet as a pattern.

3. Using the flat brush, paint each cane with a thin wash of white paint. Let dry. Clean brush in water and blot dry.

4. Place pattern under upper left candy cane. You should be able to see the stripes through the white wash.

Dip the flat brush in water, blot on paper towel, load with red paint. Work the paint into the brush by stroking it back and forth on the palette.

Paint the wide stripes. Switch to the liner brush and paint the thin stripes.

Repeat for each candy cane. Let dry.

5. Turn each sheet over, and using the stripes on the front as a pattern, paint the stripes on the back. *Note:* You do not have to paint the back white. Let dry.

6. To add the white highlight to the front of each cane, dip the flat brush in water and blot on a paper towel. Pick up a dab of white paint on a toothpick and dab in into the chisel (sharp end) of the brush. Stroke the brush on the palette to blend and soften the paint.

Place the brush at the crook end of the cane. Press and pull the brush up and over the curve of the cane. Lift brush, turn it over, and brush from the bottom of the cane, joining the highlight. Let dry.

7. To accent each cane, retrace both the front and back outline with the black marker.

8. Cut out each cane and punch a hole in the top of it.

9. Preheat the oven to 300°. Place 12 canes on a cookie sheet and put them in the oven. As they shrink, the canes will curl up and then flatten out. As soon as they are flat, remove them from the oven. If one or two are not flat, press them with a spatula while they're still warm.

Remove them from the cookie sheet.

Let cookie sheet completely cool between shrinkings.

10. Cut three 5-yard pieces of ribbon.

11. Thread one-third of the candy canes onto a piece of ribbon, positioning them 6 to 8 inches apart.

Position the first cane 8 inches from the end of the ribbon. Fold the ribbon end in half and tie an overhand knot by looping the doubled ribbon and pulling the cane through the loop.

Position the next cane approximately 4 inches from the first knot and knot it in place. Repeat until you have positioned and knotted all the canes.

Repeat with the rest of the canes and the other two pieces of ribbon.

12. Lay the candy cane ribbons on flat surface and loosely twist or braid them.

Cut the remaining ribbon into 6-inch pieces. Tie the garland together at 12-inch intervals with a small ribbon bow.

COUNTRY CLOTHESLINE

By Jan Way

MATERIALS: COUNTRY CLOTHESLINE
For Each Clothesline

¼-inch wood, 4x6 inches

Acrylic paints *: razzle red; holiday green; white; black; stoneware blue; sedona clay; devonshire cream

Paintbrushes: No. 8 and No. 4 flat; No. 2 round; fine spotter or liner

Mini gifts, four

6mm faceted beads: six red, 10 clear *for the Amish clothesline;* six red, six clear, four green *for the bear and cottages clothesline;* six red, 10 clear, four green *for the Christmas geese clothesline*

20-gauge wire, 12 inches

Yarn needle

Wire ornament hangers, six

Scroll saw

Drill with 1⁄16-inch bit

Miscellaneous items: fine sandpaper; graphite paper; tracing paper; stylus; needlenose pliers

Note: Full-size painting patterns are given on pages 34-35.

* Accent acrylic paint was used for the sample project.

1. Trace the patterns on pages 34-35 onto tracing paper. Using graphite paper and stylus, transfer pattern outlines to the wood. Use scroll saw to cut out. Sand all pieces.
Refer to photo for stringing position and drill a hole from side to side on each piece.

2. Sideload the paintbrush to add highlights and shading to each piece. To sideload, slide one side edge of brush through paint. Stroke brush back and forth over the same place on palette until paint begins to move across bristles. Apply paint with the loaded side of the brush next to the area which is to be shaded.

3. *To paint the bear and cottages clothesline,* basecoat the cottages with two coats of white; let dry. Paint cottage roof devonshire cream. Shade edges of roof with sedona clay. Paint chimneys sedona clay, doors stoneware blue, hearts razzle red, and leaves holiday green. Paint doorknobs devonshire cream.
Basecoat fat bear with two coats of devonshire cream. Shade edges with sedona clay and let dry. Lightly transfer detail lines. Sideload brush in sedona clay and paint around the muzzle. Paint eyes, nose, and mouth black. Outline inner ears and hand and foot pads with sedona clay. Paint ribbon stoneware blue, holly leaves holiday green, and berries razzle red.

4. *To paint the Amish clothesline,* mix white and sedona clay and base the hands and faces with flesh mix. Mix a little razzle red with some flesh mix and paint the cheeks. Paint hair and noses sedona clay, eyes black, and mouths razzle red. Paint hats and shoes black. Highlight edges with white. Paint dress and overalls stoneware blue. Shade edges with black. Paint shirt and apron white and shade edges with stoneware blue.
Paint house white with stoneware blue roof. Do not rinse brush, but sideload in black and paint scallops on the roof. Paint door blue; hearts, door frame, and knob sedona clay.

5. *To paint the Christmas geese clothesline,* base geese in white. Shade edges with stoneware blue. Lightly transfer detail lines. Paint beaks devonshire cream. Shade edges with sedona clay. Paint holly leaves holiday green with razzle red berries; outline in black. Highlight berries with white. Paint ribbons devonshire cream and shade edges with sedona clay. Paint eyes black with white highlights.
Paint wood heart razzle red. Do not rinse brush, but sideload in white and paint around outer edge. Paint lettering white.

6. To make each garland, use the yarn needle to make a hole from side to side through the mini gifts. *Note:* One-fourth of the package should be above the hole and three-fourths below. Make holes so two packages will hang horizontally and two vertically on each clothesline.

7. After pieces are dry, lay out the arrangement of all the pieces for each clothesline on a flat surface, alternating a mini gift between each wood jewelry piece. Two faceted beads start and end each clothesline and separate the wood pieces from the mini gifts. *Note:* There are four beads behind the heads of the geese. See the photograph.
Using needlenose pliers, bend one end of the 12-inch wire into a small loop. Thread the wood pieces, mini gifts, and beads onto the other end of the wire. When clothesline is complete, cut off excess wire so there is approximately ½ inch left, then bend this end into a small loop. Insert the loop end of a wire Christmas tree hanger into the wire loop ends of the clothesline. Bend the entire clothesline in a slightly upward curve.

FABRIC CHAIN WITH BOWS

By Marti Sandell

MATERIALS: FABRIC CHAIN WITH BOWS
For Four Garlands

Fabric: green cotton, seven different patterns, ⅛ yard each; red Christmas print, 1⅓ yards *for the "evergreen branches";* red print, ⅓ yard; white print, ⅓ yard each *for the chain*

¾-inch fusible interfacing tape, one roll

Lightweight posterboard

Hot glue gun

Miscellaneous items: scissors; threads to match fabrics; needle; 12 push pins; iron; and sewing machine

1. To make "evergreen branches," tear a ¾-inch strip across the width of each green fabric and cut into 7-inch lengths. *Note:* Tear strips for ragged edges. Set eight lengths aside and divide remaining strips into two equal groups.

To make each "branch," fold each piece of a group in half, wrong sides together, and pinch at the fold. Stitch strips continuously one to the other through the folded tip, alternating colors and sides. See the Step 1 illustration. Stitch again over the previous stitching, closing any gaps.

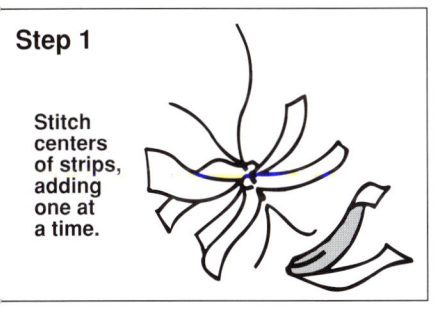

Step 1

Stitch centers of strips, adding one at a time.

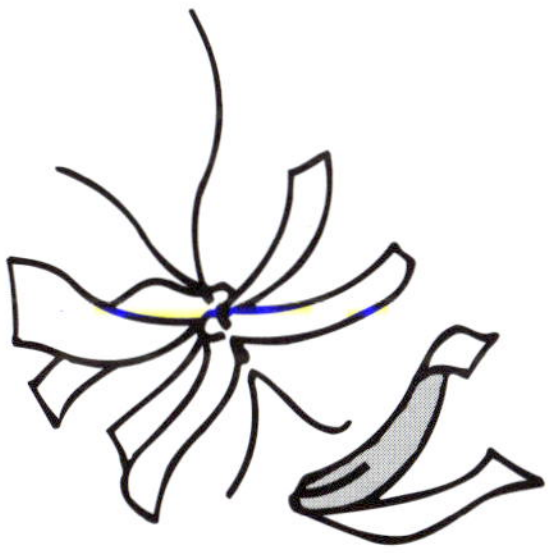

Use the eight pieces set aside to stitch a short "branch" for the center of the garland.

2. To make the rings for the chain, cut two 2-inch strips across the width of both the red and white fabrics.

From the posterboard, cut eight ¾x7½-inch strips for the red rings and 21 ¾x4-inch strips for the white rings. Place a fabric strip wrong side up and place a posterboard strip in center. Press fabric over one long edge of posterboard and cut fabric even at ends. Cut a strip of fusible interfacing the same length and place it even with the opposite long edge and under the posterboard. See the Step 2 illustration. Press this edge over, bonding the two together. Continue covering posterboard with red and white strips but do not form into rings at this point.

Step 2

Press interfacing and fabric over posterboard.

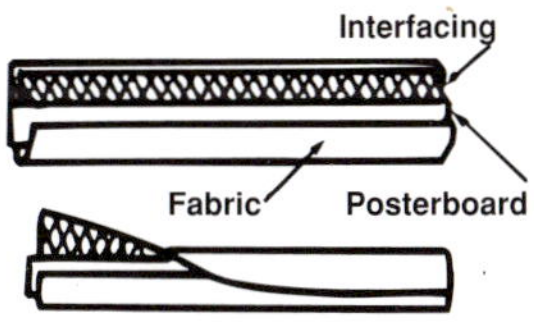

3. To make a chain, form a red ring by gluing overlapped ends, then insert a white strip through red ring and glue. Continue by gluing three white rings between two red rings.

4. To make the bow ribbons, cut three 4x38-inch pieces of red Christmas print fabric. Fold one strip in half lengthwise with right sides together. Stitch, using a ¼-inch seam allowance, tapering ends to a point and leaving an opening in center for turning. Turn right side out, slipstitch opening, and press. Repeat for remaining bow ribbons.

Tie a green fabric "branch" to each end of the chain by inserting a red bow ribbon through the red ring. Place a branch with 10 of the strips above this point and tie a half knot, then tie into a bow.

Tie a bow around the top of the center white ring, attaching the short bough in the same manner.

5. To hang this garland above a doorway, place a push pin in the center and each top corner of door frame. Slip a ring over the center pin and the back of the two end bows over the corner pins.

GINGERBREAD KIDS

MATERIALS: GINGERBREAD KIDS

Felt: brown, four 9x11-inch pieces; 8-inch white square; 3-inch red square; 2-inch pink square

⅛-inch rickrack: white, 2 yards; pink, 1½ yards

Ribbon: ¼-inch red satin, ⅓ yard; ⅝-inch red with white polka dots grosgrain, ⅔ yard

4mm wiggle eyes, 14

2¼-inch plastic candy canes, six

Red embroidery floss

Polyester fiberfill

Thick white craft glue

Miscellaneous items: air-soluble marker; tracing paper; pencil; scissors; straight pins; brown sewing thread; needle; ballpoint pen; toothpicks; paper punch

Note: Full-size patterns are given on page 35.

* Materials listed will make a garland of seven gingerbreads.

1. Trace the patterns on page 35 onto tracing paper and cut out.

2. Pin body patterns onto two thicknesses of felt and cut out four boys and three girls (14 pieces).

Trace and cut from felt: three aprons, four boy collars, and three girl collars from white; seven bows, seven bow knots, three hearts, and four buttons from red; and 14 cheeks from pink with the paper punch.

3. Using the patterns as guides, mark mouth on one head of each boy and girl with the air-soluble marker. Backstitch the mouths with three strands of knotted floss. See the Step 3 illustration. Knot and clip thread end.

Step 3

Up at A, down at B, up at C, down at A, etc.

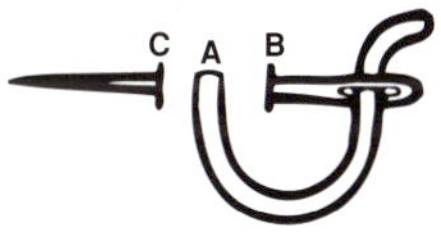

4. To stitch two body pieces together, use two strands of thread and a small overcast stitch. *Note:* Hide knot on inside of body. Begin under one arm and stitch around head to under second arm. Stuff head and arms lightly; do not overstuff. Continue stitching around body, leaving second side open for stuffing. Stuff legs and body lightly. Overcast opening. Repeat for other six gingerbread kids.

5. *To trim each boy,* cut white rickrack as follows: one 6-inch piece for the head; two 2-inch pieces for the arms; two 2¼-inch pieces for the legs; one 4-inch piece for the waist.

Glue rickrack on front of head, framing face. *Note:* Ends below neck will be covered by the collar. Wrap remaining lengths around body, checking pattern for placement as indicated by dashed lines. Overlap ends at back and glue together.

Wrap collar around neck, overlapping in back; glue ends together. Glue bow on center front of collar and bow knot at center of it. Glue button on center of chest.

Glue two eyes and cheeks on face following pattern.

6. *To trim each girl,* cut pink rickrack as follows: one 6¼-inch piece for the head; two 2-inch pieces for the arms; one 5-inch piece for the skirt hem. Cut one 4-inch piece of white for the waist.

Glue head and arm rickrack on as for the boy in Step 5.

Wrap skirt hem rickrack around body, overlapping in back; glue ends together.

Center waist rickrack along top edge of apron and glue. Place apron on doll and wrap rickrack around waist overlapping ends in back; glue ends together. Glue heart on apron following pattern.

Wrap collar around neck, overlapping ends in back; glue ends together.

Glue bow at top center of head. Glue knot on center of bow.

Glue two eyes and cheeks on face following pattern.

7. Alternating boy then girl, stitch tips of hands together, forming a garland. Glue one candy cane at center of each hand joining.

8. To make the hangers, cut two 6-inch pieces of satin ribbon. Form a circle with each one, overlapping the ends; stitch together. Tack one to the back of the hand at each end of the chain.

Cut the polka dot ribbon in half and tie each in a bow. Tack a bow in the center of each hanger.

PATTERNS

Lace Heart Pattern

Cut 32 from lace

Candy Cane Garland Pattern

Plastic Canvas Angel Garland Cutting and Stitch Graphs

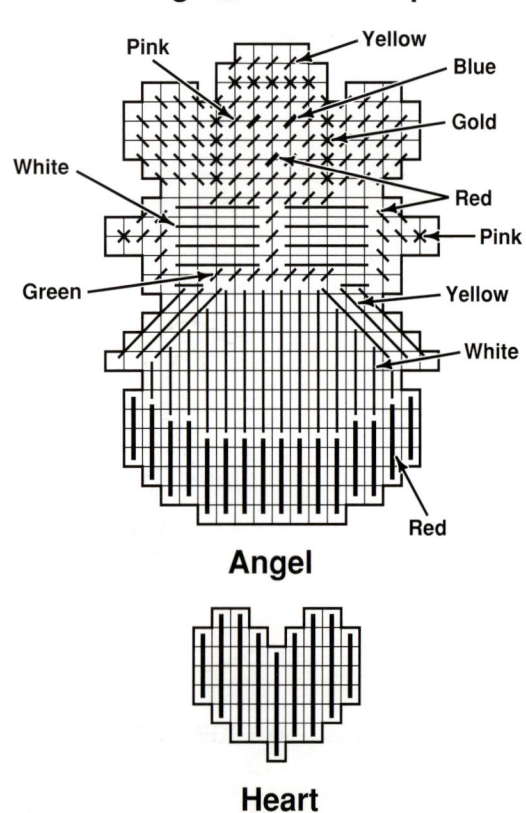

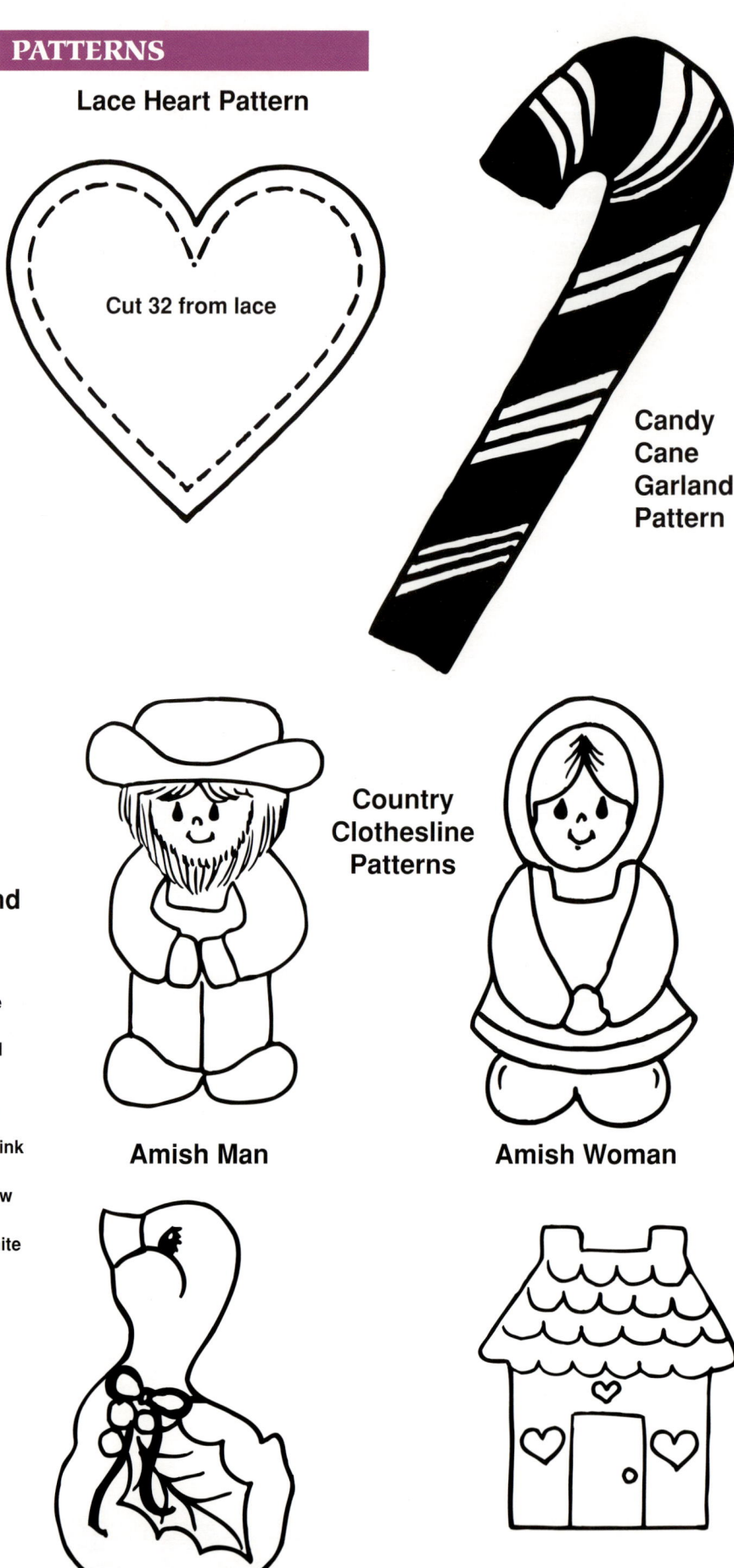

Angel

Heart

Country Clothesline Patterns

Amish Man

Amish Woman

Geese Goose

Amish House

34

Gingerbread Garland Patterns

Boy Collar

Bow Knot

Bow Tie

Girl Body
Cut from brown felt.

Boy Body
Cut from brown felt.

Heart

Apron

Girl Collar

Country Clothesline Patterns

Gingerbread Heart

Bear and Cottages Cottage

Bear and Cottages Bear

35

Quick & Easy

These super-easy ornaments were designed especially for busy people who long for beautiful hand-crafted decorations, but have little time to devote to making them.

Like the lovely **Lace Cornucopias**, many of the projects are crafted with ready-made doilies or other quickly assembled, but elegant-to-behold materials. You'll find a wide variety of choices, including three different, but easy-to-make angels—one of feathers, one of lace, and one of ribbon. All the appealing projects pictured in this chapter, from the gorgeous **Ribbon Loops** ornaments to the cute **Braided Ribbon Candy Cane**, only look time consuming!

LACE CORNUCOPIAS

By Nancy C. Hoerner

MATERIALS: LACE CORNUCOPIAS

For Each Cornucopia

5-inch white cotton doily

22-count white hardanger cloth, small piece

No. 26 tapestry needle

Fabric stiffener *

Dried naturals of your choice

Hot glue gun

For the Pink Cornucopia

Satin ribbon: ⅛-inch, rose, light rose, ⅓ yard each; ¹⁄₁₆-inch, rose, ½ yard

Embroidery floss: dark shell pink (DMC 221, Anchor 897); very light shell pink (DMC 225, Anchor 892); light shell pink (DMC 224, Anchor 893); fern green (DMC 522, Anchor 859); dark fern green (DMC 520, Anchor 862)

For the Blue Cornucopia

Satin ribbon: ⅛-inch, light blue, white, ⅓ yard each; ¹⁄₁₆-inch, light blue, ½ yard

Embroidery floss: light old gold (DMC 676, Anchor 891); medium blue violet (DMC 340, Anchor 118); light blue violet (DMC 341, Anchor 117); medium grey green (DMC 3052, Anchor 859); dark pine green (DMC 3362, Anchor 862)

For the White Cornucopia

Satin ribbon: ⅛-inch white, ⅓ yard; ¹⁄₁₆-inch ivory, 30 inches

Embroidery floss: light old gold (DMC 676, Anchor 891); yellow (DMC 3078, Anchor 292); off white (DMC 746, Anchor 386); dark pine green (DMC 3362, Anchor 862)

Miscellaneous items: cuticle scissors; wax paper; small piece of cardboard

Note: Stitch Graphs and Color Keys are given on page 43.

* Aleene's Fabric Stiffener was used in the sample project.

1. *To make each cornucopia,* lay the doily on a sheet of wax paper and place a small amount of fabric stiffener in the center. Using a small piece of cardboard, spread the stiffener over the doily; turn the doily over and cover the other side in the same manner.

Roll the doily up into a cone shape, and lay on a clean piece of wax paper, with the overlapped seam down. Make a small ball of wax paper, and insert into the top of the cone to hold the shape. Let dry. Check and reshape periodically while cornucopia is drying.

2. Refer to the Stitch Graph and Color Key on page 43, and the General Cross Stitch Instructions on page 95 to cross stitch each design with two strands of floss. If making all three cornucopias, stitch all flowers on same piece of hardanger.

Work all backstitches with one strand of floss. *For the pink cornucopia,* backstitch flower with dark shell pink and leaves with dark fern green. *For the blue cornucopia,* backstitch flower with medium blue violet and leaves with dark pine green. *For the white cornucopia,* backstitch flower with yellow and leaves with dark pine green.

3. When stitching is complete, spread fabric stiffener on front and back of design area, and let dry completely. Using cuticle scissors, carefully cut out each flower close to stitching lines. Set aside.

4. *To finish each cornucopia,* cut a 6-inch piece of ¹⁄₁₆-inch ribbon. Thread one end from front to back through top edge of cornucopia, and knot ends together in back for a hanging loop.

Hold remaining pieces of ribbon together, and tie in a bow. Hot glue bow to front of cornucopia, and glue matching flower to center of bow. Tie a knot at the end of each ribbon streamer. Fill cornucopia with dried naturals.

FELT TEDDY BEARS

By Erma Stricker

MATERIALS: FELT TEDDY BEARS

Felt: tan, two 7½x9-inch tan pieces *for each bear;* red, 4x6-inch piece *for girl bear;* 3x5-inch piece *for boy bear*

Beads: 6mm black: round, two; half-round, four; 4mm gold, two *for the boy bear*

½-inch tan pompoms, two

¼-inch green and gold metallic braid with ⅜-inch white lace trim, 7 inches *for girl bear*

⅝-inch red and green plaid craft ribbon, 2¾ inches *for boy bear*

Green flower-shaped sequin *for girl bear*

Polyester fiberfill

Air-soluble marker

Sewing thread: tan, red

White craft glue *

Miscellaneous items: sewing machine; scissors; lightweight cardboard; ruler; straight pins; sewing needle; tracing paper; graphite or carbon paper; pencil

Note: Full-size patterns are given on page 43.

* Aleene's Tacky Glue was used for the sample projects.

1. *To make each bear,* trace the body pattern on page 43 onto tracing paper and transfer to cardboard; cut out.

2. Fold tan felt in half to form a 7½x4½-inch piece and pin layers together at edges.

3. Using the air-soluble marker, trace around the cardboard pattern onto top layer of felt. Fill in lines at bases of ears, continuing line of head. See the Step 3 illustration. Mark slit lines as indicated on the pattern. Pin layers together inside the outline.

Felt Teddy Bear Boy Ornament

Felt Teddy Bear Girl Ornament

Step 3
Draw a curved line at the base of each ear.

4. Sew along marker line around body and across ear bases, leaving ears free. Trim ⅛ inch beyond stitched outline.

Trim ears to marker line and glue ear layers together.

5. Cut slit with scissors. Firmly stuff head, legs and arms. Stuff body and whipstitch opening.

6. *To finish the girl bear,* trace the dress pattern onto tracing paper and cut from red felt, cutting out neck opening and slit.

Cut lace-trimmed braid in half and glue the braid edges of the pieces to front and back dress hem lines, turning under raw edges at each end.

Slip dress over head and tack sides together below arms and at hemline.

Glue sequin to dress front at point of V neckline.

7. Glue a round black bead to center of a tan pompom and let dry. Glue pompom nose slightly below face center. Glue half-round beads slightly above pompom to each side for eyes.

8. To make a hanger, take a stitch with tan thread at top of head and knot ends at desired length.

9. *To finish the boy bear,* trace the vest pattern onto tracing paper and cut from red felt. Cut slits for armholes. Mark top of vest with air-soluble marker.

10. Put vest on bear and turn down top to form a collar. Glue the left front of the vest over the right front. Glue two gold beads for buttons close together at center front of vest.

11. To make his bow tie, fold ends of ribbon toward center, slightly overlapping them. Tightly wrap center several times with red thread and knot at back. Glue tie to neck of bear, just above neck of vest.

12. Glue on nose and eyes following Step 7 and add hanger following Step 8.

IGLOO TRIO

By Jan Way

MATERIALS: IGLOO TRIO

4-inch pinwheel doilies, three

2-inch Styrofoam balls, three

Fabric stiffener *, 4 ounces

Miniatures: painted angel; painted toy soldier; teddy bear; pine trees, candy canes, musical instruments, two each; gift-wrapped packages: one large, two medium, one small

Plastic holly sprigs with berries, four

⅛-inch satin ribbon: red, pink, white, 18 inches each

Cotton balls, three

White craft glue or hot glue

Miscellaneous items: plastic wrap; disposable bowl; three pinch clothespins; spoon; transparent tape

* Aleene's Fabric Stiffener was used in the sample projects.

1. *To make each igloo shape,* cut an 8-inch square of plastic wrap. Place the Styrofoam ball in center of square, bring ends up, and twist them together to form a tail. Tape around ends close to top of ball.

2. Pour fabric stiffener into a disposable bowl.

Immerse doily in the stiffener, completely saturating fabric. Remove doily and squeeze excess solution into bowl.

3. Holding the ball by its tail, place it in the center of doily and mold doily around ball, using fingertips to smooth scalloped edges against ball.

Attach clothespin to tail and hang doily-wrapped ball overnight or until dry.

4. Untape and untwist tail. Use a spoon to scoop out pieces of Styrofoam ball. Remove all Styrofoam and plastic wrap through the front opening, being careful not to distort the igloo shape.

5. Spread a cotton ball into a thin layer and glue to bottom of igloo.

6. *To decorate the angel igloo,* glue three holly leaves on left side, angel in center, two medium gifts on right side, and one instrument at left front.

7. *To decorate the toy soldier igloo,* glue three holly leaves in back, toy soldier in center, one pine tree at each side of soldier, and a candy cane at each side of opening.

8. *To decorate the teddy bear igloo,* glue a large gift in center of igloo and glue teddy bear on top of it. Glue three holly leaves on each side of bear, one small gift at right front of bear, and one instrument at left front.

9. *To finish each igloo,* cut a 6-inch piece of ribbon. Use pink for the angel, white for the toy soldier, and red for the teddy bear. Form it into a hanging loop, knot ends together, and glue knot to top of igloo. Use remaining ribbon to make a small bow of the same color and glue it to front of knot.

FEATHER ANGEL

By Chere Brodsky

MATERIALS: FEATHER ANGEL

- 2 x 3-inch Styrofoam cone
- White maribou feathers *, one package
- White felt, 3-inch square
- 25mm pink wooden beads
- Yellow curly chenille, ½ yard
- ⅛-inch gold metallic braid ribbon, ⅛ yard
- ½ x ¾-inch gold-tone harp mounted on wire
- Felt-tip markers: black, red
- Thick white craft glue *
- Miscellaneous items: rustproof straight pins; scissors; toothpicks; pencil

* Zucker Feather Products feathers, and Aleene's Tacky Glue were used in the sample project.

1. Trace around the base of the cone onto felt, cut out, and glue to base.

2. Using the toothpick, apply glue to the inside curve of one feather's quill. Attach feather around base of cone, butting it against felt. Repeat to cover remainder of area around base. Continue to glue and wrap feathers in this manner two-thirds of the way up cone, gently pulling the plumage of the preceding feather down to place the next feather's quill close to it.

3. To make her hair, apply glue to back half of head bead. Starting at center back, coil the chenille around head to cover glue. Cut a 5½-inch piece of chenille and glue center across forehead; curl under 1 inch on each end and glue end to each side of head to form curls. Cut a tiny piece of chenille and glue in place for bangs.

Tie ribbon into a bow and glue to side of head.

4. To make the face, use the red marker to draw two small circles for cheeks, then smudge them with your finger. Also make a small circle for the mouth. Use the black marker to make closed eyes and eyelashes above cheeks. See photo.

Glue head to top of cone.

5. Following Step 2, finish wrapping cone with feathers, lifting hair curls out of the way.

Apply glue to one long feather's quill and glue around back of head, beginning at one side of neck and ending at the other.

6. Push wire of harp into body front, one-third of the way down.

BRAIDED RIBBON CANDY CANE

By Sheryl Johnson

MATERIALS: BRAIDED RIBBON CANDY CANE

- ³⁄₁₆-inch satin picot ribbon: red, white, 1 yard each; green 6 inches
- 3mm pearl beads, four
- 18-gauge wire, 7½ inches
- White craft glue
- Miscellaneous items: scissors; ruler

1. Glue one end of white ribbon slightly overlapping one end of red ribbon to make one long piece; let dry.

2. Lay ribbon horizontally with white end at left and red end at right; mentally number the left end No. 1 and the right end No. 2. Cross No. 1 over No. 2 about 1 inch from glued center to form a loop. See the Step 2 illustration.

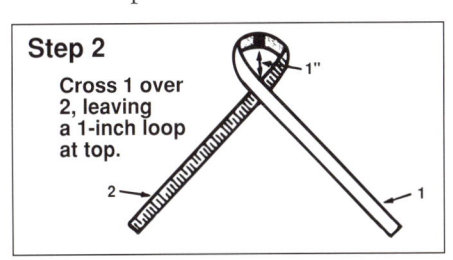

Step 2
Cross 1 over 2, leaving a 1-inch loop at top.

3. Using your right hand, fold No. 1 forward on top of itself to make a flat loop. Push it under No. 2 and up through the other loop from back to front. See the Step 3a illustration. Pull top of loop formed, then No. 2 gently until lower loop is closed snugly with upper loop laying flat. See the Step 3b illustration.

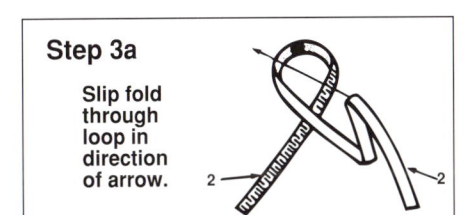

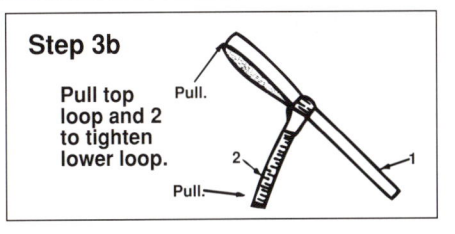

Step 3a
Slip fold through loop in direction of arrow.

Step 3b
Pull top loop and 2 to tighten lower loop.

4. Using your left hand, fold No. 2 forward on top of itself to make a flat loop. Push it under No. 1 and up through other loop from back to front.

39

Pull top of loop formed, then No. 1 gently until lower loop is closed snugly with upper loop laying flat.

5. Repeat Steps 3 and 4 alternately until braid is 7½ inches long. Make the last loop using end No. 1.

6. To end braid, pull end No. 1 through No. 2 loop then pull No. 2 so loop is snug against No. 1. Cut off No. 1 approximately ½ inch beyond braid, fold it to the wrong side, and glue to braid. Cut off No. 2 approximately ⅛ inch below loop and glue it inside the loop it exits from. See the Step 6 illustration.

Step 6

Pull 1 through 2, cut, and glue to back. Cut 2 and glue inside loop.

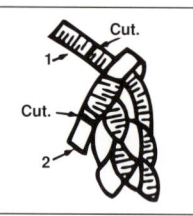

7. Run the wire up through the braid, hiding it under loops. Form into a cane shape.

8. Tie green ribbon into a bow and glue 2 inches from bottom of candy cane. Glue the beads close together over bow knot.

RIBBON LOOPS

By Lois Pritzlaff

1. *To make the lamb,* follow the Cutting Graph on page 42 to cut two lamb shapes from plastic canvas.

Thread the needle with an 18- to 24-inch length of ribbon and, referring to the Stitch Graph, stitch the sheep white and the marked areas black. To stitch, make a half cross stitch, leaving a ³⁄₁₆-inch loop on top. Keep loops even and ribbon untwisted on the right side. *Note:* If desired, make loops over small knitting needle for consistent size. To begin and end a ribbon piece, catch the tail under three stitches on the wrong side. Use the needle to lift any loops that are not flat on the wrong side. Reverse the second sheep canvas and repeat.

2. Use a toothpick to apply glue lightly to wrong sides of sheep; press together, aligning holes. Let dry.

3. Overcast the edges using white ribbon. On outside corners, make one stitch directly over corner and another stitch on each side. To end ribbon, stitch over beginning stitch and use pliers to bring needle out back. Put a dot of glue at base; trim when dry.

Use a needle to add a loop of transparent nylon thread to the top for hanging.

4. Thread needle with a 9-inch piece of plaid ribbon. Push needle from front to back at point indicated by X on graph. Thread ribbon through bell, wrap loosely under head and knot ends at the starting point. Trim ends and glue knot between loops. Tie bow with remaining

MATERIALS: RIBBON LOOPS

For the Lamb

7-mesh white plastic canvas, two 4x5-inch pieces

⅛-inch double-face satin ribbon: white, 16 yards; black, 1½ yards

⅜-inch red plaid taffeta, ½ yard

½-inch gold bell

5mm wiggle eyes, one pair

For the Horse

7-mesh red plastic canvas, two 4½ x 5-inch pieces

⅛-inch double-face satin ribbon: red, 11 yards; white, 6½ yards; royal blue, 1 yard

Felt: red, royal blue, small piece of each

³⁄₁₆-inch wood dowel, 4 inches

10mm wiggle eyes, one pair

For the Stocking

7-mesh red plastic canvas, two 5x6-inch pieces

⅛-inch double-face satin ribbon: red, 21½ yards; green, 5½ yards

For the Wreath

7-mesh green plastic canvas, two 5½-inch squares

⅛-inch ribbon: double-face green satin, 10½ yards; gold grosgrain, 6½ yards

Miscellaneous items: white craft glue; scissors; large tapestry needle; pliers; toothpick; pencil; transparent nylon sewing thread; small knitting needle (optional)

Note: Cutting and Stitch Graphs are given on page 42.

ribbon. Trim ends and glue over knot. Glue wiggle eyes in place.

5. *To make the horse,* repeat Steps 1 and 2, using red ribbon for the face and neck and white for the marked areas. Following Step 3, overcast edges with red ribbon; insert dowel at arrow on graph to protrude 2⅝ inches. Wrap ribbon tightly around base, and continue wrapping edges.

6. Cut a 7-inch piece of blue ribbon and wrap over nose, knotting and gluing under chin; trim ends. Cut a 6-inch piece of ribbon and make a bow; set aside. Wrap remaining ribbon over top of head and tie over knot under chin. Loop ends down and tie around dowel, knotting ends in both front and back. Glue knots and trim ends. Glue bow over knot on back of dowel.

7. Using the patterns in the Step 7 illustration, cut two outer ears from red felt and two inner ears from blue felt. Glue inner ears to outer, and one to each side of head at top, attaching in front of blue ribbon. Glue on wiggle eyes.

Step 7

Use these full-size patterns to cut inner and outer ears.

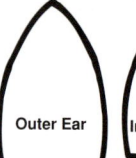

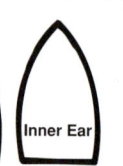

Outer Ear   Inner Ear

8. *To make the stocking,* follow Steps 1 through 3 to stitch the marked areas green and remaining areas red. Tie a small green bow and glue near top on front.

9. *To make the wreath,* follow Steps 1 through 3, stitching the front wreath piece with gold ribbon and the back piece with green. Wrap the edges using green ribbon. Tie a small green bow and glue to center top on front of wreath.

RIBBON ANGELS

By Lois Pritzlaff

MATERIALS: RIBBON ANGELS

For Each Angel

20mm wooden bead head with prepainted face

Chenille: 12-inch pink, 6-inch gold metallic stems, one each; curly, any color, 9½ inches

⅞-inch sheer stripe ribbon, 2 yards

Fine metallic gold cord, ½ yard

White craft glue

Miscellaneous items: wirecutters; compass or other sharp, pointed instrument; small piece of corrugated cardboard; ruler; and scissors

1. To make the angel's body and legs, cut an 8-inch piece from pink chenille stem and bend it in half. Glue folded end in bottom of bead head, pushing stem up to top.

2. To make the arms, bend 4-inch remainder of pink chenille stem in half and dab glue inside bend. Place bend at back of body slightly below head and wrap each end around the front to opposite sides.

3. Working on corrugated cardboard, use compass point to poke holes in center of ribbon every 3 inches, beginning 1½ inches from one end.

Thread ribbon onto body through holes, forming a loop between every two holes and turning body ⅓ of a turn each time a loop is added. See the Step 3 illustration.

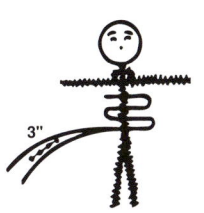

Press loops together as needed to leave 1½ inches of stem at bottom. Glue around last hole to secure it to chenille.

4. Cut curly chenille into ¼-inch pieces and glue around head for hair. Cut 3½ inches from metallic gold chenille stem, form into a circle, and twist ends together. Glue to top of angel's head, tilting slightly forward, for a halo.

5. Thread gold cord through halo and tie ends together for a hanger.

Bend arms and legs as desired.

Step 3

Insert stems through ribbon holes, looping ribbon and turning body 1/3 of a turn between holes.

VICTORIAN DOILY

By CuSToM Creations

MATERIALS: VICTORIAN DOILY

2½-inch white satin ball

10-inch ecru doily

⅛-inch rose satin ribbon, 1 yard

Tiny pink rosebuds, three

Spray of pearls

Baby's breath

Green floral tape

Miscellaneous items: scissors; ruler

1. Cut 12 inches of ribbon and thread through ball's hanger. Knot ends together near hanger to make a loop.

2. Gather doily up around ball. Tie remaining ribbon in a double knot around gathers.

3. Cluster rosebuds, pearl spray, and baby's breath together. Trim ends evenly to 2 inches and tape them together.

Position cluster on ribbon knot and tie ribbon in a bow. Trim ribbon ends to desired length and spread cluster.

RIBBON AND LACE

By Linda Lindgren

MATERIALS: RIBBON AND LACE

Ribbon: 1¼-inch plaid, 1½ yards; ¼-inch green velvet with gold edge, 2¼ yards

¾-inch white flat beading lace, 1½ yards

3-inch Styrofoam ball

½-inch red plastic berries, two

1-inch red craft bird

White craft glue

Miscellaneous items: ruler; scissors; straight pins

1. Pinning ends at top and overlapping and pinning edges, cover ball with plaid ribbon.

2. Cut lace into four equal pieces. Weave green ribbon through each piece and cut ends even with lace. Spacing strips evenly and pinning ends at top, cover ribbon seams with lace.

3. Cut 9 inches of green ribbon and pin ends to top for hanging loop. Cut remaining ribbon in half, tie pieces into small bows, and pin to top.

4. Glue small red bird and berries to center top.

LACE ANGEL

By CuSToM Creations

MATERIALS: LACE ANGEL

Ecru flat lace: 2⅜-inch, 12 inches; 1⅜-inch, 15 inches

⅛-inch rose satin ribbon, 1 yard

20mm natural wood bead

26-gauge wire, 9 inches

Miscellaneous items: ruler; scissors; needle; matching thread; fine-tip black permanent marker

1. To make the skirt, cut 12 inches of ribbon and weave it through the center holes of the 2⅜-inch lace. Do not gather or tie.

2. Tightly gather top edge of lace and knot. Sew lace ends together from the top down. Gather with the ribbon to adjust fullness of skirt. Bring ribbon ends to inside of skirt and knot; trim excess.

3. To make the collar, cut 9 inches of 1⅜-inch lace. Gather top edge tightly and knot. Sew ends together.

4. To make the hat, gather top edge of remaining 1⅜-inch lace. Knot ends of an 8-inch piece of ribbon together to make a loop. Arrange gathers of lace around knotted end and sew lace ends together, catching ribbon with a few stitches.

5. Follow the Step 5 illustration to draw face on bead with black marker. Let dry.

Step 5

Draw a face on the bead with a black marker.

6. Fold wire in half. Insert through top center of hat, catching both sides of lace through the bead, the collar, then the skirt. Make sure all seams are at the back. Twist wire ends together under skirt and trim ends.

PATTERNS

Wreath

Horse

Lamb

Ribbon Loops Cutting and Stitch Graphs

Stocking

Lace Cornucopias Stitch Graphs and Color Keys

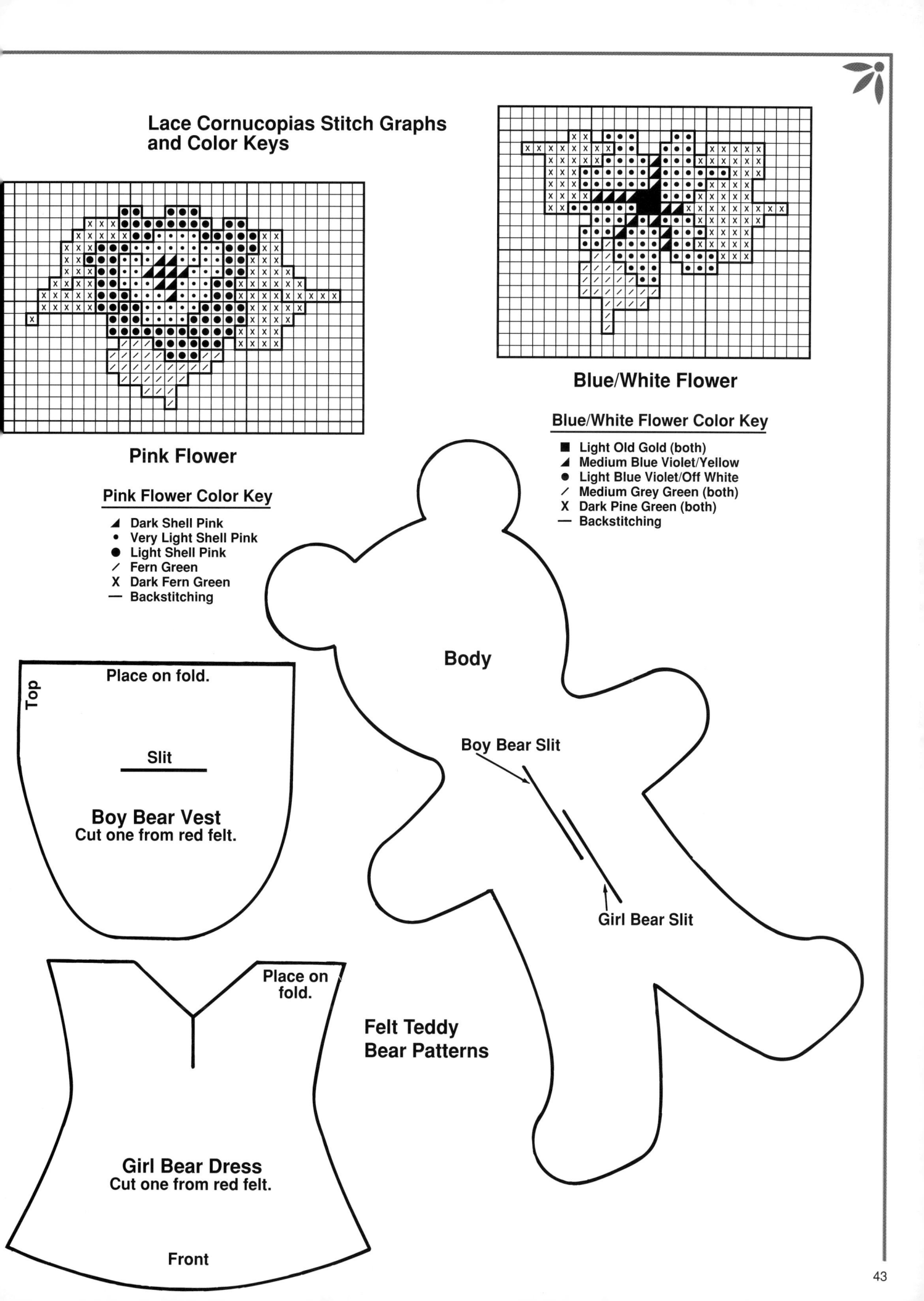

Pink Flower

Pink Flower Color Key
- ▲ Dark Shell Pink
- • Very Light Shell Pink
- ● Light Shell Pink
- ╱ Fern Green
- X Dark Fern Green
- — Backstitching

Blue/White Flower

Blue/White Flower Color Key
- ■ Light Old Gold (both)
- ▲ Medium Blue Violet/Yellow
- ● Light Blue Violet/Off White
- ╱ Medium Grey Green (both)
- X Dark Pine Green (both)
- — Backstitching

Felt Teddy Bear Patterns

Body

Boy Bear Slit

Girl Bear Slit

Boy Bear Vest
Cut one from red felt.
Top
Place on fold.
Slit

Girl Bear Dress
Cut one from red felt.
Place on fold.
Front

43

Cross Stitch Heirlooms

This appealing array of 18 cross-stitched ornaments captures a variety of holiday moods, from peaceful star-framed nativity scenes to bold designs enhanced with gold metallic thread and braid.

Reminiscent of story-book holidays, the miniature **Family Stockings** set provides the perfect place for tucking away Christmas-morning surprises for each family member. Time-conscious crafters will find the bouncy red and white snowflakes trimmed in white lace can be made in a twinkling, as can our cross-stitch **Poinsettia**. And because grandmas and grandpas are so much a part of the holiday season, we've included a set of red-framed ornaments to honor them.

Whether you lovingly hang your hand-stitched treasures on your own tree or share them with others, the ornaments included here are certain to be cherished for years to come.

Editor's note: To add a touch of holiday sparkle to any design, add one or two strands of coordinating metallic blending filament to your floss when stitching.

FAMILY STOCKINGS

By Nancy C. Hoerner

MATERIALS: FAMILY STOCKINGS

For Each Stocking

14-count ecru Aida cloth, 6-inch square

Unbleached muslin, 6-inch square

⅛-inch satin ribbon, color to match floss, 6 inches

Fusible web, ½ x 6 inches

No. 24 tapestry needle

For "Father"

Embroidery floss: red (DMC 304, Anchor 47); green (DMC 319, Anchor 246); gray (DMC 844, Anchor 401); white (Anchor 2)

3-ply gold metallic thread

For "Mother"

Embroidery floss: green (DMC 319, Anchor 246); dark pink (DMC 223, Anchor 894); pink (DMC 224, Anchor 893); yellow (DMC 677, Anchor 886); black (DMC 310, Anchor 403); white (Anchor 2)

3-ply gold metallic thread

For "Sister"

Embroidery floss: green (DMC 319, Anchor 246); dark pink (DMC 223, Anchor 894); pink (DMC 224, Anchor 893); white (Anchor 2)

⅛-inch dark pink satin ribbon, 4 inches

¼-inch white flat buttons, three

For "Brother"

Embroidery floss: red (DMC 304, Anchor 47); green (DMC 319, Anchor 246); black (DMC 310, Anchor 403)

For "Puppy"

Embroidery floss: red (DMC 304, Anchor 47); green (DMC 319, Anchor 246); gray (DMC 844, Anchor 401); brown (DMC 434, Anchor 309); beige (DMC 842, Anchor 376); black (DMC 310, Anchor 403)

3-ply silver metallic thread

For "Kitty"

Embroidery floss: red (DMC 304, Anchor 47); green (DMC 319, Anchor 246); gray (DMC 844, Anchor 401)

⅜-inch gold jingle bell

Miscellaneous items: scissors; iron; sewing machine; large tapestry needle

Note: A Stitch Graph and Color Key are given on page 52.

1. Center design on Aida cloth and stitch outline of stocking using one strand of beige floss. Refer to the Stitch Graph and Color Key on page 52 and the General Cross Stitch Instructions on page 95 to cross stitch each design with two strands of floss.

2. *To stitch "Father,"* backstitch around collar and tie with one strand of gray and stripes with one strand of green. Make tie tack with a French knot using gold thread wrapped around needle two times.

3. *To stitch "Mother,"* backstitch stripes with two strands of dark pink and around collar with one strand of dark pink. *Note:* Symbols along lower edge of collar indicate backstitching. Use one strand of green for leaves and stems and one strand of three-ply gold around brooch.

4. *To stitch "Sister,"* backstitch around collar and down center front with one strand of dark pink. Sew three buttons along center front. Tie bow with dark pink ribbon and sew at center neck edge.

5. *To stitch "Brother,"* backstitch the numerals with two strands of black and around the collar with one strand of black. Backstitch the shoulder line with two strands of red.

6. *To stitch "Puppy,"* stitch large cross stitches in the center of the collar using red for the bottom stitch and green for the top stitch. Use one strand of black to backstitch around dog tag. Use two strands of black to backstitch "K9."

7. *To stitch "Kitty,"* stitch large cross stitches along center of collar using green for the bottom stitch and red for the top stitch. Use two strands of gray wrapped two times for the toe French knots. Attach jingle bell to collar.

8. When stitching is completed, press with a warm iron. With rights sides of muslin and stocking together, stitch around outline, allowing ½ inch at the top for hem. Trim seams, clip curves, turn, and press. Turn under top hem at outline and secure with fusible web.

9. Thread corresponding ribbon on tapestry needle and attach to the stocking at the top back. Tie a knot to form a loop for hanging.

RED FRAME ORNAMENTS

By Carole Rodgers

MATERIALS: RED FRAME ORNAMENTS

For All Ornaments

No. 26 tapestry needle

For the Choir Girls

18-count white Aida cloth, 3 x 4 inches

Embroidery floss: * light brown (783); green (700); dark green (890); red (666); dark brown (938); yellow (725); flesh (951); white

Red church ornament frame *, 2 x 3½ inches

For the Teddy Bear

18-count white Aida cloth, 3 x 4 inches

Embroidery floss: * green (700); red (666); dark red (498); dark green (890); black (310); light brown (435); brown (433); dark brown (801); white

Red oval ornament frame *, 2¼ x 2¾ inches

For the Grandma and Grandpa

14-count white Aida cloth, 3½-inch square per ornament

Embroidery floss: * red (666); green (700); yellow (444)

Two red 2½-inch round ornament frames *

Miscellaneous items: scissors; iron; terrycloth towel

Note: Stitch Graphs and Color Key are given on page 49.

* DMC embroidery floss and New Berlin frames were used in the sample projects.

1. Refer to the General Cross Stitch Instructions on page 95 and the Stitch Graph and Color Key on page 49 to stitch each design with two strands of floss. Count up and over to the top left stitch to begin stitching.

2. Backstitch the choir girls with one strand of brown floss and the teddy bear with one strand of black floss. Using two strands of floss, work the backstitches on the stars of the "Grandma" ornament with red and the letters with green. Backstitch the letters of the "Grandpa" ornament with red.

3. To frame each piece, remove mounting insert from frame. Center finished work over insert and press in place. Trim excess cloth and snap into frame.

STARS

By Darla J. Fanton

MATERIALS: STARS

For Each Project

14-count white Aida cloth, 5-inch square

Gold metallic thread *

No. 24 tapestry needle

3½-inch gold star frame *

White craft glue

For the Shepherd With Baby

Embroidery floss: * black (310); light blue (794); medium blue (798); yellow gold (743); brown (433); beige (739); redwood (300); cherrywood (420); flesh (754); white

For the Angels With Baby

Embroidery floss: * black (310); light blue (794); yellow gold (743); brown (433); dark pink (962); cherrywood (420); flesh (754); white

Miscellaneous items: scissors; mild soap; terrycloth towel; iron

Note: A Stitch Graph and Color Key are given on page 50.

* DMC floss and metallic thread and New Berlin frames were used in the sample projects.

1. Using two strands of floss, refer to the General Cross Stitch Instructions on page 95 and the Stitch Graph and Color Key on page 50 to stitch each design.

2. Backstitch the star and Baby's hair with one strand of metallic thread. Work all remaining backstitches and one-wrap French knots with one strand of black.

3. Center and glue design on mounting board provided with frame. Trim excess fabric and insert in frame.

METALLIC THREAD ORNAMENTS

By Lois Winston

MATERIALS: METALLIC THREAD ORNAMENTS

14-count white Aida cloth, three 6-inch squares

Embroidery floss: * carmine rose dark (44); carmine (47); juniper dark (218); spring green dark (239); topaz dark (308)

Metallic blending filament: * crimson (031); red (003); green (008); chartreuse (015); gold (002HL)

4-inch round self-adhesive mounting board, three

⅛-inch flat gold metallic braid, 2 yards

1¼-inch double-loop gold metallic braid, 2 yards

Red or green adhesive felt, three 4-inch squares

White craft glue *

No. 24 tapestry needle

Miscellaneous items: scissors; pencil; tape measure; masking tape

Note: Stitch Graphs and Color Key are given on pages 50-51.

* Susan Bates embroidery floss, Balger metallic blending filament, and Aleene's Tacky Glue were used in the sample projects.

1. Refer to the General Cross Stitch Instructions on page 95 and the Stitch Graph and Color Key on pages 50-51 to stitch each design with two strands of floss.

Use two strands of floss with two strands of blending filament for all stitching. Knot the blending filament to the needle first as follows: Cut a piece twice the length needed. Fold in half and thread the loop through the eye of the needle. Pull the filament through the loop and tighten the loop at the end of the eye. Thread the needle with floss.

2. Work in rows beginning from the left, completing each color or section. *Note:* The outer star of design No. 1 is the same for designs 2 and 3.

3. To finish each design, trace the mounting board onto the paper backing of the felt. Cut out felt circle. Center and mount stitched design onto mounting board according to manufacturer's instructions.

4. Apply a thin line of glue around the back of the mounted ornament. Starting at the bottom, attach the gold double-loop braid, letting the loops extend beyond the circle. Trim excess and let dry.

5. Cut a 9-inch piece of flat gold braid. Fold it in half and press the ends to the back of the ornament. Cover the back with a felt circle.

6. Apply a thin line of glue to the outer front edges. Starting at the bottom, wrap flat gold braid around the edge, slightly overlapping the ends. Trim excess.

POINSETTIA

By Chris Middleton

MATERIALS: POINSETTIA

18-count beige Aida cloth, 5-inch square

Embroidery floss: * dark pink (335); light pink (899); red (326); green (320)

Yellow glass beads, five

Lightweight paper twist *, 1 yard

Mediumweight paper twist *, 2½ yards

1/16-inch rose stain ribbon, 2½ yards

Self-adhesive white felt, one 3½-inch circle

White craft glue

Miscellaneous items: tapestry needle; scissors; aluminum soft-drink can; terrycloth towel; iron; ruler

Note: A Stitch Graph and Color Key are given on page 49.

* DMC embroidery floss and MPR Creative Twist™ were used for the sample project

1. Using two strands of floss, refer to the General Cross Stitch Instructions on page 95 and the Stitch Graph and Color Key on page 49 to stitch the design.

Work the backstitching with one strand of floss.

2. Using one strand of dark pink floss, attach the five yellow beads in the center with half cross stitches.

3. To make the frame, wrap the medium twist around an aluminum soft-drink can. Slip off can, holding rings together. With other hand, slip half of the 1 yard of light twist through center of rings. Tie a knot with the two ends,

47

leaving tails of equal length on each side. Wrap tails in opposite directions around the wreath, ending back at original knot. Weave ends under knot to hold.

4. To make a tassel, cut nine 6-inch pieces of ribbon. Fold them in half together and tie near fold with end of one piece. Slide tassel to center of 1 yard of ribbon. Wrap ribbon around frame so ends meet at the top; tie in a bow.

5. Center and glue back of wreath over cross stitch design. Let dry. Adhere felt to back of wreath. Trim fabric and felt even with frame.

SNOWFLAKES

By Kathleen Hurley

MATERIALS: SNOWFLAKES

14-count red Aida cloth, 10x14 inches

White linen, 10x14 inches

White embroidery floss

⅝-inch white flat cluny lace, 1½ yards

⅛-inch white satin ribbon, 1 yard

Polyester fiberfill

Miscellaneous items: tracing paper; white and lead pencils; scissors; compass; ruler; tapestry and sewing needles; white sewing thread

Note: Stitch Graphs are given on page 51.

1. Divide the Aida cloth into four 5x7-inch sections with basting stitches.

2. Using two strands of floss, refer to the General Cross Stitch Instructions on page 95 and the Stitch Graph on page 51 to stitch each design.

3. Using the compass and a white pencil, draw a 3-inch diameter circle around each design, then a 3¾-inch circle for the seam allowance.

4. Cut lace into four 13-inch lengths. Gather each piece to 11 inches. Stitch ends together. Baste gathered edge to inside pencil line on each ornament.

5. Cut ribbon into four 8-inch pieces. Fold each one in half and tack ends to seam allowance.

6. Cut out snowflakes along outer circles.

7. Using a lead pencil, draw four 3-inch circles, then 3¾-inch circles outside them on the linen. Cut out along outer pencil lines.

8. Pin one each linen and Aida cloth circles right sides together with ribbon and lace extending to center. Stitch around inner circle, leaving an opening. Turn, stuff, and slipstitch opening. Repeat for remaining ornaments.

Editor's note: For a special touch, add crystal seed beads as you stitch.

PATTERNS

Red Frame Ornaments Stitch Graphs and Color Keys

Grandma and Grandpa

Grandma and Grandpa Color Key

- ● Green
- + Red
- ○ Yellow
- — Backstitching

Teddy Bear Color Key

- ○ Green
- + Red
- / Dark Red
- I Dark Green
- □ White
- ■ Black
- − Light Brown
- ● Brown
- X Dark Brown
- — Backstitching

Choir Girls Color Key

- I Light Brown
- □ White
- ○ Green
- X Dark Green
- + Red
- ● Dark Red
- / Dark Brown
- − Yellow
- U Flesh
- — Backstitching

Teddy Bear

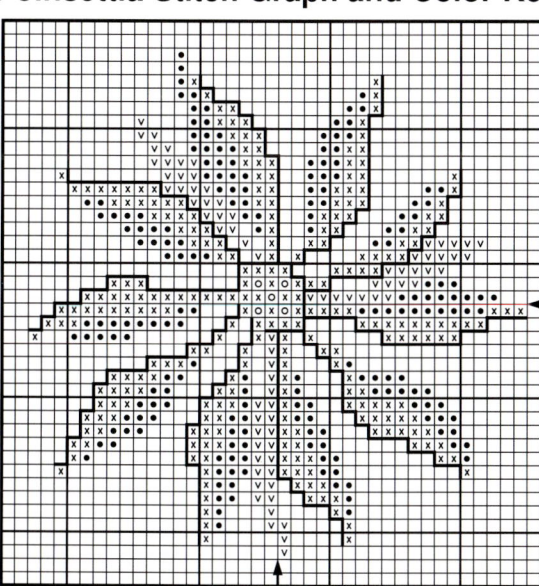

Choir Girls

Poinsettia Stitch Graph and Color Key

Color Key

- X Dark Pink
- ● Light Pink
- V Green
- ○ Yellow Bead
- — Red Backstitchin

49

Stars Stitch Graphs and Color Key

Angels With Baby

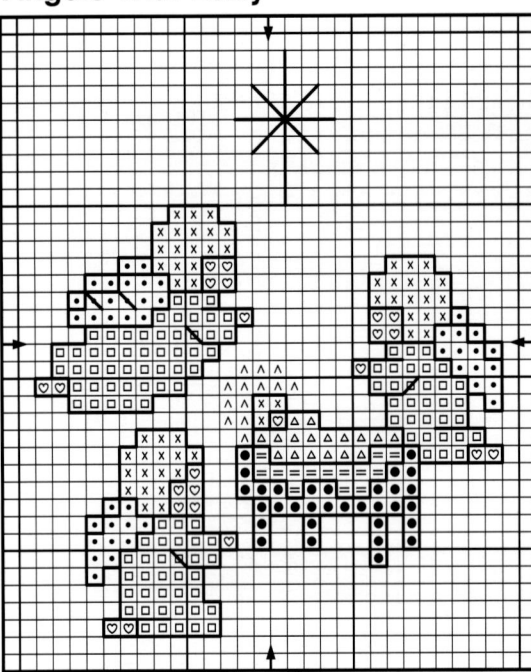

Shepherd With Baby

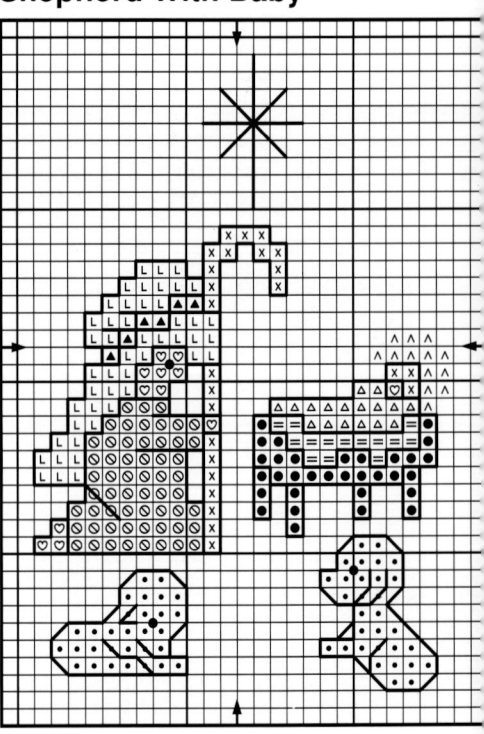

Color Key

- △ Light Blue (794)
- = Yellow Gold (743)
- ● Brown (433)
- L Beige (739)
- ▲ Redwood (300)
- ◒ Medium Blue (798)
- X Cherrywood (420)
- ♡ Flesh (754)
- ∧ Gold Metallic
- • White
- □ Dark Pink (962)
- — Backstitching
- ✦ French Knot

Metallic Thread Ornaments Stitch Graphs and Color Key

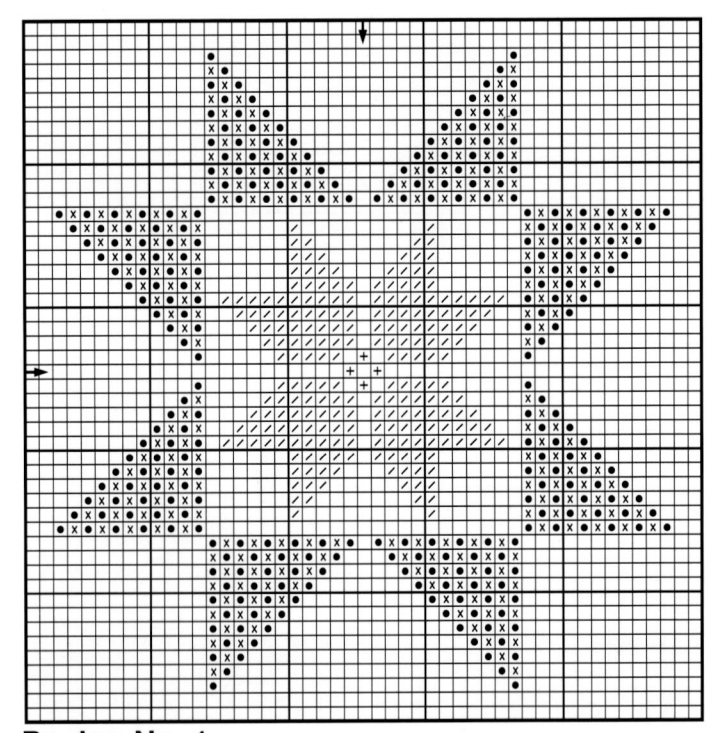

Color Key

- X Carmine Rose Dark Floss and Crimson Filament
- ● Juniper Dark Floss and Green Filament
- ╱ Carmine Floss and Red Filament
- ○ Spring Green Dark Floss and Chartreuse Filament
- + Topaz Dark Floss and Gold Filament

Design No. 1

50

Cross Stitch Snowflakes Stitch Graphs

Metallic Thread Ornaments Stitch Graphs

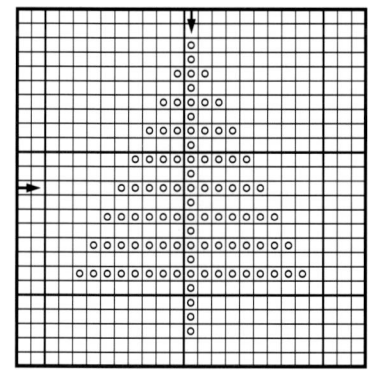

Design No. 2

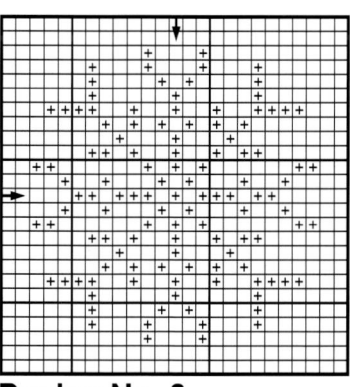

Design No. 3

Family Stockings Stitch Graphs and Color Key

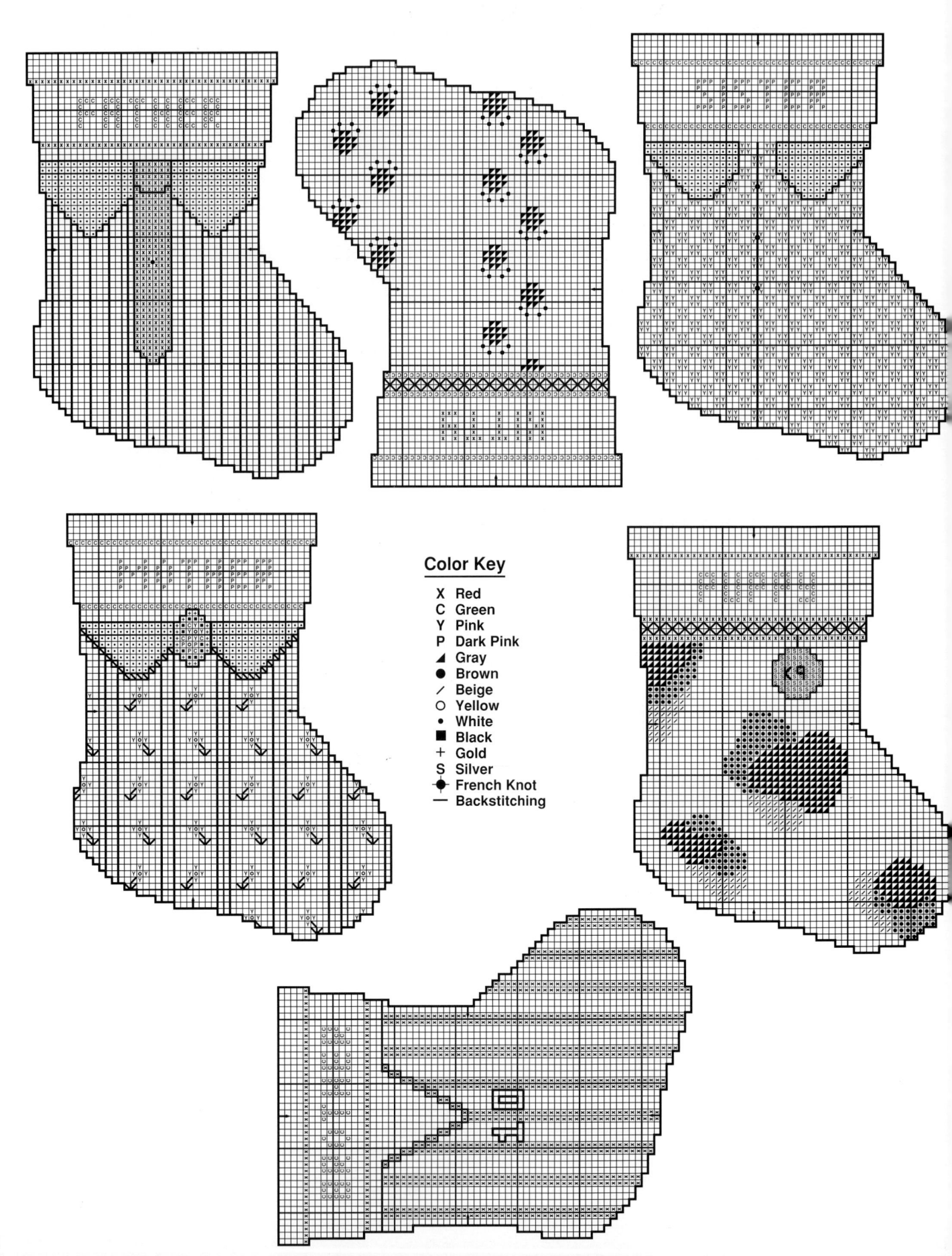

Color Key

- X Red
- C Green
- Y Pink
- P Dark Pink
- ◢ Gray
- ● Brown
- ╱ Beige
- ○ Yellow
- · White
- ■ Black
- + Gold
- S Silver
- ⬤ French Knot
- — Backstitching

Especially for Kids

Little hands are always eager to share in the Christmas decorating spirit, and your child would be proud to hang one of his very own hand-crafted ornaments on the holiday tree. These ornaments range from very easy, suitable for preschoolers, to more challenging for advanced young crafters. Mostly, though, these projects are fun and simple to make.

Let your kids try their hands at the colorful **Pom Pom Cookie Cutters**, pretty **Paper Punch** ornaments, or fun-to-watch **Sun Catchers**. The elegant **Paper Doily Angel** only looks difficult to make, she's really just a creative combination of three doilies. Beginning cross stitchers will delight in stitching the **Simmering Spice Bag**, while Rudolph lovers will have fun assembling and using the **Rudolph and Rhoda Reindeer Clip-Ons**.

Kids will especially enjoy twisting and rolling the **Christmas Angels** made with metallic and iridescent paper twist. But don't forget, little hands also like to paint, and the attractive **Marbleized Wooden Cutouts** provide a creative lesson in using paints. There are so many kids projects to choose from that you may wonder where to begin!

PAPER PUNCH

By Cindy Groom Harry

MATERIALS: PAPER PUNCH

Lightweight paper: 4x5 inches each: dark green, light green *for the tree;* gold, yellow *for the bell;* dark blue, light blue *for the angel;* medium green, light green *for the wreath;* black, white, 4-inch square each *for the bear;* white, red, 3x5-inch piece each *for the candy cane*

⅛-inch satin ribbon, ⅓ yard *per ornament:* yellow *for the tree;* green *for the bell and candy cane;* white *for the angel;* red *for the wreath and bear*

White craft glue *

Miscellaneous items: paper punch; pencil; tracing paper; transfer paper

Note: Full-size patterns are given on page 62.

* Aleene's Tacky Glue was used in the sample projects.

1. Trace, transfer, and cut the patterns on page 62 from the appropriate colors of paper. Inside lines are for the top paper punched piece; outside lines are for the back mounting piece.

2. Using a paper punch, punch holes in the top piece of paper only, as indicated by the circles on the pattern.

Center and lightly glue punched piece onto back mounting piece.

3. To finish each ornament, cut a 3-inch piece of ribbon, fold it into a loop, and glue ends to the top back. Tie remaining ribbon into a bow and glue to the ornament as indicated by the X on the pattern.

SUN CATCHER

By Carol Mittal

MATERIALS: SUN CATCHER

Heavyweight construction paper, posterboard, or vinyl wallpaper, choice of colors: two 6-inch squares per small snowflake, two 8-inch squares per large snowflake

Colored cellophane

Craft glue

Heavy black thread

Wire ornament hangers

Miscellaneous items: pencil; sharp pointed scissors; tracing paper

Note: Full-size patterns are given on page 63.

1. Trace patterns on page 63 and cut two per ornament from paper.

2. *To make each ornament,* cut pieces of cellophane large enough to cover the cut out areas of the snowflakes. Place small dots of glue around each cut out area on the wrong sides of the snowflakes and press cellophane pieces into place. *Note:* Use glue sparingly so it doesn't run onto the cellophane window.

With wrong sides together and aligning edges and cut out areas, attach snowflakes by applying a small amount of glue to the wrong side of one snowflake. Let dry.

3. Referring to the pattern, cut a small hole in the ornament at the X. Add a wire hanger through the hole.

4. *To make a mobile,* make one large and two small ornaments. Referring to the pattern, make two holes at the bottom of the large snowflake as indicated by the Xs. Cut three 12-inch pieces of black thread. Thread one piece through the hole at the top of the large ornament, knotting ends to make a hanging loop. Attach small snowflakes with loops of black thread tied between holes of small snowflakes and bottom holes of large snowflake.

POM POM COOKIE CUTTERS

By Cindy Groom Harry

1. *To make each ornament,* apply a line of glue around the inside of the cutter, ¼ inch from the cutting edge. For the bottom layer of pompoms, place cutting side down on plastic wrap and gently press pompoms along cutter edge. See the Step 1 illustration. To fill the middle of the bottom layer, apply a small amount of glue to sides of pompoms and press into middle to fill. Refer to individual instructions for color placement.

Step 1
Glue along inside of cutter, ¼ inch from edge.

Repeat for the top layer of pompoms, placing line of glue ¼ inch from smooth top edge, and repeating color order.

To add a hanger, cut a 3-inch piece of ribbon, form a loop, and glue ends of the loop to the top back between the inside edge of the cutter and a pompom.

2. *To make the bear,* fill with pompoms, add loop, and tie remaining ribbon in a bow around neck.

3. *To make the candy cane,* alternate red and white pompoms, beginning and ending with red. Add loop and tie remaining ribbon in a bow around curve of cane.

MATERIALS: POM POM COOKIE CUTTERS

For the Bear
2 ½ x 3-inch bear cookie cutter with open center
¾-inch brown pompoms, 28
⅛-inch red satin ribbon, ½ yard

For the Candy Cane
2 ¼ x 3 ½-inch candy cane cookie cutter with open center
¾-inch pompoms: red, 10; white, eight
⅛-inch green satin ribbon, ½ yard

For the Tree
3 x 4-inch tree cookie cutter with open center
¾-inch pompoms: yellow, two; brown, two; green, 48
⅛-inch red satin ribbon, ⅔ yard

For the Star
3-inch star cookie cutter with open center
¾-inch pompoms: yellow, 12; gold, 10
⅛-inch yellow satin ribbon, ¼ yard

For the Candle
3 ¼ x 4-inch cookie cutter with open center
¾-inch pompoms: green, six; yellow, four; gold, 18
⅛-inch yellow satin ribbon, ⅔ yard

For the Bell
2 ¼ x 2 ¾-inch bell cookie cutter with open center
¾-inch pompoms: red, 20; green, two
⅛-inch green satin ribbon, ½ yard

For the Rocking Horse
2 ½-inch rocking horse cookie cutter with open center
¾-inch pompoms: white, 16; red, 10
⅛-inch white satin ribbon, ⅔ yard

For the Santa
2 ½ x 4 ¾-inch Santa cookie cutter with open center
¾-inch pompoms: green, 10; red, 14; white, 18; pink, two
⅛-inch green satin ribbon, ½ yard
White craft glue *

Miscellaneous items: plastic wrap; scissors

* Aleene's Tacky Glue was used for the sample projects.

4. *To make the tree,* place a yellow pompom at the top, brown at the bottom, and fill in with green. Add loop; cut remaining ribbon into 6-inch pieces and tie into bows. Glue bows to front of the tree.

5. *To make the star,* place yellow pompoms in the points, add gold in between the yellow, and place a yellow pompom in the center. Add loop; tie remaining ribbon in bow and glue to front.

6. *To make the candle,* fill in base with gold pompoms, the candle stick with green, and the flame with yellow. Add loop; tie remaining ribbon around handle, making a bow at top front.

7. *To make the bell,* place green pompom at center bottom and fill in with red. Add loop; tie remaining ribbon in a bow around top of bell.

8. *To make the rocking horse,* place a row of white pompoms along the top edge of the horse. Make the legs by placing a row of white, red, and white pompoms in the middle. Place a row of red along the rocker. Add a loop of green ribbon; tie remaining green ribbon in a bow around neck. Cut white ribbon in half, make two bows, and glue to front at each end of the rocker.

9. *To make the Santa,* place white pompoms for his hat, beard, and coat trim; add pink for his face, red for his hat and coat, and green for his bag and boots. See the Step 9 illustration. Add

Step 9
Glue appropriate colors of pom poms in Santa cutter.
Color Key
1 White
2 Pink
3 Red
4 Green

loop; tie remaining ribbon in a bow around the hat top.

DOILY ANGEL

By Cindy Groom Harry

MATERIALS: DOILY ANGEL

8-inch paper doilies, solid center with 2-inch design border, three

⅛-inch mauve satin ribbon, ½ yard

White craft glue *

Stapler

Scissors

* Aleene's Tacky Glue was used in the sample project.

1. To make the angel's dress, fold one doily in half and curl into a cone with the design border at the bottom. Overlap edges slightly and staple twice, 2½ inches from lower edge of the cone.

2. For the wings, fold a doily in half. Beginning at the folded edge, make four ½-inch accordion folds, leaving the center curved edge unfolded. Staple in the center through all folds. See the Step 2 illustration.

Step 2

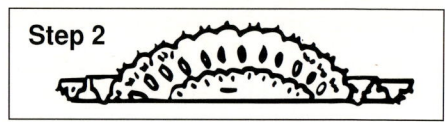

Begin at folded edge to make four folds.

Glue design side of the wings to the dress back, placing the folded edge ½ inch from the top of the cone covering the staples.

3. To make the head, cut the remaining doily in half. Cut along the 2-inch design border of one half; discard solid center and other half. With the remaining design border make a fan with ½-inch accordion folds on the inside curve and ¾-inch folds on the outside curve. See the Step 3 illustration. Staple through folds close to the lower edge of the fan.

Step 3

Beginning at straight edge, pleat head.

4. Cut ⅛-inch off the top of the dress and apply a dot of glue in the opening. Gently spread fan head and place stapled edge into dress opening.

5. Tie the ribbon in a bow and glue to the dress front at the base of the head.

SIMMERING SPICE BAG

By Nancy Hoerner and Suzanne Weyer

MATERIALS: SIMMERING SPICE BAG

For the Bag

18-count Aida cloth *, 5x11 inches

Embroidery floss: green (DMC 699/Anchor 923); red (DMC 304/Anchor 47)

Muslin, ⅛ yard

Needles: No. 24 tapestry, sewing

For the Spice Mixture

Whole cloves, ¼ cup

Cinnamon sticks, four

Orange, one half

Lemon, one half

Miscellaneous items: scissors; masking tape; sewing thread; ruler; sharp knife; embroidery hoop (optional)

Note: A Stitch Graph and Color Key are given on page 61.

* Fiddler's Lite fabric from Charles Craft Inc. was used for the sample project.

1. Tape the edges of the fabric to prevent raveling. Fold the Aida cloth in half width-wise to measure 5x5½ inches. Fold in half again in the opposite direction. Unfold and begin stitching the tree trunk on the second fold line, 20 squares up from the bottom.

2. Cut floss into 18-inch pieces and use two strands for all stitching. Cross stitch the trees and backstitch the letters, referring to the General Cross Stitch Instructions on page 95.

3. Carefully remove tape from edges. If necessary, soak needlework in cool water to soften the tape residue. Fringe ½ inch of each 5-inch side.

4. Fold Aida cloth in half widthwise, with the stitched design on the inside. With sewing thread, stitch the sides of he bag using a ½-inch seam allowance. Turn right side out.

5. Thread a 12-inch piece of six-strand red floss into the needle. Starting in the center front, 1 inch from the top edge, sew around bag using large stitches to form a drawstring.

6. To make a spice bag insert, cut a 4½ x 8-inch piece of muslin and fold in half widthwise. Using a ½-inch seam allowance, stitch the two side seams, leaving the top open. Turn right side out.

7. *Note:* Spice mixture will be enough for two bags. Prepare the spice mixture by quartering the orange and lemon; slice each very thin. Let them air dry or dehydrate in warm oven. Combine with cloves and broken cinnamon sticks. Fill spice bag with one-half of the mixture. Fold top edges of bag under ½ inch and slipstitch together. Place inside stitched bag, draw string to close, and tie ends in bow.

8. Add a gift card with the following instructions: Remove spice bag, place in saucepan, and cover with water. Simmer. Bag can be used several times.

GLUE ORNAMENTS

By Cindy Groom Harry

MATERIALS: GLUE ORNAMENTS

Acrylic paints *: green, red, brown, yellow

White craft glue *

Glue syringes *, four

Craft sticks, four

Heavy sandwich bag, one per design

Medium paintbrush

Paper cups, four

White candle, 3 x 6 inches (optional)

Clear acrylic spray (optional)

Miscellaneous items: tracing paper; pencil; scissors; paper towels; masking tape; old measuring spoons; newspapers (optional)

Note: Full-size Painting Patterns and a Color Key are given on **page 64**.

* Delta Ceramcoat acrylic paints and Aleene's Tacky Glue and glue syringes were used in the sample projects.

1. Trace each pattern on page 64 onto a separate piece of tracing paper.

2. Squeeze approximately three tablespoons glue and one tablespoon paint into a paper cup and mix thoroughly with craft stick. Cut ¼ inch off the end of a syringe and use a craft stick to fill with paint. Wipe top off with a paper towel and insert plunger. Repeat to fill each syringe with a different color.

3. To paint each design, insert the pattern into a plastic bag and tape corners of bag to table. Referring to the Color Key, follow the pattern lines and squeeze an even line of the main color onto the bag. Add detail lines, then dots, making certain that all lines and dots connect to another color. *Note:* To change or correct a line, either wipe while wet with a paintbrush, or let dry, cut out, and repaint.

4. Let designs dry for two days and carefully peel off plastic. Turn shapes over and let back dry thoroughly. *Note:* To maintain shape for hanging, let designs dry for one week.

5. Use scissors to trim points on poinsettia and cut away any errors.

For a shiny appearance, place designs on newspapers and spray lightly with clear acrylic spray.

6. Place designs on a candle if desired, or use on a wreath, window, or as a tree decoration.

57

PINWHEELS

By Carole Rodgers

1. Press fabric squares. With edges even, place the fusible web between wrong sides of the fabric squares. Follow the manufacturer's instructions to adhere fabric to the web. Let cool.

2. Trace and cut out the pattern on page 64. Center over fabric square and pin in place. Using pinking shears, cut around pattern edge, being careful not to cut the pattern.

Using scissors, follow lines on pattern to cut from each corner toward the center. *Note:* Do not cut too close to center.

MATERIALS: PINWHEELS

Cotton fabric, contrasting prints or print and solid, two 6-inch squares

Fusible web, 5-inch square

⅜- to ¾-inch button or bead

Needles: sewing, darning

Gold elastic cord, 8 inches

Miscellaneous items: tracing paper; pencil; pinking shears; scissors; pins; sewing thread; iron

Note: A full-size pattern is given on page 64.

---

3. Determine which side of square will be the inside of the pinwheel and which will be the outside.

Thread sewing needle, knotting and trimming ends. Insert needle through the center of the square, from outside to inside and pull until the knot rests firmly against the square. Bring corner No. 1 up and over to center, insert needle through corner from inside to outside, and pull thread tightly. Repeat for each corner, working in numerical order.

Thread bead or button onto needle and sew tightly onto center of pinwheel. Knot and trim thread.

4. Thread darning needle with decorative cord, sew through one corner of the pinwheel and knot ends to make a hanging loop.

MARBLEIZED WOODEN CUTOUTS

By Carole Rodgers

MATERIALS: MARBLEIZED WOODEN CUTOUTS

4-inch wood cutouts, Christmas shapes

Lacquer-based spray paints: white, metallic gold, green, red

Gesso or white paint

Sponge paintbrush

Clear acrylic spray

Gold cord, 8 inches *per ornament*

Miscellaneous items: drill with 1/16-inch bit (for cutouts without holes); heavy thread or thin cord; disposable bucket or deep pan for water; newspapers; paper towels; sticks for paint stirrers

---

1. Cover work surface with newspapers and work in a well-ventilated area. Fill bucket or pan with water to 1 or 2 inches from the top.

2. Use the sponge brush to paint cutouts on both sides and edges with white paint or gesso and let dry.

If cutouts do not have holes, use drill to make holes where desired for hanging.

Cut a 10-inch piece of heavy thread or thin cord for each cutout and insert through hole; tie ends into a knot.

3. Using white, metallic gold, and another paint color of your choice, spray each color onto the surface of the water. Hold the can 8 inches from the water and spray for several seconds. Stir with a stick to swirl the paint.

4. Holding cutout by the cord, immerse in paint water and turn slowly as you remove it. *Note:* If the cutout is too lightweight to sink, carefully place on water surface, then turn to cover with paint. Hang to dry.

5. Remove excess paint from water by stirring with stick or placing paper towel on water surface and quickly removing it.

Repeat process as desired to marbleize cutouts.

6. Spray ornaments with several coats of clear acrylic spray and let dry.

7. Remove heavy thread or cord and replace with an 8-inch piece of gold cord. Knot ends to make a hanging loop.

CHRISTMAS ANGELS

By Cindy Groom Harry

1. For each angel, cut one 18-inch and one 6-inch piece of metallic twist and one 12-inch piece of iridescent twist. Carefully unwrap long metallic and iridescent twist by starting at one end and gently unwrapping toward the other. *Note:* Do not unwrap short metallic piece.

2. Bring ends of opened metallic twist together without creasing fold. Gather ends and twist on bead, placing it 2 inches from the top. See the Step 2 illustration.

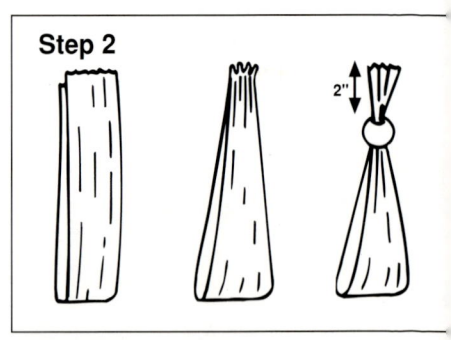

Step 2

Fold twist in half; slide bead on ends.

MATERIALS: CHRISTMAS ANGELS

To Make One Angel

Paper twist *: metallic: gold, silver, blue, or mauve, 24 inches; iridescent: 12 inches

38mm wood bead, natural or white

Chenille tinsel stems, gold or silver, two

Miscellaneous items: scissors; craft cutter; pinking shears; tape measure

* MPR Creative Twist was used in the sample projects.

3. Separate twist ends and wrap around sides of bead, overlapping at back and gathering at neck. Squeeze neck firmly and wrap center of one chenille stem around front of neck. See the Step 3 illustration. Pull stem ends tightly and twist several times to hold at back of neck.

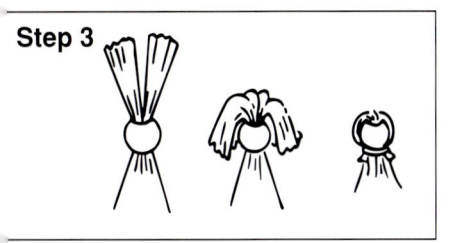

Step 3

Wrap ends around head; secure with stem.

4. To make arm unit, lay angel front side down on table and place 6-inch metallic twist across back of neck, below twisted chenille stem.

For wing unit, gather opened iridescent twist in center and place on top of arm unit; pinch on front and back to hold. With other hand, wrap one chenille stem end over wing unit, under left arm, and over right shoulder.

Wrap other stem end over wing unit, under right arm, and over left shoulder, creating an X on the front. See the Step 4 illustration. Twist ends together again at back of neck, twisting out to the ends.

Open twist arms to create full sleeves.

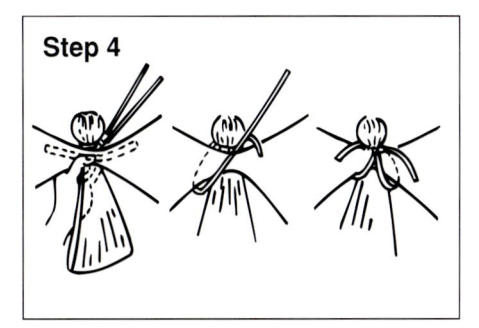

Step 4

Wrap stem halves around wings to form an X.

5. Shape a halo by bending one end of the other chenille stem into a 1 ½-inch circle, twisting end to hold. Bend stem end down. See the Step 5 illustration.

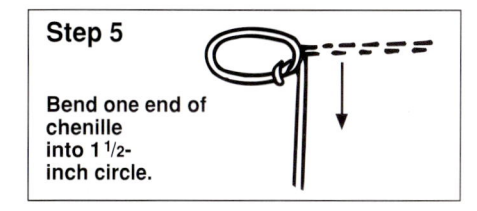

Step 5

Bend one end of chenille into 1 ½-inch circle.

6. Position halo 1 ½ inches above head and twist the halo stem and the neck stem together with two or three turns. Place finger between stems and twist together again around finger, twisting out to ends to make a loop. Use craft cutter to cut off end ¼ inch beyond loop and bend up. See the Step 6 illustration.

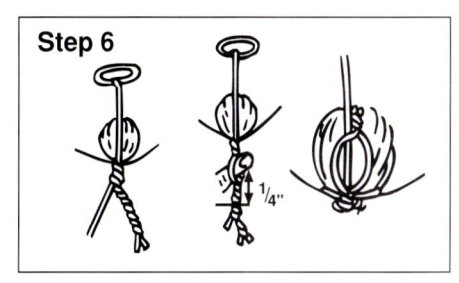

Step 6

Twist stems below finger; bend up loop.

7. To trim the wings, hold angel upside down, smooth outside edge of twist, and cut three scallops diagonally inward. See the Step 7 illustration.

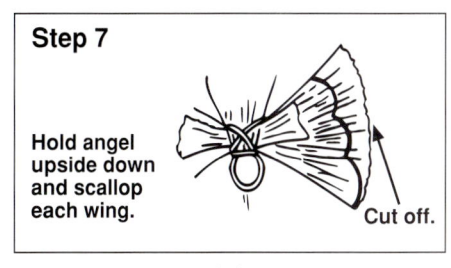

Step 7

Hold angel upside down and scallop each wing.

Cut off.

59

RUDOLPH AND RHODA REINDEER CLIP-ONS

By Cindy Groom Harry

MATERIALS: RUDOLPH AND RHODA REINDEER CLIP-ONS

For Each Project

Pompoms: 2-inch: tan; ¾-inch: tan; pink, two; ¼-inch: red

Brown felt, 1½x2 inches

Natural wired Creative Twist, 15 inches

Wood spring clothespin

12mm wiggle eyes, two

12mm gold jingle bell

White craft glue *

Hot glue gun

For Rudolph

Green Christmas print craft ribbon, 2½-inch square

White loopy junior chenille stem, 6 inches

Polyester fiberfill, small amount

For Rhoda

⅜-inch red Christmas print craft ribbon, 10 inches

Brown felt, ¾-inch square

Red acrylic paint

Small brush

Miscellaneous items: scissors; paper plates; paper towels; craft or wire cutters; water bucket

* Aleene's Tacky glue was used in the sample projects.

1. *For each reindeer,* cut brown felt into two 1x1½-inch pieces for ears and two ⅜x¾-inch pieces for Rhoda's eyelashes. Cut a 10-inch piece from the ⅜-inch ribbon and tie in bow for Rhoda. Cut green ribbon into 2½-inch squares for Rudolph's hat, and cut 6-inch pieces of loopy chenille for Rudolph's hatband. Cut 4-, 5-, and 6-inch pieces of Creative Twist for the antlers.

2. Paint slanted ends of clothespin red for Rhoda's mouth. See the Step 2 illustration.

Step 2
Paint slanted ends red for the mouth.

3. To make either reindeer, cut ears by tapering one end to a curved point. See the Step 3 illustration. Apply glue to ear bottom and fold in half. Repeat with other ear. Set aside on paper plate to dry.

Step 3
Cut curve; glue and fold bottom in half.

Glue

4. Apply a ½-inch circle of glue to the ¾-inch tan pompom muzzle and glue it to the 2-inch pompom head. Glue two ¾-inch pink pompoms on each side of the muzzle for cheeks and the red pompom on top of muzzle for the nose.

5. Cut three snips in one long edge of each felt eyelash. Fan out and glue to back of eyes for Rhoda. Glue eyes on reindeer heads on either side of nose touching cheeks.

6. To make the antlers, align the three pieces of twist. Grasp pieces in center and twist several times. Bend ends up into curves. Spread fur apart on top of head and glue antlers to head.

7. Glue ears into the fur of the head pompom just below the antlers.

8. To make Rudolph's hat, round off one corner of ribbon square. See the Step 8 illustration. Apply glue to one edge of ribbon and fold into cone by overlapping opposite side ¼ inch. Pinch to hold.

Step 8
Round off one corner of the ribbon square.

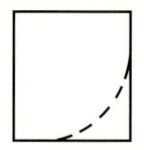

Bend a chenille hat band into a circle and twist together ¼-inch at ends to retain shape. Check fit of chenille by placing over top of hat and dropping it in place at hat bottom; do not glue. Gently stuff hat with fiberfill. Apply glue to bottom inside edge of hat and place on top of head, between antlers. Shape and glue the chenille hatband to hat.

Lay Rudolph flat to glue bell to point of hat. Let dry.

9. Glue bow and bell to top of Rhoda's head. Let dry.

10. To finish reindeer clip-ons, place clothespin on paper plate and apply glue across top from front end back to spring. Place reindeer on glue surface so muzzle aligns with front end of clothespin. Let dry. *Note:* If Rudolph is top heavy, glue back of hat band to clothespin.

4. *To make a mobile,* make one large and two small ornaments. Referring to the pattern, make two holes at the bottom of the large snowflake as indicated by the Xs. Cut three 12-inch pieces of black thread. Thread one piece through the hole at the top of the large ornament, knotting ends to make a hanging loop. Attach small snowflakes with loops of black thread tied between holes of small snowflakes and bottom holes of large snowflake.

POM POM COOKIE CUTTERS

By Cindy Groom Harry

1. *To make each ornament,* apply a line of glue around the inside of the cutter, ¼ inch from the cutting edge. For the bottom layer of pompoms, place cutting side down on plastic wrap and gently press pompoms along cutter edge. See the Step 1 illustration. To fill the middle of the bottom layer, apply a small amount of glue to sides of pompoms and press into middle to fill. Refer to individual instructions for color placement.

Step 1
Glue along inside of cutter, ¼ inch from edge.

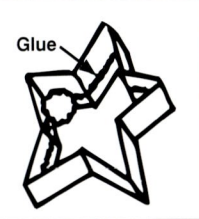

Repeat for the top layer of pompoms, placing line of glue ¼ inch from smooth top edge, and repeating color order.

To add a hanger, cut a 3-inch piece of ribbon, form a loop, and glue ends of the loop to the top back between the inside edge of the cutter and a pompom.

2. *To make the bear,* fill with pompoms, add loop, and tie remaining ribbon in a bow around neck.

3. *To make the candy cane,* alternate red and white pompoms, beginning and ending with red. Add loop and tie remaining ribbon in a bow around curve of cane.

MATERIALS: POM POM COOKIE CUTTERS

For the Bear
2½ x 3-inch bear cookie cutter with open center
¾-inch brown pompoms, 28
⅛-inch red satin ribbon, ½ yard

For the Candy Cane
2¼ x 3½-inch candy cane cookie cutter with open center
¾-inch pompoms: red, 10; white, eight
⅛-inch green satin ribbon, ½ yard

For the Tree
3 x 4-inch tree cookie cutter with open center
¾-inch pompoms: yellow, two; brown, two; green, 48
⅛-inch red satin ribbon, ⅔ yard

For the Star
3-inch star cookie cutter with open center
¾-inch pompoms: yellow, 12; gold, 10
⅛-inch yellow satin ribbon, ¼ yard

For the Candle
3¼ x 4-inch cookie cutter with open center
¾-inch pompoms: green, six; yellow, four; gold, 18
⅛-inch yellow satin ribbon, ⅔ yard

For the Bell
2¼ x 2¾-inch bell cookie cutter with open center
¾-inch pompoms: red, 20; green, two
⅛-inch green satin ribbon, ½ yard

For the Rocking Horse
2½-inch rocking horse cookie cutter with open center
¾-inch pompoms: white, 16; red, 10
⅛-inch white satin ribbon, ⅔ yard

For the Santa
2½ x 4¾-inch Santa cookie cutter with open center
¾-inch pompoms: green, 10; red, 14; white, 18; pink, two
⅛-inch green satin ribbon, ½ yard
White craft glue *

Miscellaneous items: plastic wrap; scissors

* Aleene's Tacky Glue was used for the sample projects.

4. *To make the tree,* place a yellow pompom at the top, brown at the bottom, and fill in with green. Add loop; cut remaining ribbon into 6-inch pieces and tie into bows. Glue bows to front of the tree.

5. *To make the star,* place yellow pompoms in the points, add gold in between the yellow, and place a yellow pompom in the center. Add loop; tie remaining ribbon in bow and glue to front.

6. *To make the candle,* fill in base with gold pompoms, the candle stick with green, and the flame with yellow. Add loop; tie remaining ribbon around handle, making a bow at top front.

7. *To make the bell,* place green pompom at center bottom and fill in with red. Add loop; tie remaining ribbon in a bow around top of bell.

8. *To make the rocking horse,* place a row of white pompoms along the top edge of the horse. Make the legs by placing a row of white, red, and white pompoms in the middle. Place a row of red along the rocker. Add a loop of green ribbon; tie remaining green ribbon in a bow around neck. Cut white ribbon in half, make two bows, and glue to front at each end of the rocker.

9. *To make the Santa,* place white pompoms for his hat, beard, and coat trim; add pink for his face, red for his hat and coat, and green for his bag and boots. See the Step 9 illustration. Add

Step 9
Glue appropriate colors of pom poms in Santa cutter.
Color Key
1 White
2 Pink
3 Red
4 Green

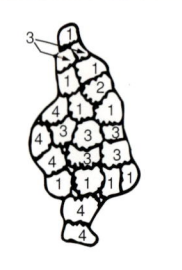

loop; tie remaining ribbon in a bow around the hat top.

DOILY ANGEL

By Cindy Groom Harry

MATERIALS: DOILY ANGEL

8-inch paper doilies, solid center with 2-inch design border, three

⅛-inch mauve satin ribbon, ½ yard

White craft glue *

Stapler

Scissors

* Aleene's Tacky Glue was used in the sample project.

1. To make the angel's dress, fold one doily in half and curl into a cone with the design border at the bottom. Overlap edges slightly and staple twice, 2½ inches from lower edge of the cone.

2. For the wings, fold a doily in half. Beginning at the folded edge, make four ½-inch accordion folds, leaving the center curved edge unfolded. Staple in the center through all folds. See the Step 2 illustration.

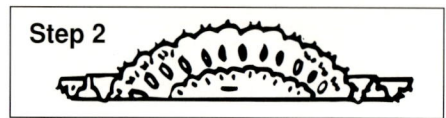

Step 2

Begin at folded edge to make four folds.

Glue design side of the wings to the dress back, placing the folded edge ½ inch from the top of the cone covering the staples.

3. To make the head, cut the remaining doily in half. Cut along the 2-inch design border of one half; discard solid center and other half. With the remaining design border make a fan with ½-inch accordion folds on the inside curve and ¾-inch folds on the outside curve. See the Step 3 illustration. Staple through folds close to the lower edge of the fan.

Step 3

Beginning at straight edge, pleat head.

4. Cut ⅛-inch off the top of the dress and apply a dot of glue in the opening. Gently spread fan head and place stapled edge into dress opening.

5. Tie the ribbon in a bow and glue to the dress front at the base of the head.

SIMMERING SPICE BAG

By Nancy Hoerner and Suzanne Weyer

MATERIALS: SIMMERING SPICE BAG
For the Bag
18-count Aida cloth *, 5x11 inches

Embroidery floss: green (DMC 699/Anchor 923); red (DMC 304/Anchor 47)

Muslin, ⅛ yard

Needles: No. 24 tapestry, sewing

For the Spice Mixture
Whole cloves, ¼ cup

Cinnamon sticks, four

Orange, one half

Lemon, one half

Miscellaneous items: scissors; masking tape; sewing thread; ruler; sharp knife; embroidery hoop (optional)

Note: A Stitch Graph and Color Key are given on page 61.

* Fiddler's Lite fabric from Charles Craft Inc. was used for the sample project.

1. Tape the edges of the fabric to prevent raveling. Fold the Aida cloth in half width-wise to measure 5x5½ inches. Fold in half again in the opposite direction. Unfold and begin stitching the tree trunk on the second fold line, 20 squares up from the bottom.

2. Cut floss into 18-inch pieces and use two strands for all stitching. Cross stitch the trees and backstitch the letters, referring to the General Cross Stitch Instructions on page 95.

3. Carefully remove tape from edges. If necessary, soak needlework in cool water to soften the tape residue. Fringe ½ inch of each 5-inch side.

4. Fold Aida cloth in half widthwise, with the stitched design on the inside. With sewing thread, stitch the sides of

56

HOLIDAY GIFT BAGS

	DMC	Color
x	321	Christmas red
z	699	Christmas green
•	white	white
∕	436	tan
bs	938	coffee brown, ultra dark

NOTE: Cut fabric (refer to individual instructions for stitch counts and fabric sizes needed). For each design, measure up 2" from bottom of fabric and mark. This line marks placement for bottom of cross stitch design. Fold fabric in half lengthwise to find center.

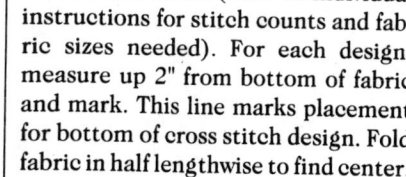

CANDY CANES

Fabric used for model: 14-count antique white Aida
Stitch count: 12H x 39W
Fabric size: 6½" x 6"
Approximate design size:
　14-count—⅞" x 2¾"

Instructions: Cross stitch using two strands of floss. Backstitch using one strand 699.

DO NOT OPEN

Fabric used for model: 14-count antique white Aida
Stitch count: 11H x 39W
Fabric size: 6½" x 6"
Approximate design size:
　14-count—¾" x 2¾"

Instructions: Cross stitch using two strands of floss. Backstitch using one strand of floss unless indicated otherwise.
Backstitch (bs) instructions:
　699　Do not open
　321　*until Dec. 25th* (two strands)

GINGERBREAD MEN

Fabric used for model: 14-count antique white Aida
Stitch count: 16H x 35W
Fabric size: 6½" x 5½"
Approximate design size:
　14-count—1¼" x 2½"

Instructions: Cross stitch using two strands of floss. Backstitch using one strand of floss. Make French knots using two strands of floss, wrapping floss around needle twice.
Backstitch (bs) instructions:
　white　bands on arms and legs of gingerbread men
　938　gingerbread men
French knots:
　938　buttons
　699　eyes

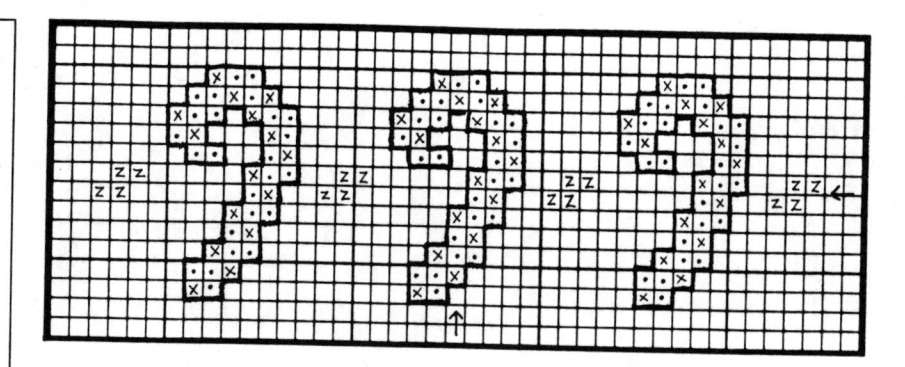

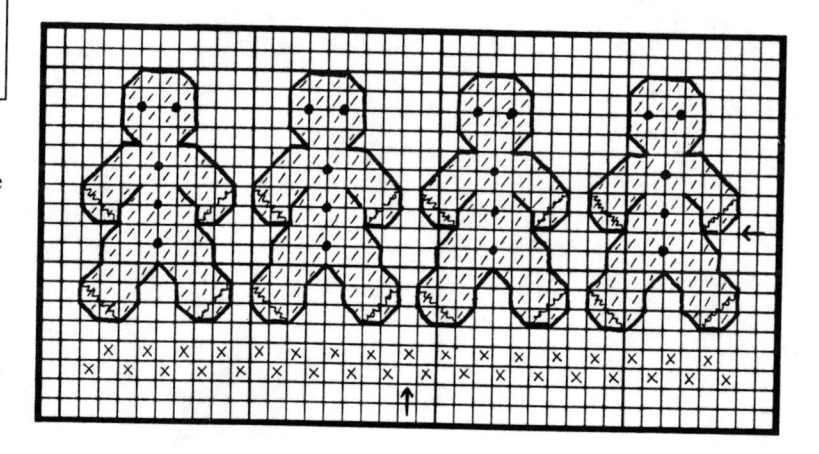

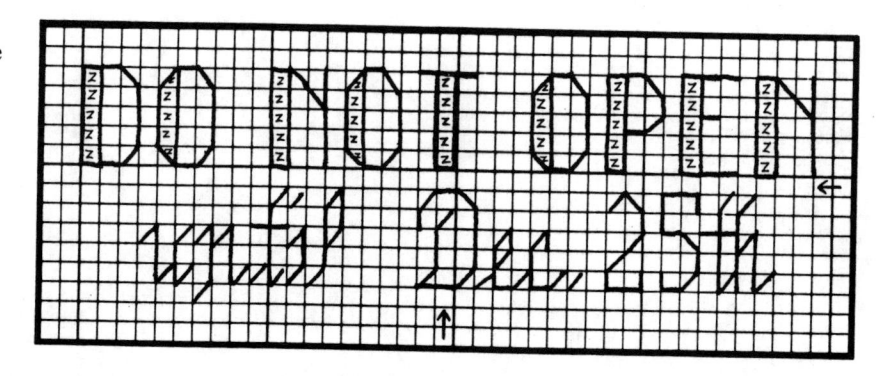

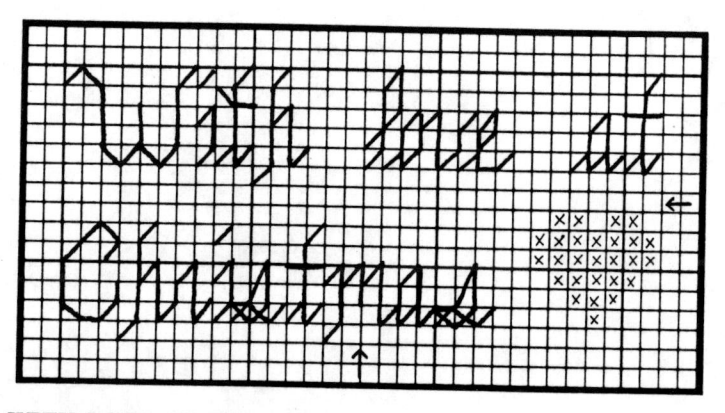

WITH LOVE AT CHRISTMAS

Fabric used for model: 14-count antique white Aida
Stitch count: 13H x 32W
Fabric size: 6½" x 5½"
Approximate design size:
　14-count—1" x 2¼"

Instructions: Cross stitch using two strands of floss. Backstitch (bs) lettering using two strands 699.

Designed by Robyn Taylor

CHENILLE CANDY CANES

By Lois Pritzlaff

MATERIALS: CHENILLE CANDY CANES

For Both Ornaments

⅛-inch chenille stems: one each: red, white

⅛-inch green satin ribbon, 12 inches

Black felt, small piece

For the Mouse

Gray felt, small piece

Pompoms: ⅜-inch gray, two; ⅝-inch gray, four; 5mm black

½-inch black stiff paintbrush bristles

For the Bear

Brown felt, small piece

Pompoms: ⅜-inch beige, two; ⅝-inch brown, five; 7mm brown

Miscellaneous items: wirecutters; scissors; white craft glue; pencil; tracing paper

1. Cut each chenille stem in half. Hold one white and one red half together with ends even and twist. Bend top over, forming a candy cane. Repeat with the other two halves.

2. *To make each ornament,* glue one ⅝-inch pompom to the top bend of a candy cane, placing it slightly closer to the short end. Glue the other ⅝-inch pompom behind the first and let dry. Glue a ⅜-inch pompom on each side of the back one and where the larger ones meet.

3. Trace the pattern in the Step 3 illustration and cut two ears from felt. Glue the base of each ear to the head. Cut two tiny black felt rectangles and glue to face for eyes. Glue the 5mm black or 7mm brown pompom to the candy cane at the base of the face for a nose.

Step 3
Cut two ears from matching felt.

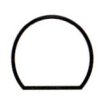

4. Make a bow from 6 inches of ribbon, trimming ends at an angle, and glue to the back of the neck.

5. *To finish the bear,* trim the ⅝-inch brown pompom and glue it to back pompom for a tail.

6. *To finish the mouse,* glue three paintbrush bristles on each side of the nose. Cut a 1 ¼-inch long narrow strip of gray felt, rounding one end and cutting the other end to a point. Glue rounded end to bottom, bringing tail to one side and up on top of mouse.

PATTERNS

Simmering Spice Bag Stitch Graph and Color Key

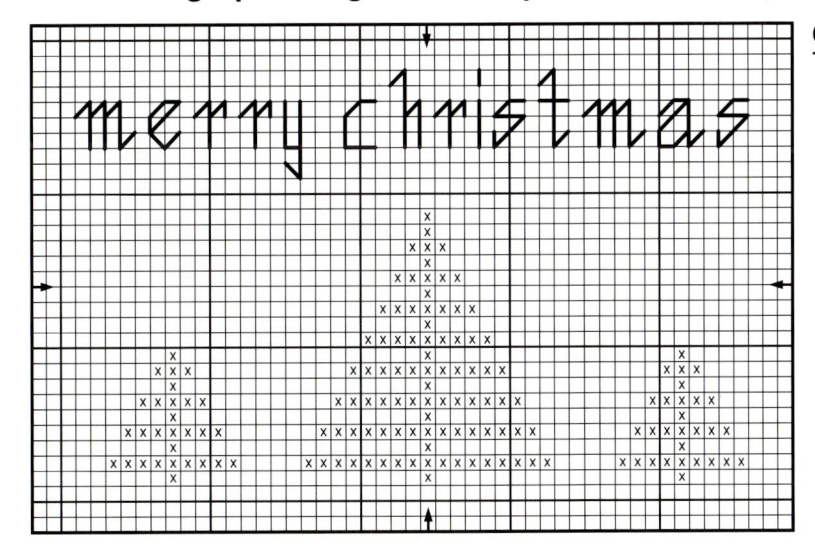

Color Key

X Green
— Red Backstitching

Paper Punch Ornaments Patterns

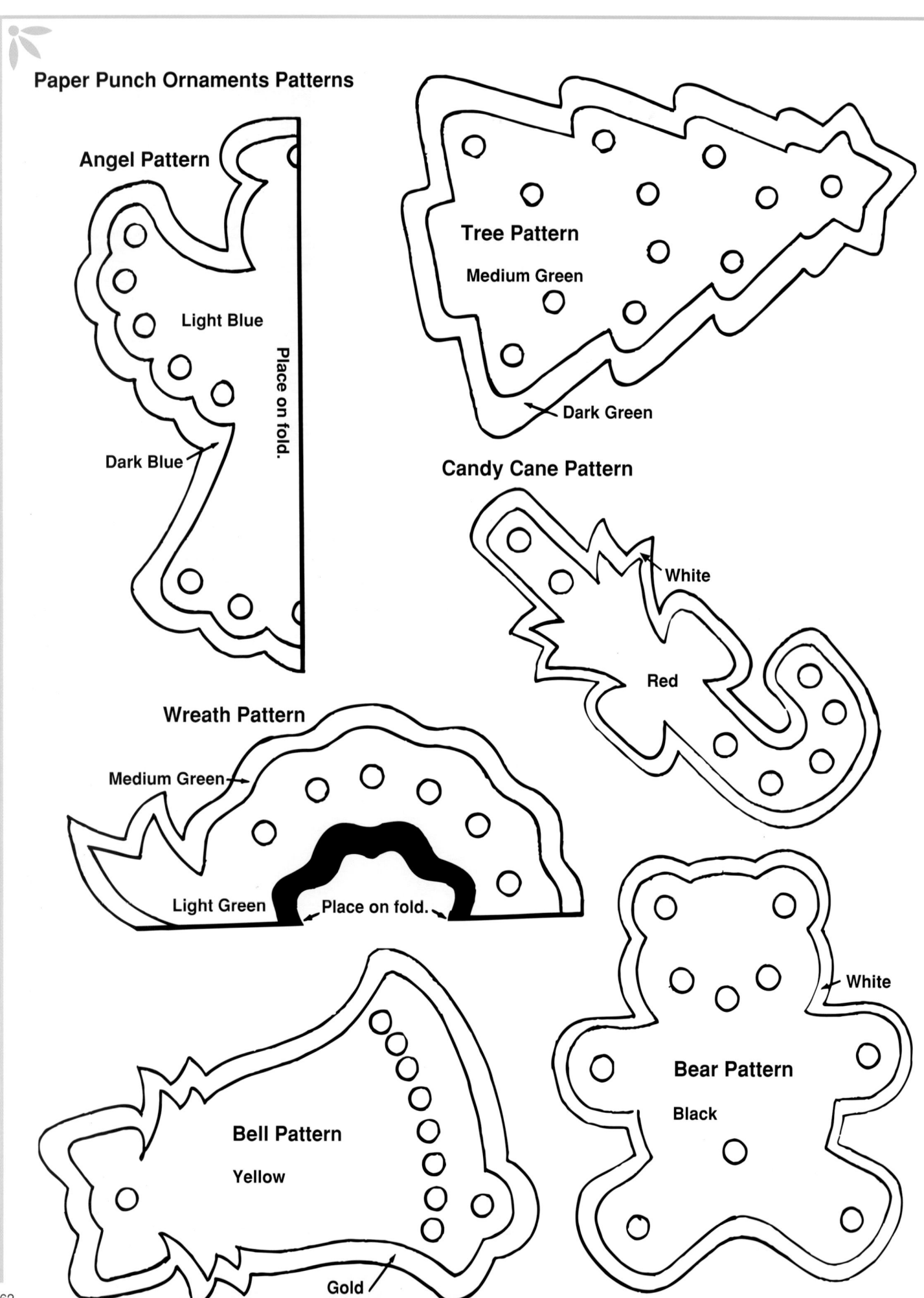

Angel Pattern

Light Blue

Dark Blue

Place on fold.

Tree Pattern

Medium Green

Dark Green

Candy Cane Pattern

White

Red

Wreath Pattern

Medium Green

Light Green

Place on fold.

Bell Pattern

Yellow

Gold

Bear Pattern

White

Black

Sun Catcher Ornaments Patterns

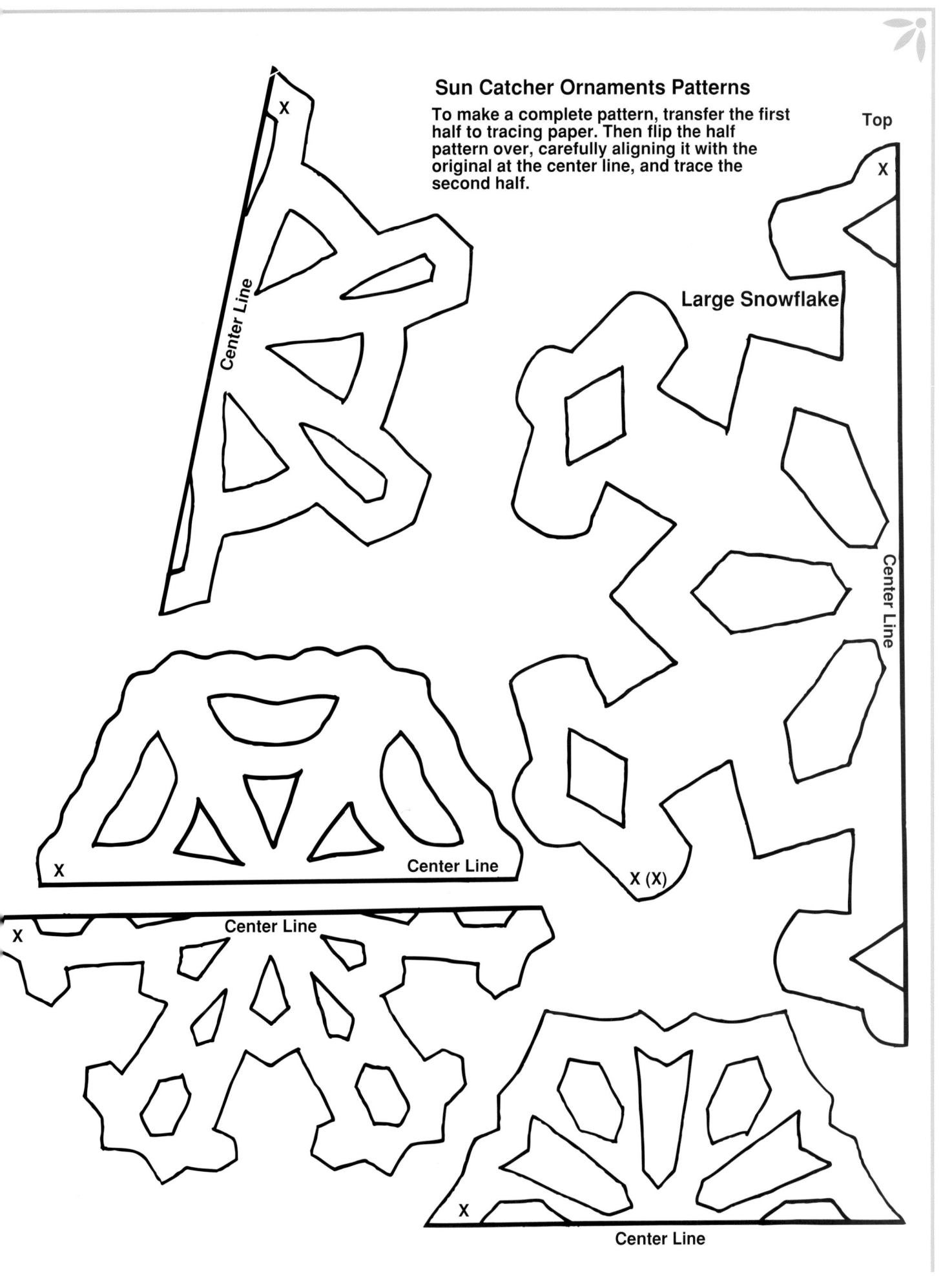

To make a complete pattern, transfer the first half to tracing paper. Then flip the half pattern over, carefully aligning it with the original at the center line, and trace the second half.

Large Snowflake

63

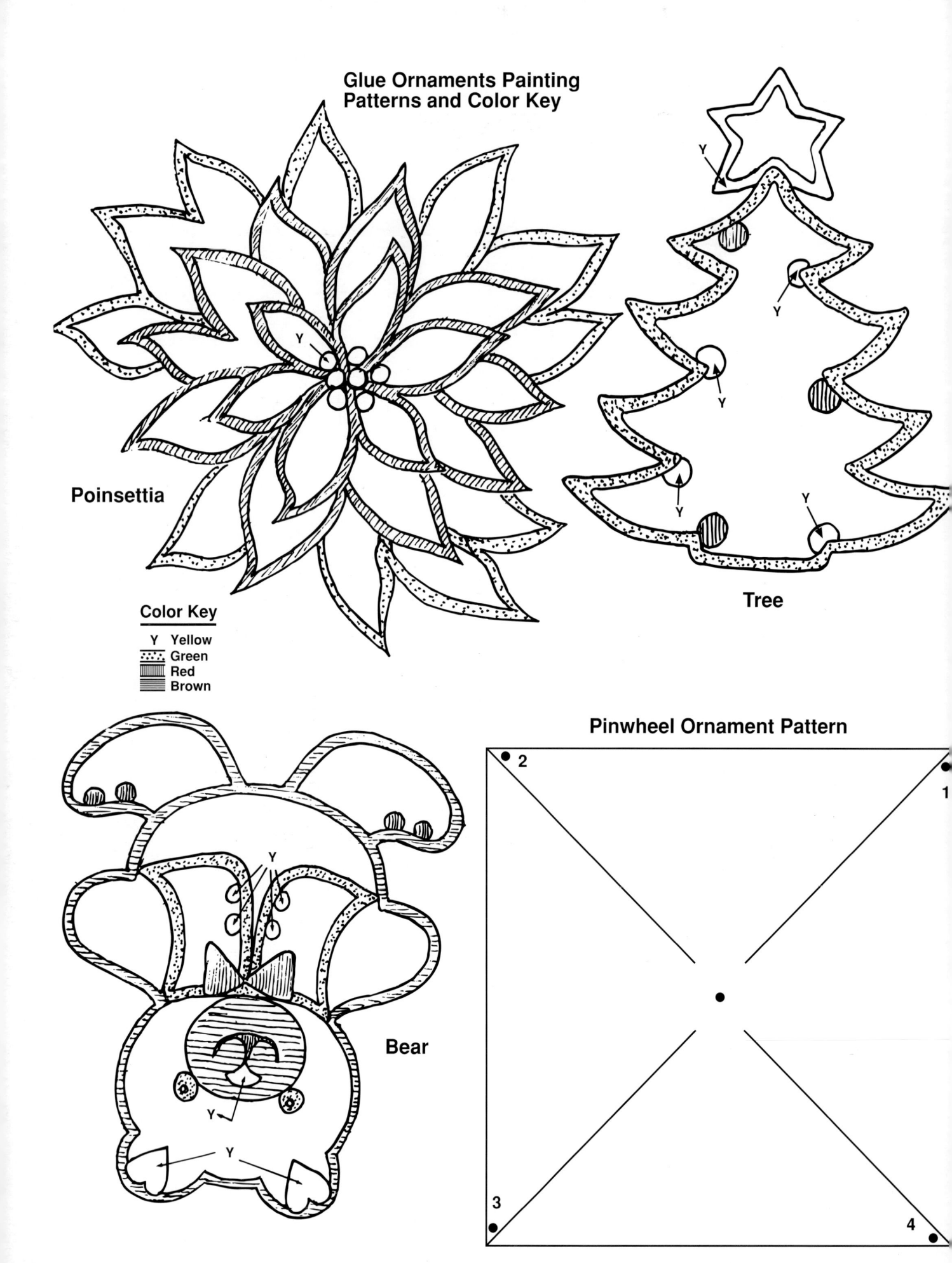

Glue Ornaments Painting Patterns and Color Key

Poinsettia

Tree

Color Key
- Y Yellow
- Green
- Red
- Brown

Bear

Pinwheel Ornament Pattern

1
2
3
4

Fanciful Victoriana

Elegant and appealing are the magical holiday decorations inspired by the Victorian era. The Victorians were the first to elevate the Christmas tree to superstar status, and with good reason—their tree-trimming creations were absolutely awe inspiring.

    Recapturing the delicate, romantic look of 19th century England is this assortment of lace- and ribbon-trimmed ornaments. Soft colors—ivory, white, pink, and mauve—are the hallmark of the era, but it's really the trimmings that say "Victorian." Consider the pearls, satin ribbon roses, small bows, dried flowers, and crystal beads that give this ornament medley its character. And who but the Victorians would cap iridescent balls with crochet caps for an alluring look?

BATTENBERG LACE SNOWFLAKES

By Susan Ray and Susan Price

MATERIALS: BATTENBERG LACE SNOWFLAKES

White Battenberg tape, 1⅓ yards per snowflake

No. 5 white pearl cotton, one skein per snowflake

Needles: sewing; No. 24 tapestry

Fabric glue

Monofilament line, 1 yard

Spray starch

Miscellaneous items: scissors; pencil; iron; straight pins; tape measure; wax paper; white thread; heavy tracing paper

Note: Full-size patterns are given on pages 78-80.

1. Trace the Battenberg lace patterns on pages 78-80 onto separate pieces of tracing paper.

2. With needle and thread, baste the Battenberg tape directly onto the paper, following the pattern and specific instructions.

• The tape has a coarse thread woven into both edges. By pulling the thread along one edge, the tape shortens on that side causing the opposite edge to curve outward. See the Step 2a illustration.

Step 2a
Pull thread from inner edge to shape curve.

• The thread may be pulled in two places: at the beginning of a tape section or within the section where the curve appears or tape changes direction.

• Use the tip of your needle to pull up a loop of the coarse thread to form the necessary curve or curves. Clip the loop and tie the ends in a knot. Conceal the cut ends in the lace stitches. See the Step 2b illustration.

Step 2b
Pull up a loop of thread. Clip and tie in a knot.

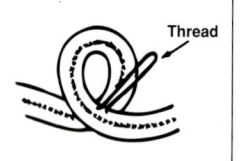

• Turn all cut edges under, and secure with glue. Apply fabric glue very sparingly to hold cut ends and folds, and overlapped areas of tape. Be careful not to glue the tape to the paper.

3. Using pearl cotton and a tapestry needle, follow the Battenberg Stitch Chart on page 95 to work the stitches between the tape for each snowflake. Work stitches through tape edges only, do not work through paper. Begin and end with a knot at the back.

4. *To make the star,* baste star points to paper first, and cut tape. Baste circle over star, and tack with thread at inside points. Work three rows of single net stitch around inside of center circle. Fill in center with wheel stitch. Work 9 woven leaf stitches inside each star point.

5. *To make the six-petal flower,* baste petals to paper first. Make six rings, and tack one ring between each petal with sewing thread. See the Step 5 illustration.

Step 5 
Wrap thread around finger 10 times. Work buttonhole stitches over all threads until covered.

Fill in the center of each petal with branched bars.

6. *To make the four-petal flower,* baste inside flower first. With second piece of tape, form outer loops and baste to paper. Tack where tape edges meet. Work a spider web stitch inside each small outer loop. Work double net stitch inside each petal. Fill in spaces between petals with Russian Foundation stitch.

7. To finish each snowflake, cut the basting threads from the back of the paper and carefully pull out, releasing each snowflake.

Lay flat on a piece of wax paper, saturate with spray starch, and iron. Turn and repeat for other side. Let dry. Thread an 8-inch piece of monofilament line through each snowflake, and knot ends for a hanging loop. ♡

PERFORATED PAPER

By Carol Krob

1. *To make each ornament,* cut two 4-inch squares of perforated paper. Stitch two identical pieces for each ornament.

MATERIALS: PERFORATED PAPER

Ivory perforated paper, 4x8 inches per ornament

Embroidery floss *: two skeins each: dark seafoam green (561), dark Christmas red (498); one skein each: medium seafoam green (563), medium salmon (3328)

Glass seed beads *: old gold (557); garnet (367); emerald (332)

Quilting thread

Needles: No. 24 tapestry; No. 10 crewel

Miscellaneous items: scissors; pencil; ruler

Note: Cutting and Stitch Graphs and a Color Key are given on page 82.

* DMC embroidery floss and Mill Hill seed beads were used in the sample projects.

2. Each square on the Stitch Graph represents one square over four holes in the paper. Refer to the General Cross Stitch Instructions on page 95 and the Stitch Graphs and Color Key on page 82 to stitch each design, using three strands of floss for cross stitch and one strand of quilting thread to attach beads with half cross stitches.

3. Locate the center of the paper square, and mark lightly on the back with a pencil (back of paper has a dull finish and rough feel). Count from the center to find your starting point.

Use the "stab-stitch" method, bringing the needle straight up and down through holes in paper. Do not carry thread across unstitched areas.

4. To finish stitched ornament, carefully trim away excess paper around design, following cutting line on the graph.

Thread tapestry needle with two -yard strands of floss in a coordinating color. Sew front to back, wrong sides together, matching edges. Begin at top center, and sew a running stitch around design, sewing through all thicknesses and following outline of stitched design.

End with a loop of thread at the top for hanging.

ELEGANT WREATH

By Judy Tripp

MATERIALS: ELEGANT WREATH

No. 1 round basket reed, 7 feet

Satin ribbon: ¼-inch mauve picot, ⅝ yard; ⅛-inch burgundy, ½ yard

9mm mauve ribbon roses, two

1-inch green velvet rose leaf

Pearl string, ½ yard

Gold cord, 8 inches

Acrylic paint, white or ivory

Hot glue gun

Floral wire

Miscellaneous items: container of water; scissors; wax paper; ruler

1. Cut two 16-inch pieces and five 10-inch pieces of basket reed. Soak the reeds 10 to 15 minutes in warm water.

Grasp all reeds together in one hand with ends even. With other hand, grasp the 16-inch reeds together, and wrap around the 10-inch reeds to within 1½ inches of ends. Bring ends together to form a circle, overlap, and continue wrapping over overlap. Tuck remaining long reeds into wreath to secure. Let dry.

2. Mix a small amount of white paint in a bowl of water. Dip wreath into mix to dye. Place on wax paper to dry.

3. Cut a 3-inch piece of pearl string and a 7-inch piece of mauve ribbon; set aside.

Wrap burgundy ribbon around wreath, gluing ends at top center. Repeat with remaining pearl string.

4. Fold 7-inch ribbon piece in half and glue to top center of wreath to form streamers. Glue the leaf, pointing up, above streamers. Fold remaining mauve ribbon into a six-loop bow and wire center. Glue bow below the leaf.

Join ends of 3-inch pearl string to form loop and glue to the bottom of the bow. Glue the two roses to the bow center.

5. Knot ends of cord together and glue the knot to the back of the leaf for a hanging loop.

LACE HAT

By Judy Tripp

MATERIALS: LACE HAT

3½-inch white or ivory lace hat

¼-inch burgundy satin picot ribbon, ⅝ yard

Wired pearl clusters, four

18mm mauve ribbon roses, two

1-inch green velvet rose leaves, four

Gold cord, 8 inches

Hot glue gun

Floral wire

Miscellaneous items: scissors; ruler

1. Cut a 6-inch piece of ribbon, wrap around crown of hat, and glue at center back. From remaining ribbon, make a six-loop bow with tails and wire center.

2. Glue the bow to the center back. Glue two leaves and a rose on each side of bow. Glue two pearl loops to center of bow, and one pearl loop on each side, directly above each rose.

3. Fold gold cord in half, and knot ends together. Glue to underside of brim at center top for a hanger.

67

POTPOURRI BALL

By Judy Tripp

MATERIALS: POTPOURRI BALL

White or ivory lace fabric, 8-inch square

Satin ribbon: ⅛-inch burgundy, ¼ yard; ¼-inch picot: mauve, ¼ yard; burgundy, ⅓ yard

1 ½-inch white or ivory gathered lace, ⅓ yard

18mm mauve ribbon rose

1-inch green velvet rose leaf

Wired pearl clusters, three

Pearl string, 3 inches

Rose-scented potpourri, ⅓ cup

Hot glue gun

Floral wire

Miscellaneous items: scissors; ruler

1. Place potpourri in the center of the lace square. Draw corners up around potpourri to form a "bag", and wrap with floral wire.

2. Knot ends of ⅛-inch ribbon together to form a loop. Tuck knotted end into top of gathered lace and glue.

3. Thread wire through bound edge of gathered lace trim, wrap around gathered neck of ornament with gathers up, and twist wire securely.

4. Wrap and glue burgundy ribbon around neck, covering edge of lace trim, and tie ends tightly in a bow.

Fold mauve ribbon into bow, and tack at center. Glue to center of burgundy bow.

Glue ends of the pearl string to form a loop and glue the pearl loop just below the bows.

Glue the leaf, pointing down, in the center of the loop. Glue the ribbon rose over the center of the bows, and the three pearl clusters directly below the rose.

LACE TREE

By Judy Tripp

MATERIALS: LACE TREE

White posterboard, 4x8-inch piece

⅛-inch burgundy satin ribbon, ½ yard

White or ivory lace, 1 ½-inch gathered scallop, ½ yard; 1-inch flat, ¼ yard

White pearl flower stamens, one package

Pearl clusters: white, six; pink, four

18mm crystal star beads, five

¾-inch green rose leaves, two

9mm mauve ribbon roses, two

Pink pearl string, ½ yard

Gold cord, 8 inches

Floral wire

Hot glue gun

Miscellaneous items: needle; white thread; scissors; ruler; tracing paper; pencil; graphite paper

Note: A full-size pattern is given on page 81.

1. Trace the pattern on page 81, transfer to poster board, and cut out. With pattern lines on outside, fold into a cone. Overlap edges to make a bottom diameter of 2 ½ inches, and glue.

2. Glue flat lace to bottom of cone, slightly extending beyond bottom edge.

3. From gathered lace, cut a 7 ½-inch, 5 ½-inch, and 3 ½-inch piece.

Use needle and thread to gather 7 ½-inch piece to fit around cone following first dashed line from bottom. Glue gathers along line, overlapping ends.

Gather 5 ½-inch piece and glue along second dashed line of cone.

Gather 3 ½-inch piece as tightly as possible and glue around top of cone, leaving a tiny point of cone exposed. Glue a star bead to point.

4. Wire nine pearl stamens together at center and fold down to make a fan-shaped cluster. Repeat to make nine more clusters. Glue clusters, with pearls down, evenly spaced around tree. Glue two to top and four each to other two tiers.

Cut 10 1½-inch pieces of pearl string. Join the ends to form loops, and glue a loop over each stamen cluster.

5. Cut ribbon in half, and tie each piece into a bow with 2-inch streamers. Glue bows to top of tree, one on each side.

Thread gold cord through the center of top star. Tie cord between points of star and knot ends together for hanging loop.

Glue pink pearl clusters over the holes of remaining stars, then glue stars evenly spaced, around bottom ruffle of tree.

To finish top of tree, glue three pearl clusters above each burgundy bow and a leaf and rose between each bow.

PARASOL

By Judy Tripp

1. Place lace and taffeta together, draw a 5-inch circle on fabric, and cut out. With craft glue, glue fabric circles together.

Gather lace trim to fit, and glue around edge of circle, placing on lace side with scalloped edges of trim slightly beyond edge of circle.

MATERIALS: PARASOL

Fabric, 6-inch square each: pink taffeta; white or ivory lace

Mauve satin ribbon, ½ yard each: ⅛-inch, ¼-inch

1½-inch white or ivory gathered scallop lace, ⅓ yard

Wired pearl clusters, five

12mm crystal drop beads, three

Mauve ribbon roses: 18mm; 9mm

1-inch green velvet rose leaf

Gold cord, 8 inches

6-inch chenille stem

Floral wire

Hot glue gun

White craft glue

Miscellaneous items: needle; white thread; scissors; ruler; pencil; compass

2. Cut a 12-inch piece of ¼-inch ribbon. Glue to top of the chenille stem, and wrap down and around entire length of stem, completely covering it. Glue at bottom.

3. Fold circle in half, then in half again. Crease with fingers, and open up.

On taffeta side, make a light pencil mark at the center and at each fold line near the outside edge.

At center mark, cut a small opening, just large enough to insert the ribbon-wrapped stem. Push stem through taffeta side of circle, until about ⅛ inch protrudes. Apply glue to taffeta around stem, pinch from the outside, forming gathers, and hold until glue sets.

Apply glue to four pencil marks near edge of taffeta, and attach to stem, forming four folds. Let dry. Place another dot of glue along edge, between each fold, and attach to center, forming eight equal folds in the parasol. Let dry.

4. With ⅛-inch ribbon, make a double-loop bow, wiring center and leaving 3½- and 4½-inch streamers. Knot the end of each streamer.

5. Glue a crystal drop to the end of each streamer and to the bottom of the parasol. Tie a 2-inch piece of ¼-inch ribbon around bottom of parasol where crystal bead is attached. Glue a pearl cluster on each side of ribbon knot.

6. Bend top of stem down to form a curved handle.

Knot ends of gold cord together and hot glue to the front of the handle curve.

Glue four-loop bow over cord knot, and the small ribbon rose and two pearl clusters to center of bow. Glue large ribbon rose to left of small rose, then glue leaf to left of large rose, with tip pointing down and out. Glue third pearl cluster to base of leaf next to rose.

NOSEGAY

By Judy Tripp

MATERIALS: NOSEGAY

4-inch white or ivory flat lace, ⅓ yard

⅛-inch pale pink satin ribbon, 1 yard

Mauve ribbon roses: 18mm, one; 9mm, three

1-inch iridescent white silk flowers, three

1-inch rose leaves: iridescent white, three; green velvet, three

Pearl string, 6 inches

Hot glue gun

Floral wire

Miscellaneous items: scissors; ruler

1. Thread a 12-inch piece of floral wire lengthwise through the center of the lace. Fold the lace in half along wire, and gather tightly to form a double ruffle. Twist to fasten, and cut off ends of wire. Glue ends of lace together, forming a circular ruffle.

2. Place the 18mm rose in the center of the silk flowers, and twist the stems together. Insert stems through center hole of ruffle. Do not cut stems.

3. Glue three iridescent leaves, evenly spaced, just under flower petals. Repeat with the three green leaves.

4. Cut three 6-inch pieces of ribbon, form into loop bows, and glue to the base of each iridescent leaf.

Cut three 2-inch pieces of pearl string, form into single loops, and glue to top of bows.

69

5. Glue a 9mm rose on top of each green leaf at the base.

6. Trim stems at back of nosegay, and glue to lace.

Cut remaining ribbon in half. Make a loop from one piece, and glue ends to center back for hanger. Tie a bow in the remaining piece, and glue over the ends of the hanging loop.

3. Cut one loop from the bottom of two pearl stems.

Arrange the four pearl stems evenly across fan, following the fan shape; glue stem bottoms to fan point.

Glue the ⅜-inch ribbon bow slightly up from bottom point of fan. Glue 6-inch ribbon piece under bow for streamers. Glue the six-loop bow to center of larger bow.

Glue two leaves, pointing up, at the top of the bows, and one leaf, pointing down, at the bottom. Glue the ribbon roses in the center, and glue a pearl loop to each top leaf.

4. Tie a knot at each end of the gold cord, and glue to the ribs on the back of the fan for a hanging loop.

IRIDESCENT BALL

By Judy Tripp

1. Cut two 7½-inch pieces each of white and mauve ribbon. Using craft glue, start at top and glue white ribbon completely around ball. Glue second white piece perpendicular to first, dividing it into fourths. Glue mauve ribbon pieces between white pieces, dividing ball into eighths.

MATERIALS: IRIDESCENT BALL

2½-inch clear glass ball ornament

Satin ribbon: ⅛-inch mauve, ⅝ yard; ⅜-inch white picot, ½ yard

1-inch iridescent white silk flowers, two

1½-inch iridescent white silk leaves, two

2½-inch pearl filament sprays, six

18mm ribbon roses, two

Pearl string, ½ yard

Hot glue gun

Floral wire

Miscellaneous items: scissors; ruler

2. At top of ball, glue an iridescent flower on each side of the hanger over white ribbon. Glue a leaf, pointing down, to ribbon under each flower.

Cut pearl string in half, and fold into two bows, wiring center. Glue pearl bows, standing up, over the remaining white ribbons between the flowers. Glue three pearl filaments under center of each pearl bow, then glue a ribbon rose to the center of each.

3. Thread remaining mauve ribbon through hanging loop, tie a knot at wire, then knot the ends together.

LACE FAN

By Judy Tripp

MATERIALS: LACE FAN

3-inch white or ivory lace fan

Mauve satin picot ribbon: ¼-inch, 1 yard; ⅜-inch, ½ yard

Wired pearl loop sprays, four stems

18mm mauve ribbon roses, two

1-inch velvet leaves, three

Gold cord, 8 inches

Hot glue gun

Floral wire

Miscellaneous items: scissors; ruler

1. Spread fan open and remove tassel.

2. Cut a 6-inch piece of ⅜-inch ribbon. Tie a bow with the remaining piece, and set both aside.

Make a six-loop bow with the ¼-inch ribbon, secure at center with wire, and set aside.

70

FROSTED BALL

By Judy Tripp

MATERIALS: FROSTED BALL

2½-inch frosted glass ball ornament

Satin ribbon: ⅛-inch burgundy, ½ yard; ⅜-inch mauve picot, ¼ yard

Mauve ribbon roses, two each: 18mm, 9mm

1-inch green velvet rose leaves, six

Wired pearl clusters, three

Pearl string, 3 inches

Hot glue gun

White craft glue

Miscellaneous items: scissors; ruler

1. Cut the ⅜-inch ribbon in half. Use white craft glue to glue both pieces across the top of the ornament with the hanger in the center, forming a "V" on each side.

2. Glue two leaves, pointing up and out, to each side where picot ribbon ends meet.
  Cut two 8-inch pieces of burgundy ribbon, fold each into a bow, and glue over base of each leaf pair.
  Glue an 18mm ribbon rose over center of each bow and three pearl clusters above each rose.

3. Glue the pearl string around the base of the ornament hanger.

4. Glue a leaf, pointing down, to the ribbon on each side of the hanger. Glue a 9mm rose to base of each leaf. See the Step 4 illustration.

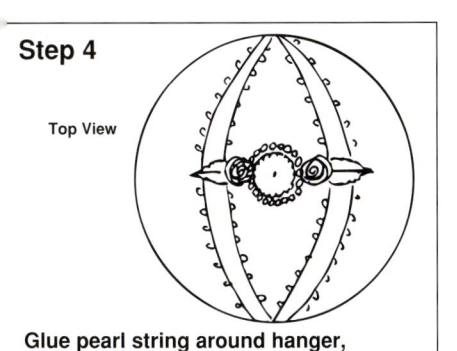

Step 4

Top View

Glue pearl string around hanger, leaves to ribbon, and roses to leaves.

5. Slip remaining piece of ribbon through the hanging wire, and knot ends.

CROCHET COVERED GLASS BALLS

By Mary Buse Melick

MATERIALS: CROCHET COVERED GLASS BALLS
For Each Ball Cover

3-inch iridescent glass ball

Size 7 steel crochet hook

Extra thick white craft glue *

Fine gold cord, ⅓ yard

3-inch styrofoam ball

Spray starch

Rustproof pins

For the Ecru Ball

Bedspread weight crochet thread *

⅜-inch mauve ribbon roses, three

¹⁄₁₆-inch mauve ribbon, 1 yard

3mm white pearl beads string, ⅔ yard

For the White Ball

Bedspread weight crochet cotton *

1-inch rose leaves, three

⅜-inch peach ribbon roses, three

1½-inch star flower pearl centers, three

¹⁄₁₆-inch peach satin ribbon

Note: A Crochet Stitch Chart is given on page 96.

* Aleene's Designer Tacky Glue, Susan Bates crochet thread, and Lily crochet cotton were used in the sample projects.

1. Use a gauge of 9 ch = 1 inch; 9 sc = 1 inch; and 9 dc = 1 inch. Refer to the Crochet Stitch Chart on page 96 for abbreviations and stitch illustrations.
  Note: If your crochet is too loose or too tight, it will not fit a 3-inch glass ball. If your gauge is off, try using a No. 10 thread and a No. 8 hook or a No. 20 thread and a No. 9 hook.

2. *To crochet the ecru ball,* use the following instructions:
  Rnd 1: Ch 16, sl st in 1st sc to form a ring.
  Rnd 2: Ch 1, sc in 1st ch (joining st), 2 sc in next ch; (sc in next ch, 2 sc in next ch) 7 times; sl st in 1st sc to join. (24)
  Rnd 3: Ch 1, 2 sc in 1st sc (joining st), sc in next 2 sc; (2 sc in next sc, sc in next 2 sc) 7 times; sl st in 1st sc to join. (32)

Rnd 4: Ch 1, sc in 1st 8 sc, ch 3; (sc in next 8 sc, ch 3) 3 times; sl st in 1st sc to join. (4 ch-3 sps)

Rnd 5: Sl st in next sc, ch 1, sc in same st, sc in next 5 sc; (sk next sc, ch 3, sc in ch-3 sp, ch 3; sk next sc, sc in next 6 sc) 3 times; sk next sc, ch 3, sc in ch-3 sp, ch 3; sl st in 1st sc to join.

Rnd 6: Sl st in next sc, ch 1, sc in same st; sc in next 3 sc; (sk next sc, ch 3, sc in next ch-3 sp, ch 7; sc in next ch-3 sp, ch 3; sk next sc, sc in next 4 sc) 3 times; sk next sc, ch 3, sc in ch-3 sp, ch 7, sc in ch-3 sp, ch 3; sl st in 1st sc to join.

Rnd 7: Sl st in next sc, ch 1, sc in same st, sc in next sc; (sk next sc, ch 3; sc in next ch-3 sp, ch 3; 8 sc in ch-7 sp, ch 3; sc in next ch-3 sp, ch 3; sk next sc, sc in next 2 sc) 3 times; sk next sc, ch 3, sc in next ch-3 sp, ch 3, 8 sc in ch-7 sp, ch 3, sc in next ch-3 sp, ch 3, sl st in 1st sc to join.

Rnd 8: Sk next sc, sl st in next ch-3 sp, ch 1, sc in same sp, ch 4; (sk next ch-3 sp, sk next sc, sc in next 6 sc; sk next sc, sk next ch-3 sp, ch 4, sc in next ch-3 sp, ch 4; sk next 2 sc, sc in next ch-3 sp, ch 4) 3 times; sk next ch-3 sp, sk next sc, sc in next 6 sc, sk next sc, sk next ch-3 sp, ch 4, sc in next ch-3 sp, ch 4; sl st in 1st sc to join.

Rnd 9: Sl st in next ch-4 sp, ch 1, sc in same sp; *ch 4, sk next sc, sc in next 4 sc; sk next sc; (ch 4, sc in next ch-4 sp) 3 times *; rep between *'s 3 times. Ch 4, sk next sc, sc in next 4 sc, sk next sc; (ch 4, sc in next ch-4 sp) 2 times, ch 4; sl st in 1st sc to join.

Rnd 10: Sl st in next ch-4 sp, ch 1, sc in same sp; *ch 4, sk next sc, sc in next 2 sc; sk next sc, ch 4; sc in ch-4 sp, ch 4; (6 sc in next ch-4 sp) 2 times; ch 4, sc in next ch-4 sp *; rep between *'s 3 times. Ch 4, sk next sc, sc in next 2 sc; sk next sc, ch 4; sc in ch-4 sp, ch 4; (6 sc in next ch-4 sp) 2 times, ch 4; sl st in 1st sc to join.

Rnd 11: Sl st in next ch-4 sp, ch 1, sc in same sp, *ch 4, sk next 2 sc, (sc in next ch-4 sp, ch 4) 2 times; sk next sc, sc in next 10 sc; sk next sc, (ch 4, sc in next ch-4 sp) 2 times *; rep between *'s 3 times. Ch 4, sk next 2 sc, (sc in next ch-4 sp, ch 4) 2 times; sk next sc, sc in next 10 sc; sk next sc, (ch 4, sc in next ch-4 sp) 1 time, ch 4; sl st in 1st sc to join.

Rnd 12: Sl st in next ch-4 sp, ch 1, sc in same sp, ch 4; (sc in next ch-4 sp, ch 4) 2 times; *sk next sc, sc in next 8 sc, sk next sc; (ch 4, sc in next ch-4 sp) 5 times, ch 4 *; rep between *'s 3 times. Sk next sc, sc in next 8 sc, sk next sc; (ch 4, sc in next ch-4 sp) 2 times, ch 4; sl st in 1st sc to join.

Rnd 13: Sl st in next ch-4 sp, ch 1, sc in same sp, ch 4; (sc in next ch-4 sp, ch 4) 2 times; *sk next sc, sc in next 6 sc, sk next sc; (ch 4, sc in next ch-4 sp) 6 times, ch 4*; rep between *'s 3 times. Sk next sc, sc in next 6 sc, sk next sc; (ch 4, sc in next ch-4 sp) 3 times, ch 4; sl st in 1st sc to join.

Rnd 14: Sl st in next ch-4 sp, ch 1, sc in same sp, ch 4; (sc in next ch-4 sp, ch 4) 2 times; *sk next sc, sc in next 4 sc, sk next sc; (ch 4, sc in next ch-4 sp) 7 times, ch 4 *; rep between *'s 3 times. Sk next sc, sc in next 4 sc, sk next sc; (ch 4, sc in next ch-4 sp) 4 times, ch 4; sl st in 1st sc to join.

Rnd 15: Sl st in next ch-4 sp, ch 1, sc in same sp, ch 4; (sc in next ch-4 sp, ch 4) 2 times; *sk next sc, sc in next 2 sc, sk next sc; (ch 4, sc in next ch-4 sp) 8 times, ch 4 *; rep between *'s 3 times. Sk next sc, sc

in next 2 sc, sk next sc; (ch 4, sc in next ch-4 sp) 5 times, ch 4; sl st in 1st sc to join.

Fasten off and weave in ends.

3. *To crochet the white ball,* follow the following instructions:

Rnd 1: Ch 16, sl st in 1st sc to join.

Rnd 2: Ch 1, sc in 1st ch (joining st), ch 5; (sk next ch, sc in next ch, ch 3) 7 times; sk last ch, ch 3, sl st in 1st sc to join.

Rnd 3: Sl st in ch-5 sp, ch 1, sc in same sp; ch 4, *sc in next ch-3 sp, ch 4; rep from * around; sl st in 1st sc to join (8 ch-4 sps).

Rnd 4: Ch 1, sc in 1st sc (joining st); *in next ch-4 sp work (hdc, 3 dc, hdc) (shell made); sc in next sc, rep from * around, sl st in 1st sc to join.

Rnd 5: Sl st in next hdc and in next dc; ch 1, sc in 2nd dc, ch 7; *sc in 2nd dc of next shell, ch 7; rep from * around; sl st in 1st sc to join.

Rnd 6: Ch 15 (9 counts as 1st dc and ch 12), dc in 1st sc (joining st); work dc, ch 3, dc (V-st) in 4th ch of next ch-7 sp; *in next sc work (dc, ch 12, dc); work V-st in 4th ch of next ch-7 sp; *rep from * around; sl st in 3rd ch of beg ch-15 to join.

Rnd 7: Sl st in next ch, ch 1; in same ch 12-sp work (sc, ch 3; sc, ch 3; sc, ch 6; sc, ch 3; sc, ch 3; sc); ch 2, sc in next V-st, ch 2; *in next ch 12-sp work (sc, ch 3; sc, ch 3; sc, ch 6, sc, ch 3; sc, ch 3, sc); ch 2, sc in next V-st, ch 2, rep from * around; sl st in 1st sc to join.

Fasten off and weave in ends.

4. *To block each ball cover,* dampen both sides with spray starch. Stretch and pin cover over 3-inch Styrofoam ball. Let dry. Unpin and carefully remove from ball.

To secure cover to glass ball, apply a thin line of glue around inside of top two rounds. Carefully position over glass ball and press into place. Then stretch and glue edges, one at a time. Hold each edge to ball until glue dries.

5. *To decorate the ecru ball,* use 6 inches of ribbon to make four small 1-inch wide figure-8 bows. Glue each one to the ball using the photo as a guide. Cut stems off roses and glue one to center of each bow.

Cut bead string into four 4-inch pieces. Glue the end of one to a rose and the other end to the next rose. Repeat for each piece.

Using single pearls, cut from the string, glue one to the top of each rose and to each pair of 2 scs. Glue

remaining string pearls in a ring around the top of the ball.

Slip gold cord through hanger of glass ball and knot ends to form a loop.

6. *To decorate the white ball cover,* cut ribbon into 8-inch pieces and make three bows following the Step 6 illustration. Glue them evenly spaced around the top of the ball cover.

Step 6
Make four small loops and large center loop.

Cut off stems and glue a rose to the center of each bow. Glue leaves at a slant between each bow. While pushing bow loops upward, glue white flowers on top of leaves. Glue point A of ribbon loop underneath each rose to make two more loops.

Slip gold cord through hanger of glass ball and tie ends together to form a loop. ♡

STIFFENED SPIDER WEB

By Mary Buse Melick

1. Refer to the Crochet Stitch Chart on page 96 for stitch abbreviations and illustrations.

2. *To crochet each spider web,* ch 40, sl st to form a ring.

Rnd 1: Ch 1, sc in joining st; sc in next 3 chs, 2 sc in next ch; *sc in next 4 chs, 2 sc in next ch; rep from * around; sl st in 1st sc to join (48)

Rnd 2: Ch 1, sc in joining st, ch 4; *sk next 2 sc, sc in next sc, ch 5; sk 2 sc, sc in next sc, ch 4; rep from * around; sl st in 1st sc to join. (16 ch sps)

Rnd 3: Sl st in next ch-4 sp, ch 1, in same sp work (sc, ch 4, sc); *ch 4, sc in next ch-5 sp, ch 4; in next ch-4 sp work (sc, ch 4, sc); rep from * around, sl st in 1st sc to join. (24 ch sps)

Rnd 4: Sl st in next ch-4 sp, ch 1, in same sp work (sc, ch 4, sc); *ch 5, sk ch-4 sp, sc in next sc; ch 5, sk next ch-4 sp; in next ch-4 sp work (sc, ch 4, sc); rep from * around; sl st in 1st sc to join. (16 ch-5 sps)

MATERIALS: STIFFENED SPIDER WEB

For Each Project

Size 7 steel crochet hook

Thick white craft glue *

Fabric stiffener *

Hot glue gun (optional)

For the Suncatcher

Bedspread weight ecru crochet thread

1/16-inch light green double-face satin ribbon, 1 yard

3/8-inch pink satin ribbon roses

Beads: 10x18mm faceted crystal teardrop; 5mm iridescent round glass, three

Gold sewing thread

For Picture Frame

Bedspread weight Williamsburg blue crochet thread

1/16-inch peach double-face satin ribbon, 1/2 yard

3/8-inch satin ribbon roses, one each: off white, mauve, light blue, one each

Bleached gypsophila, three small sprigs

For the Open Center Web

Bedspread weight Williamsburg blue crochet thread

1/8-inch light green double-face satin ribbon, 1 yard

3/8-inch satin ribbon roses, three each: mauve, off white, peach

4mm white pearl beads, six

Miscellaneous items: scissors; tape measure; white paper; compass; pencil; cardborad; rust-proof straight pins; plastic wrap; self-sealing sandwich bags; monofilament thread (optional)

* Aleene's Designer Tacky Glue and Fabric Stiffner were used in the sample projects.

On back of frame, place a thin line of glue around Rnds 1 and 2. Center over picture and press. Let dry, then trim excess picture.

If desired, hang with monofilament thread.

6. *To finish the open center web,* follow Step 4 to make a hanging loop and to weave remaining ribbon through Rnds 2 and 5. Glue a cluster of three roses, one of each color, in three places on Rnds 2 and 3. Glue one bead between each clump. Along outer edge, glue three more beads evenly spacing them.

Rnd 5: Sl st in ch-4 sp, ch 1, in same sp work (sc, ch 4, sc); *ch 11, sk next 2 ch-5 sps; in next ch-4 sp work (sc, ch 4, sc); rep from * around; sl st in 1st sc to join. (8 ch-11 sps)

Rnd 6: Sl st in ch-4 sp, ch 1, in same sp work (sc, ch 4, sc); *ch 6, sc in middle of next ch-11 sp, ch 6; in next ch-4 sp work (sc, ch 4, sc); rep from * around; sl st in 1st sc to join (16 ch-6 sps)

Rnd 7: Sl st in ch-4 sp, ch 1, in same sp work (sc, ch 4, sc); *ch 6, sk ch-6 sp, in next sc work (sc, ch 4, sc); ch 6, sk next ch-6 sp, in next ch-4 sp work (sc, ch 4, sc); rep from * around; sl st in 1st sc to join.

Fasten off and weave in ends.

3. Cut a 3-inch circle from paper and tape to cardboard beneath plastic wrap. Use this circle as a guide to keep center circle of suncatcher round when pinning. Follow manufacturer's instructions to stiffen, pinning out ch-4 sps in last Rnd onto board, keeping inside circle round. Let dry and unpin.

4. *To finish the suncatcher,* cut 5 inches of ribbon and glue ends to back of one point to make a hanging loop. Beginning at back beneath hanger, weave remaining ribbon over ch-11 sps of Rnd 5 and back through ch-4 sps of Rnd 2. Glue ends together in back.

Cut off stems and glue roses evenly spaced around Rnd 3 or 4. Glue glass beads in between roses. Hang teardrop bead in center with thread.

5. *To finish the picture frame,* make a four-loop bow with ribbon and glue to center bottom of Rnds 3 and 4. Glue roses to center of bow. Glue gypsophila sprigs among roses.

From Top: Diamond Suncatcher, Spider Web Suncatcher and Wallhanging, Diamond Ornament, and Spider Web Picture Frame

STIFFENED DIAMONDS AND SQUARES

By Mary Buse Melick

MATERIALS: STIFFENED DIAMONDS AND SQUARES

For Each Project

Size 7 steel crochet hook

Thick white craft glue

Fabric stiffener *

Hot glue gun (optional)

For the Suncatcher

Bedspread weight ecru crochet cotton *

1/16-inch Williamsburg blue double-face satin ribbon, 1/2 yard

3/8-inch satin ribbon roses: off white, peach, mauve, one each

Bleached gypsophila, three small sprigs

10x18mm crystal faceted teardrop bead

Gold sewing thread

For the Ornament With Pearls

Bedspread weight ecru crochet cotton *

1/8-inch pink double-face satin ribbon, 1 yard

3/8-inch mauve satin ribbon roses, three

Pearl beads: 4mm white; 2 1/2mm white string, 1/4 yard

Miscellaneous items: scissors; ruler; graph paper; cardboard; rust-proof straight pins; plastic wrap; self-sealing sandwich bags

* Aleene's Designer Tacky Glue and Fabric Stiffener and Lily 18th Century crochet thread were used in the sample projects.

1. Refer to the Crochet Stitch Chart on page 96 for stitch abbreviations and illustrations.

2. *To crochet the diamond shape,* ch 64, sl st to form a ring. *Note:* V-stitch equals dc, ch 1, dc; shell equals 3 dc, ch 2, 3 dc.

Rnd 1: Ch 3 (counts as 1st dc), dc in next 15 chs, ch 4; (dc in next 16 chs, ch 4) 3 times; sl st in 3rd ch of beg ch-3 to join.

Rnd 2: Ch 4 (counts as 1st dc and ch 1), dc in joining st; °(sk 2 dc, V-st in next dc) 5 times; in ch-4 sp work (V-st, ch 2, V-st); V-st in next dc; rep from ° around, sl st in 3rd ch of beg ch-4 to join.

Rnd 3: Sl st in ch-1 sp, ch 1, sc in same sp, ch 3; work (sc, ch 3) in each V-st and ch-2 sp around; sl st in 1st sc to join.

Rnd 4: Sl st in ch-3 sp, ch 1, sc in same sp, ch 3; (sc in next ch-3 sp, ch 3) 5 times; sc in next ch-3 sp, ch 4; °(sc in next ch-3 sp, ch 3) 8 times; sc in next ch-3 sp, ch 4; rep from ° around; sl st in 1st sc to join.

Rnd 5: Sl st in ch-3 sp, ch 2 (counts as 1st hdc), in same sp work (2 dc, hdc); in each ch-3 sp around work (hdc, 2 dc, hdc), and in each ch-4 sp (corners) work (hdc, 5 dc, hdc); sl st in 2nd ch of beg ch-2 to join.

Fasten off and weave in ends.

3. Following manufacturer's instructions to stiffen, use graph paper under plastic wrap to stiffen and pin pieces, stretching edges straight and square. Let dry and remove pins.

4. *To finish the suncatcher,* turn shape so it is a diamond. Hang teardrop bead in a corner of center with thread. Make a four-loop bow with ribbon and glue above bead.

Glue roses in middle of bow. Glue gypsophila sprigs between roses. Cut 5 inches of ribbon and glue ends to back of top point for a hanging loop.

5. *To finish the ornament with pearls,* turn shape so it is a diamond. Tie a four-loop ribbon bow with 4-inch streamers. Glue bow above top, inside corner of diamond. Glue ends of remaining ribbon to back of top point for a hanger.

Cut beaded string into a 5 ½-inch and a 3 ½-inch piece. Make loops with both and glue ends to center of bow.

Glue roses to center of bow. Glue pearl between two roses at upper right of bow.

QUILLED POINSETTIAS

By Sandy Rollinger

MATERIALS: QUILLED POINSETTIAS
For Both Projects
Slotted quilling tool *
White glue *
For the Ball
⅛-inch quilling paper, 24-inch lengths: gold, one; red, green two each
2 ½-inch satin ball
¼-inch white satin picot ribbon, ¼ yard
For the Bell
⅛-inch quilling paper, 24-inch lengths: white, 24; red, gold, olive green, one each
2 ½-inch foam bell
⅛-inch white satin picot ribbon, ½ yard
Miscellaneous items: scissors; toothpicks; wax paper; small plastic bags

* Quill Art quilling tool and Bond Tacky White Cement were used in the sample projects.

1. To make each ornament, tear paper into specified lengths. Follow the Quilling Chart at right and roll each shape as instructed. Glue end securely and let dry. Store rolled shapes in plastic bags.

Put a small amount of glue on the wax paper. Use a toothpick to apply glue to each piece and put on ornament. Use another toothpick for positioning shapes, using photo as a guide.

2. *To make the poinsettia ball,* use 4 ½-inch pieces of paper to roll the following shapes: 10 green marquises, six red marquises, and three gold tight rolls.

Glue six green marquises with points touching into a flower shape on one side of ball. Glue two green marquises with ends touching to the upper left and the lower left side of the flower.

Glue six red marquises on top of the six green ones with petals in between lower layer.

Glue tight circles on top of center. Tie ribbon through top for a hanging loop.

3. *To make the bell,* use 4-inch pieces of paper to roll the following shapes: approximately 53 white loose circles, 80 white teardrops, six green and six red marquises, and three gold tight circles.

Glue five loose circles around top of ball. With pointed ends facing down, glue a row of teardrops around the loose circles.

Glue the next row of teardrops with points facing up so they fit between the

Quilling Chart

Tight Circle
Roll paper tightly, remove it from the tool, and glue end.

Loose Circle
Roll tight circle; loosen it to twice its size and glue end.

Teardrop
Roll a loose circle and pinch one side.

Marquise
Roll a loose circle and pinch opposite sides.

previous row. Glue additional rows, changing direction of points on each row to fit shape.

At curve of bottom edge, begin gluing on rows of loose circles. Continue to fill bottom and let dry.

On one side of bell, make a poinsettia flower as in Step 2, eliminating the extended leaves. Tie 9 inches of ribbon in a bow and cut ends at an angle. Glue bow to top of ornament. Tie remaining ribbon through top for a hanging loop.

CROCHET BALLS

By Karen Nordhausen and Joan Green

MATERIALS: CROCHET BALLS
For Each Ball

Ecru crochet cotton *

No. 9 steel crochet hook

2- to 2½-inch plain satin ball

1/16-inch satin ribbon: color to match ball, 6 to 18 inches

White craft glue *

Miscellaneous items: scissors; straight pins

* DMC Cebilia crochet cotton and Aleene's Tacky glue were used in the sample project.

1. Refer to the Crochet Stitch Chart on page 96 for stitch instructions and abbreviations.

To crochet design No. 1, ch 8 and join with sl st. Ch 4 (counts as 1st tr), 2 tr, ch 3, and 3 tr in ring. *Ch 5, turn, sh in sh (3 tr, ch 3, 3 tr in ch-3 space), long dtr (yo 4 times) in same ch-3 space. Repeat from * until long enough to fit around ball. End off.

2. *To crochet design No. 2*, ch 15, join with sl st. Make two.

Rnd 1: Ch 1, 30 sc in ring, sl st to 1st sc.

Rnd 2: Ch 1, sc in same st. *Ch 8, sk 2 sc, sc in next sc. Repeat from * 9 more times. Ch 4, dtr (yo 3 times) in last sc.

Rnd 3: *Ch 6, sl st in 4th ch from hook, ch 9, sl st in 4th ch from hook, ch 2, sc in next lp. Repeat from * around. End off.

3. *To crochet design No. 3*, ch 5, join with sl st, ch 1. Make two.

Rnd 1: 8 sc in ring, sl st to 1st sc.

Rnd 2: (Ch 5, sc in next sc) 7 times, ch 3, tr in 1st sc.

Rnd 3: *Ch 5, sc in next lp. Repeat from * around.

Rnd 4: *3 sc in ch-5 lp, ch 11, remove hook from chain, insert in last sc made, and sl st in last ch of ch-11, making long loop. In long loop, sc, hdc, 7 dc, ch 3 (1 picot made), 7 dc, hdc, sc. 3 sc in same ch-5 loop. Repeat from * around. End off.

4. *To crochet design No. 4*, ch 10, join with sl st. Make two.

Rnd 1: 16 sc in ring, sl st to 1st sc.

Rnd 2: Ch 12, 1 long tr (yo 6 times) in next sc. (Ch 5, long tr in next sc) 14 times. Ch 5, sl st in 7th ch of ch-12.

Rnd 3: Sl st over 2 ch, sc under next ch. (Ch 6, 2 sc in next lp) around. End with 1 sc, sl st to 1st sc. End off.

5. *To crochet design No. 5*, ch 10, join with sl st. Make two.

Rnd 1: Ch 3, 23 dc in ring, sl st to ch-3.

Rnd 2: (Ch 4, sk 1 dc, sc in next dc) 11 times, ch 2, dc in beg st.

Rnd 3: (Ch 6, sc in next lp) 11 times, ch 3, tr in top of dc ending previous rnd.

Rnd 4: (Ch 15, sc in next lp) 11 times, ch 7, long tr (yo 6 times) in beg of rnd. End off.

6. *To crochet design No. 6*, ch 5, sl st to form a ring. Ch 3, 2 dc, ch 3, 3 dc in ring. *Ch 10, turn. Sh st (3 dc, ch 3, 3 dc) in ch-3 space. Repeat from * until long enough to fit around ball. End off.

7. *To finish each ball*, stretch, pin, and glue designs 4 and 5 over the top and bottom of the balls; designs 1 and 6 around the center, and designs 2 and 3 on the front and back.

Tie the ribbon into bows and glue to the balls or weave it through the crochet.

LITTLE STITCHES

By Sandi Kassnel

Design No. 3
Design No. 1
Design No. 4
Design No. 2

MATERIALS: LITTLE STITCHES

For Four Ornaments

White satin fabric, four 6-inch squares

¼-inch white gimp braid, 38 inches

¾-inch white gathered lace, 38 inches

⅛-inch white satin ribbon, 26 inches

White pearl beads: 3x6mm oval, 44; round: 2½mm, 305; 3mm, 50

1- to 2-inch pre-embroidered appliques: heart, flower motifs, four

Self-adhesive padded mounting board *, 8-inch square

Self-adhesive red velour, 8-inch square

Miscellaneous items: scissors; 4-inch embroidery hoop; water-soluble pen; needle; white thread; iron; towel; press cloth; craft knife; carpet tape; ruler; thick white craft glue

Note: Full-size patterns are given on pages 78-79.

* Press-On Products mounting board was used for the sample projects.

1. Place a fabric square wrong side up into the hoop, centering and stretching fabric taut. Turn the hoop over, center it over the pattern on page 78-79, and transfer the pattern markings to the fabric with a water-soluble pen. Turn the fabric right side up in the hoop.

2. Center an applique onto the fabric, as indicated by the broken line on the pattern. Pin in place. Using a 16-inch single thread, tack the edges of the applique to the fabric. See the Step 2 illustration.

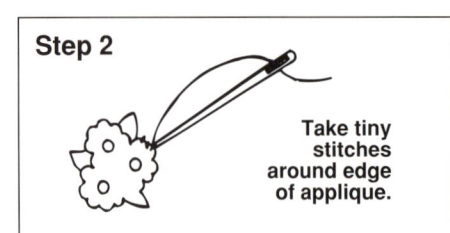

Step 2

Take tiny stitches around edge of applique.

3. *Note:* If your applique varies in size from those used in the projects, add or subtract pearls from the pattern as needed. Working with a single 16-inch length of thread, stitch individual pearls to designs No. 1 and 2. Dots represent round pearls and dashes represent oval pearls. Bring needle up from the wrong side of the fabric at one side of a marked symbol. Slide a pearl onto the needle, center it over the mark, and reinsert the needle at the opposite side of the symbol. See the Step 3 illustration. Adjust stitch width as needed so pearl lies flat against the fabric.

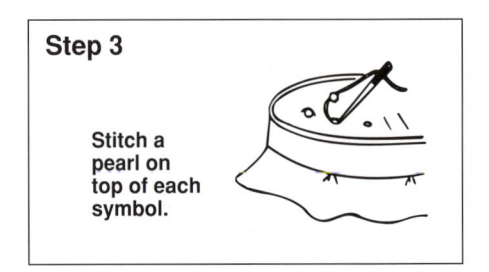

Step 3

Stitch a pearl on top of each symbol.

4. Working with a single 20-inch length of thread, stitch pearl rings to designs No. 3 and 4. Bring needle up through the X, thread on 48 2½mm pearls, reinsert needle through the X, and secure thread end. See the Step 4 illustration. Center the ring onto the marked circle or oval and tack it in place by taking tiny stitches over the thread between every third pearl.

5. Working with a single 20-inch length of thread, stitch pearl loops around the pearl rings of designs 3 and 4. Bring the needle up from the back between two pearls at the outside edge of the circular or oval pearl ring. Thread

Step 4

Come up at X, string beads, go down at X, forming a ring.

on two oval pearls for design No. 3 or eight 2½mm pearls for design No. 4. Count over three pearls on the ring of design No. 3 or four pearls on the ring of design No. 4 and reinsert the needle to form a loop. See the Step 5 illustration. Bring the needle back up through the fabric very close to the last stitch and repeat the procedure, adding a pearl loop for every group of three or four pearls around the circular or oval ring.

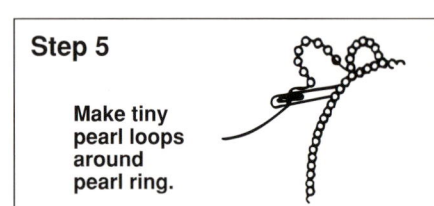

Step 5

Make tiny pearl loops around pearl ring.

6. Sew a bead to each flower center, stitching them as in Step 3.

7. Remove fabric from hoop. Cut ¾ inch beyond design edge. Lightly sponge each piece with cold water to remove pen marks and pat between towels to remove excess water. Using a warm iron, press pieces between towels and press cloth, stretching the fabric slightly.

8. Transfer the pattern for the ornament shape to the back of the mounting board and the back of the self-adhesive velour and cut out. Cut the board with a craft knife by first scoring the cardboard backing several times and then cutting through the foam.

Attach one side of the carpet tape around the cardboard shape so there is at least a ¾-inch border of tape around the edge. Trim excess tape, following the shape of the ornament.

Peel the paper backing from the foam and center the back of the stitched design onto it. Turn the board over and remove the backing from the carpet tape. Pull the fabric over the edge, securing it to the adhesive at the top, bottom, and sides of the design. Continue working around the design, clipping and trimming the fabric as needed for the design to lie smoothly.

9. For each ornament, cut 9½ inches each of lace and braid and 6½ inches of ribbon.

Apply a thin line of glue to the wrong side of the braid. Starting at the bottom front of the ornament, wrap the braid around the edge. Overlap the ends ½ inch and trim excess.

Apply a thin line of glue around the back edge of the ornament. Starting at the bottom, position the straight edge of the lace onto the glue. Overlap the ends ½ inch and trim excess.

Fold the ribbon in half. Positioning the loop at the top of the design, glue the ends to the back of the ornament. Let dry.

10. Remove the backing from the velour. Carefully center it over the back of the ornament and press firmly in place.

PAINTED FOLK ART BALLS

By Mona Kochendorfer

1. Trace patterns on page 81 onto tracing paper. Transfer to desired ornament by chalking the back of the traced pattern and tracing with the stylus.

2. *To paint the Bavarian tulip*, use the No. 5 brush and cherry royale to paint the basic tulip shape. Load the No. 3 brush with cherry royale, tip in icy white, and paint the overstrokes. See the Step 2 illustration.

Step 2
Follow numbers to paint overstrokes from top to bottom.

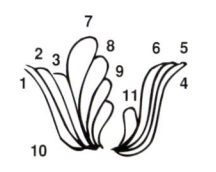

Load the No. 3 brush with slate blue and paint scallops. Outline top edge of the scallops with the No. 1 brush and thinned old ivy. Mix small amount of slate blue and icy white and outline lower edges of scallops. Use the stylus and icy white to dot the scallop points.

MATERIALS: PAINTED FOLK ART BALLS

3-inch matte glass ornaments: mauve, blue, red, white

Acrylic paints *: white; slate blue; indigo; icy white; chocolate cherry; cherry royale; old ivy; licorice; Christmas red; lemonade; kim gold

Round paintbrushes, Nos. 1, 3, and 5

⅛-inch satin ribbon, choice of color, ½ yard per ornament

White craft glue *

Miscellaneous items: disposable palette; tracing paper; white and colored chalk; stylus; soft paper towels; scissors; ruler; container of water

Note: Full-size painting patterns are given on page 81.

* Plaid Folk Art and Delta Ceramcoat acrylic paints and Aleene's Designer Tacky Glue were used for the sample projects.

Using the No. 3 brush, paint the leaves and outline their lower edges with old ivy. Load the No. 1 brush with icy white to paint overstrokes across the top of the leaves.

Use licorice and the stylus to paint graduated dots between petals, leaves, and scallops. Also paint dot below tulip and dot above bottom leaves. Refer to the photo.

3. *To paint the Dutch tulip and flower*, use the No. 5 brush and thin washes of paint. Paint the tulip chocolate cherry, the flower and flower center indigo, and the leaves, stems, and background comma strokes with old ivy.

Using the No. 1 brush and unthinned paint, add overstrokes to the tulip with chocolate cherry, the flower with indigo, and the stems and leaves with old ivy. See the Step 3 illustration. Add indigo dots around the flower center.

Step 3
Follow numbers to paint overstrokes as indicated by shaded areas.

4. *To paint the large blossom*, use the No. 5 brush and paint the petals and buds white, and the leaves with old ivy. Mix white with lemonade and paint the center. With a very small amount of paint on the brush, dab a few areas of white around the blossom.

Using the No. 1 brush, paint the stems and add accent strokes between leaves with old ivy. Outline the flower petals, buds, and leaves; add veins to the leaves and accent lines to the buds with chocolate cherry. See the Step 4 illustration.

Step 4
Use liner to outline petals and leaves and to add veins.

Use the stylus to add chocolate cherry, white and kim gold dots to the center. Add dots around blossom with kim gold.

5. *To paint the small blossom*, follow Step 4. Paint the petals and buds Christmas red and add accent strokes on petals with white.

6. *To finish each ornament*, tie ribbon in a bow around top of ball.

77

PATTERNS

Battenberg Lace Star Pattern

Little Stitches Patterns

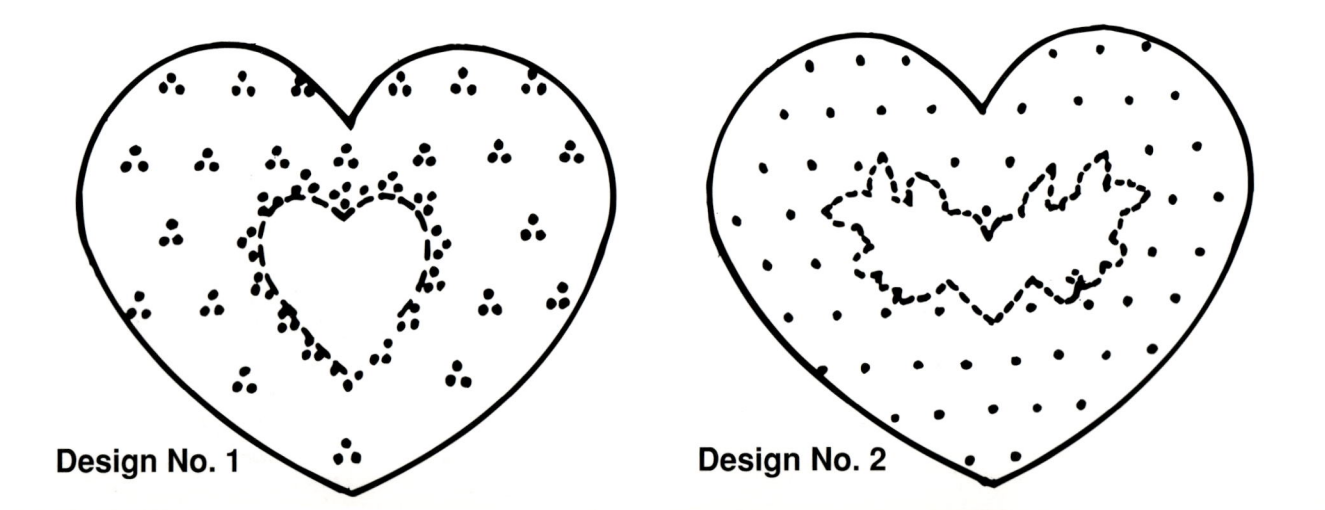

Design No. 1

Design No. 2

Battenberg Lace Four-Petal Flower Pattern

Little Stitches Patterns

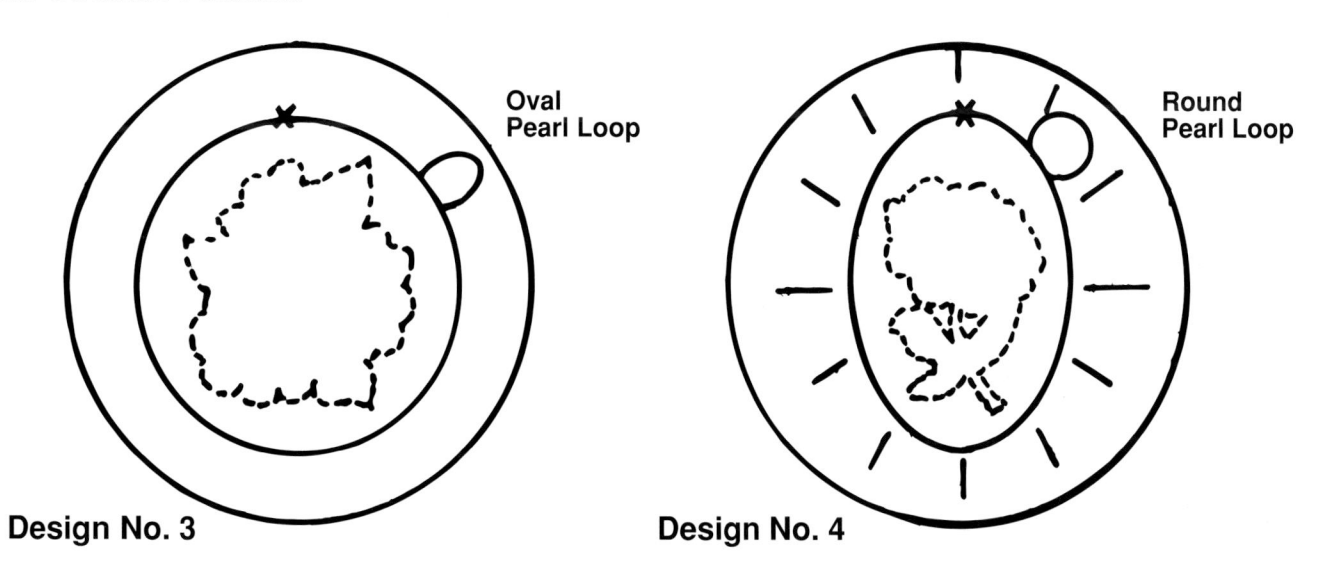

Oval Pearl Loop

Round Pearl Loop

Design No. 3

Design No. 4

Battenberg Lace Six-Petal Flower Pattern

Painted Folk Art Balls Painting Patterns

Lace Tree Pattern

Lace Placement

Cut one from posterboard.

Bottom

Bavarian Tulip On Ball

Dutch Tulip And Flower On Ball

Small Blossom On Ball

Large Blossom On Ball

Perforated Paper Ornament Cutting and Stitch Graphs and Color Key

Design No. 1

Color Key

- ✱ Dark Seafoam Green
- \> Medium Seafoam Green
- X Dark Christmas Red
- = Medium Salmon
- O Old Gold Bead
- ● Garnet Bead
- Ø Emerald Bead

Design No. 2

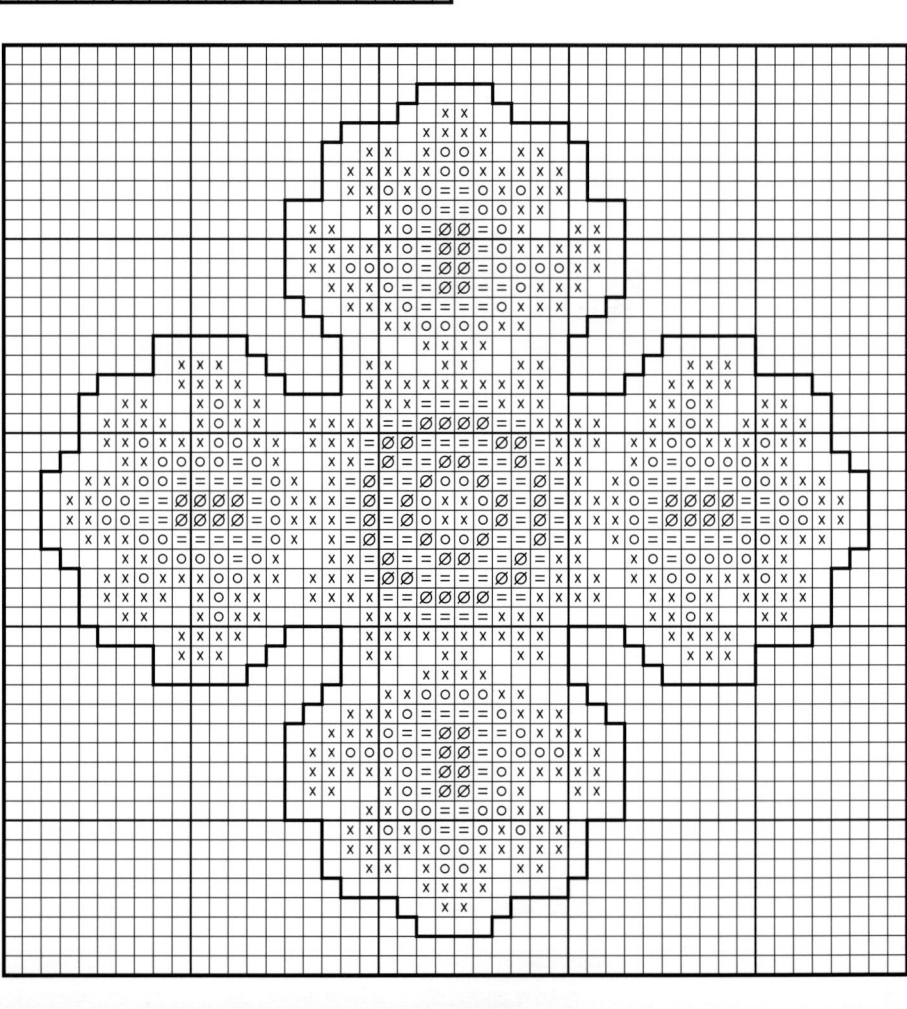

82

Decorator Trees

Each of our six stunning decorator trees captures a theme from top to bottom, including alluring treetop angels and matching tree skirts.

If you're mesmerized by the romantic look of lace, then you'll appreciate the delicate **Paper Lace** tree ornaments. Each ornament is crafted with lacy paper ribbon, set off with delicate ribbons and bows. Three Victorian-look trees will capture the fancy of satin, beads, and lace lovers, while country fans will appreciate the appeal of the patchwork and wheat bedecked **Country Calico** tree.

Designed especially for small places, the mini **Perforated Paper** tree, with its dainty 1-inch square ornaments and matching tree skirt, is the perfect holiday decoration for apartments or offices.

PAPER LACE

By Fran Queen and Lynette Goode

1. *To make each snowflake,* fold the 11-scallop piece of paper lace accordion style, making a fold between and in the center of each scallop (24 pleats). Bring ends together to form a circle; overlap and glue.

2. Lay pleated circle wrong side up. Wrong side of snowflake has a hole in center where pleats meet. Place a dot of glue in hole to hold pleats together.

Turn snowflake over and glue rose to center front.

3. Thread mauve ribbon through two holes at top of any scallop, and tie ends in a bow, forming a 3-inch hanging loop.

4. *To make each fan,* refer to Step 1 to fold the 6-scallop piece of paper lace. Pinch pleats together at one edge to form a fan, and place glue on the back between the pleats to secure.

MATERIALS: PAPER LACE
For Each Project
Hot glue gun, low melt

For Each Snowflake
1 ⅜-inch white Queen Anne Paperlace *, 11-scallop section
⅛-inch mauve satin ribbon, ⅓ yard
¼-inch aqua ribbon rose

For Each Fan
2 ⅜-inch white Queen Mary Paperlace *, 6-scallop section
Mauve satin ribbon, ¼-yard each: ⅛-inch, ¹⁄₁₆-inch
¼-inch aqua ribbon roses, two
White baby's breath, small amount

For Each Angel
2 ⅜-inch white Queen Mary Paperlace *, 11-scallop section
2 ⅜-inch silver Paperibbon, 5 inches
Mauve satin ribbon, ⅓-yard each: ⅛-inch, ¹⁄₁₆-inch inch
½-inch white pompom

For Each Pocket
Paperlace ®*: 2 ⅜-inch white Queen Anne, 10-scallop section; Queen Mary, small piece for stencil
White embroidery floss, ½ yard
Tapestry needle

Acrylic paints: mauve, green
Dried naturals: white baby's breath; starflowers: mauve, green
Small stencil brush
Polyester fiberfill, small amount
White craft glue
Paper towels
Container of water

For Tree Top Angel
White Queen Anne paperlace: 2 ⅜-inch, 4 yards; 1 ⅜-inch, ¼ yard
Creative Twist ®*: untwisted: iridescent, 7 inches; white, 9 inches; wired white, 19-inch pieces
2 ⅜-inch Paperibbon ®*: white, ⅜ yard; silver, 1 ¼ yards
⅛-inch mauve satin ribbon, 1 ½ yards
1 ½-inch styrofoam ball
24-gauge spool wire
8 ½x11-inch piece white construction paper
8x12-inch piece white posterboard
Drinking straw
White craft glue

Miscellaneous items: scissors; ruler

Note: A full-size pattern is given on page 94.

* MPR Associates Paperlace, Paperibbon, and Creative Twist were used in the sample projects.

5. Thread the 1/16-inch ribbon through the holes along top edge of fan. Glue at each edge, and cut ribbon even with edge of fan.

6. Glue baby's breath and roses to bottom front of fan. Tie the 1/8-inch ribbon in a bow and glue directly below roses at point.

7. *To make each angel,* cut a 7-scallop and a 4-scallop piece from paper lace. Refer to Step 4 to fold and glue the 7-scallop piece into a fan shape. Fold the 4-scallop piece into four pleats and set aside.

8. Fold silver paper ribbon into four 4-inch pleats, place four-scallop paper lace piece on top, matching pleats, and pinch together at center to form wings. Place glue on back, between pleats to secure center. Cut corners of silver on a curve.

9. Invert paper lace fan for a skirt, and glue wings over skirt top.
   Make a loop with the 1/16-inch ribbon, and glue ends to top center of wings. Glue pompom over ends of ribbon.
   Tie remaining ribbon in a bow, and glue to front of angel below pompom.

10. *To make each pocket,* fold cut ends of 10-scallop paper lace down 1 inch (one scallop) for a hem. Fold paper in half lengthwise, matching scallops, with hem to the inside.
    Thread tapestry needle with 18-inch piece of floss. Beginning at top edge, "sew" sides of pocket together through innermost holes of paper lace, carrying floss across the bottom in back. Leaving two equal tails of floss at top edge, tie together for a 2-inch hanging loop and then tie in a bow.

11. To finish the pocket, use a small section of "Queen Mary" paper lace for a stencil. On pocket front, stencil the flower with mauve and the stem and leaves with green. Fill pocket half-full with fiberfill. Insert baby's breath and starflowers into the top.

12. *To make the tree-top angel,* fold the white posterboard into a cone, measuring 6 inches from top to bottom and 4 inches across bottom opening. Leave a small opening at the top of the cone. Glue overlapped edges and trim bottom edge so angel will sit flat.

13. To make the head and collar, push one end of the straw into the foam ball, and secure with glue. Cut a 7-inch circle from iridescent Creative Twist, center over the ball, and bring down and around to cover ball. Gather with wire and twist securely. Set aside.

14. To make the body, trim one scalloped edge off the 2 5/8-inch paper lace and set edge aside. Beginning at the top of the cone, pleat paper lace along the trimmed edge with fingers, and glue down and around outside of cone. Overlap rows of paper lace, scalloped edge down, until cone is covered completely.

15. To make the arms and hands, shape the wire twist into a circle and twist ends together. With the ends in the center, flatten the circle, and twist length together, leaving loops on each end for the hands. See the Step 15 illustration.

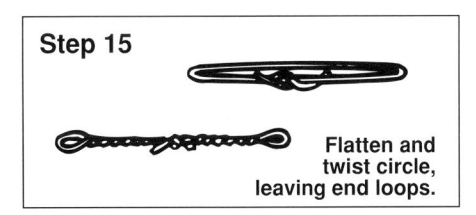

Step 15

Flatten and twist circle, leaving end loops.

16. To make the sleeves, cut two 4 1/2-inch pieces of white Creative Twist. For each arm, overlap and glue 4 1/2-inch edges together, with wrong sides out, to form a tube. Place tube end over hand and wire at wrist. Carefully invert the twist to cover the wire twist. See the Step 16 illustration. Repeat for other arm. Overlap the ends in the center and wrap with wire to secure.

Step 16

Wire arm to wrist; turn and pull over wire twist.

17. Cut three 8-inch pieces of white paper ribbon. Overlap and glue 8-inch edges together to form a tube. Fold under and glue a 1/2-inch hem at each open end.
    Cut 1 3/8-inch paper lace in half lengthwise. Glue one length around inside of each hemmed sleeve edge, with scallops out. Slip over arm/sleeve assembly. Center and glue to top back of body. See the Step 17 illustration.

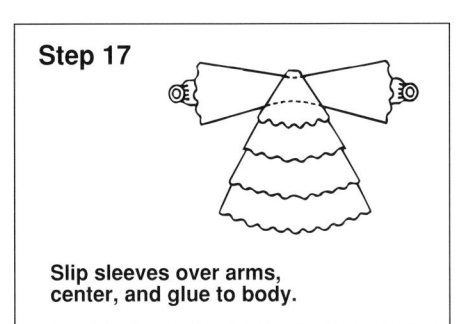

Step 17

Slip sleeves over arms, center, and glue to body.

18. Insert straw into opening at top of body until head rests in proper position, with gathered edge of iridescent Creative Twist forming a collar. Glue underneath collar to secure.

19. To make the wings, trace the pattern on page 94 and cut from white construction paper. Use white craft glue to cover wings completely with silver paper ribbon. Let dry and trim edges even. Fold wings horizontally into accordion pleats. Fold pleated wings at center, and secure with glue. See the Step 19 illustration.

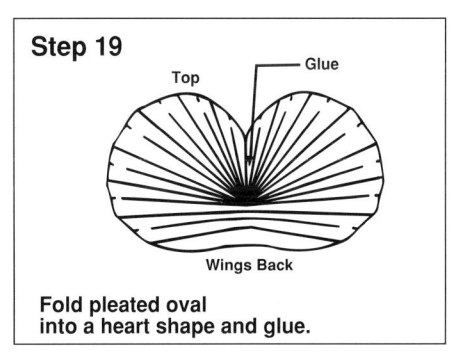

Step 19

Top — Glue
Wings Back

Fold pleated oval into a heart shape and glue.

20. To make the ribbon heart, cut three 12-inch pieces of mauve ribbon. Holding all ends even, measure down 2 inches and tie a knot. Beginning at knot, braid until 2 inches from opposite end; tie in knot.
    Cut a 7-inch piece of wire and weave through back of ribbon braid. Bend into a heart shape with knots meeting at the bottom, and twist wire ends together at point of heart. See the Step 20 illustration.

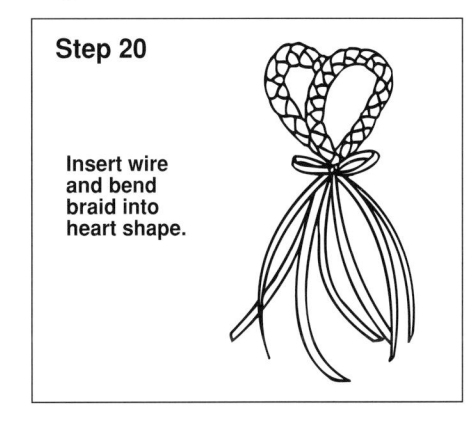

Step 20

Insert wire and bend braid into heart shape.

21. Glue a sprig of baby's breath and a rose to front of heart. Cut a 3-inch piece of ribbon, and thread through the hands. Pull ribbon taut, bringing hands to the front until 1 inch apart, and knot. Glue top of heart to ribbon.
    Cut remaining ribbon in half and tie two bows. Glue one bow to the heart, just below the rose, and the other at the neck.

PERFORATED PAPER TREE

By Carol Krob

MATERIALS: PERFORATED PAPER TREE

Perforated paper, three 8½x11-inch sheets

Embroidery floss *: cherry (2530); sage (5125)

Glass seed beads *: old gold (557), cream (123), emerald (332), garnet (367), two tubes each; jet (81), coral (275), one tube each

Felt: white 13-inch circle; adhesive-backed, one sheet each: dark red, dark green

³⁄₁₆-inch gold metallic adhesive-backed rickrack, one package

Needles: No. 24 tapestry, No. 10 crewel

Miscellaneous items: white sewing or quilting thread; scissors; pencil; ruler; tracing paper; shallow container; masking tape; graphite paper

Note: Full-size patterns are given on page 94. A Stitch Graph and Color Key are given on page 94.

* Coats & Clark Royal Mouline embroidery floss and Mill Hill beads were used in the sample projects.

---

1. *To make the ornaments,* cut the perforated paper into 48 2-inch squares. *Note:* If desired, stitch several designs on a half sheet of paper, leaving 1 inch unstitched between them, then cut apart. Stitch two identical pieces for each ornament. Stitch a complete set of 12 each of the red and green ornaments. Refer to the Stitch Graphs and Color Key on page 94 and the General Cross Stitch Instructions on page 95 to stitch each design and attach beads.

2. Thread tapestry needle with three strands of red or green embroidery floss and work cross stitches. Use the stab stitch method, bringing needle straight up then straight down. Do not skip across areas that will remain unstitched or floss will show through holes. Weave ends of floss through stitching on back and clip close.

3. After completing all cross stitches, thread crewel needle with sewing or quilting thread and weave it through stitching on back to secure end. Pour a few beads of each color into a shallow container. Attach beads one at a time with half cross stitches. *Note:* Use emerald beads with red cross stitch designs and garnet beads with green cross stitch designs. Beginning at top of design, work from left to right, making all stitches in the same direction.

4. Trim excess paper around designs, leaving one row of empty holes for joining on all four sides of design. Place matching front and back pieces wrong sides together, aligning holes. Thread tapestry needle with three strands of red floss for green designs and three strands of green floss for red designs. Leaving a 2-inch tail and beginning at one corner, work a running stitch through outer row of empty holes to connect both pieces. See the Step 4 illustration. Tie ending and beginning thread with a double knot close to ornament and a second knot 1 inch up to form a hanging loop.

Step 4
Come up at 1, down at 2, up at 3, etc., along edges.

5. *To make the angel,* cut two 2½x3¼-inch pieces of perforated paper. Referring to the Stitch Graphs, Color Key, and General Cross Stitch Instructions, stitch front and back pieces entirely with beads.

Cut around designs as close to beads as possible without cutting into the stitching.

6. To make the fringe, thread crewel needle with thread and weave it through stitching on back to secure end. For the front piece, bring needle up through hole at lower left corner, marked by a triangle on the graph. Thread three garnet beads, one gold bead, and three garnet beads. Insert needle through next hole to the right, marked by a triangle. Repeat two more times, then make a series of four cream loops and three more garnet loops, stringing a gold bead at the center of each one. For the back piece, make a series of 10 garnet loops, placing a gold bead at center of each one.

7. To assemble, thread crewel needle with thread and weave through stitching on wrong side of one piece near bottom to anchor thread end. Hold front and back pieces wrong sides together, aligning the holes. Work a running stitch through both pieces along outer row of beads, leaving bottom open.

Wrap top branch of tree with masking tape and fit angel down over treetop.

8. *To make the skirt,* cut two 4-inch slits, crossing them to make an X, at center of the felt circle.

9. Separately trace the diamond and the center square patterns on page 94 onto tracing paper. Using graphite paper, transfer four squares onto paper side of green adhesive-backed felt; cut out. Repeat with red felt. Repeat to cut four diamonds each from red and green felt. Cut 16 2-inch strips of rickrack. Remove backing and firmly press two strips crosswise on top of each felt diamond. Remove backing from red felt squares and attach to centers of green diamonds on top of rickrack intersections. Mount green squares in centers of red diamonds.

Alternating red and green, attach felt diamonds, one at a time, at regular intervals around the outer edge of the felt circle.

10. Detach tree base, slip on tree skirt, and attach base. Drape gold trim garland around tree and decorate with ornaments.

VICTORIAN PINK AND MAUVE TREE

By Cindy Groom Harry

Note: Materials box is on page 88.

1. *To make the tree skirt,* work on a large hard surface. Mark center of felt with pen. Tie string around pen and hold it with finger at center 18 inches from knot. Keeping string taut, rotate pen around finger-held center and draw a 36-inch circle; cut out.

2. Using yardstick as a guide, draw a solid line from one edge of circle to center point for skirt opening; do not cut.

Position yardstick to extend this line from the center to opposite edge. Beginning 1 inch from edge, draw a 5-inch, 4-inch, and 3-inch line, leaving 1 inch between lines. See the Step 2a illustration. Innermost line will end 3 inches from center.

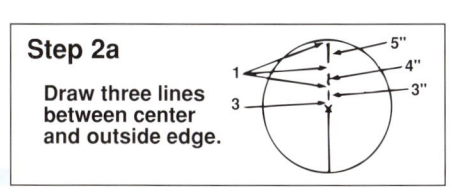

Perpendicular to this line draw another series of 5-, 4-, and 3-inch lines on each side of the center; dividing circle into quarters.

Measure and mark the center of one quarter section, as shown in the Step 2b illustration, then align yardstick and draw the series of three measured lines from each edge. Repeat to divide the circle into 32 sections.

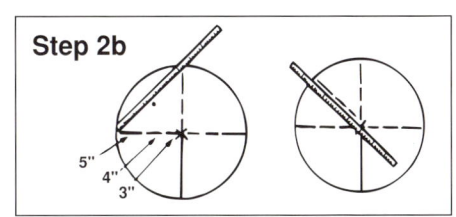

3. In the two outer rows, also divide the distance between marks. Measure midpoints between ends of all 4-inch lines and draw additional lines. See the Step 3 illustration. Divide the distance between ends of all 5-inch lines into thirds; draw additional lines.

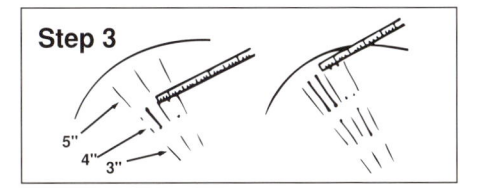

4. Cut skirt opening along solid line. Cut each measured line on skirt. Pinch felt near one end of line, snip with scissors, insert scissors point, and cut line.

Draw a 3-inch circle with the compass at center of skirt and cut it out.

5. Turn skirt over so unmarked side faces up. Follow the guidelines below to weave the pattern following the sequence in Step 6.

• Begin at the outer edge of skirt and work toward the center. Keep edges of skirt opening aligned as you work.

• Fold each specified length of ribbon in half and mark center with tape. Pull ribbon through the slit directly across from skirt opening to tape; remove tape.

• Weave first ribbon row over and under the felt background strips. Work from center to opening then weave the other half, keeping ribbon toward outside edge. Weave through six or seven slits before pulling ribbon flat and even out puckering. Pull ribbon tightly, but do not distort the felt background.

• Beginning at the center and working out along each side, glue ribbon to back of each strip of felt.

• Reverse the weaving sequence for each consecutive row. Do not leave any space between rows.

6. Weave and glue the following ribbon through the 5-inch slits:
Row 1: ⅜-inch pink, 3¼ yards
Row 2: ¼-inch burgundy, 3 yards
Row 3: ⅜-inch white, 3 yards
Row 4: ¼-inch burgundy, 3 yards
Row 5: ⅜-inch pink, 2¾ yards
Row 6: ¼-inch burgundy, 2¾ yards
Row 7: ⅜-inch white, 2¾ yards
Row 8: ¼-inch burgundy, 2½ yards
Row 9: ⅜-inch pink, 2½ yards

Weave and glue the following ribbon through the 4-inch slits:
Row 10: ⅜-inch white, 2¼ yards
Row 11: ¼-inch pink, 2 yards
Row 12: ⅜-inch white, 2 yards
Row 13: ¼-inch pink, 1¾ yards
Row 14: ⅜-inch white, 1¾ yards
Row 15: ¼-inch pink, 1¾ yards
Row 16: ⅜-inch white, 1¾ yards

Weave and glue the following ribbon through the 3-inch slits:
Row 17: ¼-inch pink, 1 yard
Row 18: ¼-inch burgundy, 1 yard
Row 19: ¼-inch white, 1 yard
Row 20: ¼ inch pink, 1 yard

MATERIALS: VICTORIAN PINK AND MAUVE TREE

For Each Project

Hot glue gun

White craft glue *

For the Tree Skirt

36-inch white felt, 1 yard

Satin craft ribbon: ⅝-inch: pink, 8 ½ yards; white, 13 ½ yards; ¼-inch: pink, 8 ¼ yards; burgundy, 14 yards; white, 2 yards

2 ½-inch white gathered lace, 3 ¼ yards

18mm burgundy satin ribbon roses, 12

For the Treetop Angel

Porcelain doll parts: 4 ½-inch head; 3 ½-inch arms

12-inch foam cone

White satin fabric: 15-inch square; 8-inch circle

Lace: white: ¼-inch gathered, 1 yard; 2 ½-inch double-edged with off-center gathering, 2 ½ yards

⅛-inch satin ribbon: pink, 2 ¾ yard; white, ½ yard

Satin ribbon roses: 9mm white, 12; 18mm: white, eight; burgundy, two; mauve, two

Small sprigs of white illusion gypsophila

Green leaves: small cluster on 2-inch stem, three; any size, two

Green floral tape, 6 inches

Jumbo white chenille stems, four

Polyester fiberfill, small amount

For Each Victorian Doll

5-inch china or plastic doll

Lace: ⅝-inch pink gathered, ⅓ yard; 2 ½-inch white double-edged with off-center gathering, ⅔ yard

⅛-inch pink satin ribbon, ⅔ yard

Curly brown chenille, 21 inches

For Each Swan

8-inch white medallion doily

Fabric stiffener

⅜-inch pink, mauve, or burgundy craft ribbon, ⅔ yard

⅜-inch white pearl beads, two

Silk flowers: 1 ½-inch white carnations, five; small sprigs: burgundy, three; mauve or pink, two

For Each Parasol

8-inch white medallion doily

Fabric stiffener

⅜-inch pink, mauve, or burgundy craft ribbon, ⅔ yard

Jumbo white chenille stem

⅜-inch white pearl bead

Silk flowers: 2-inch white mums, two; small sprigs, color to match ribbon, two

For Each Hat

8-inch white medallion doily

Fabric stiffener

2-inch foam ball

⅜-inch pink, mauve, or burgundy craft ribbon, 1 yard

Small sprigs of white, mauve, and burgundy or pink silk flowers, 16

1 ½-inch green silk flower leaves, four

For Each Flower Bouquet

6-inch white medallion doily

Fabric stiffener

⅜-inch craft ribbon: mauve, ¼ yard; pink, 1 yard

Silk flowers: 1 ½-inch mauve, four; medium sprigs: pink, two; white, three

1 ½-inch green silk flower leaves, 12

For Each Satin Ball

3-inch white satin ball

⅜-inch pink, mauve, or burgundy craft ribbon, 3 ¼ yards

⅜-inch white pearl beads, seven

For Each Heart

Plastic white heart frame

⅜-inch burgundy craft ribbon, 1 ⅓ yards

Small silk flowers: light pink, four; dark pink, four

4-inch sprig white gypsophila

For Each Bow

1-inch mauve or pink craft ribbon with lace edge, ⅔ yard

⅛-inch satin ribbon, color to match craft ribbon, ¼ yard

Miscellaneous items: ballpoint pen; scissors; 30-inch string; yardstick; compass; masking tape; foam coffee cup; straight pins; serrated knife; plastic warp; bowl; rubber band; pop bottle; paper towel or toilet tissue cardboard roll core

* Aleene's Tacky glue was used in the sample projects.

Row 21: ¼-inch burgundy, 1 yard
Row 22: ¼-inch white, 1 yard
Row 23: ¼-inch pink, ¾ yard
Row 24: ¼-inch burgundy, ¾ yard

7. Glue lace around side of skirt edge.

Cut 32 bows with 8-inch pieces of ¼-inch pink ribbon. Refer to the photo and glue bows evenly spaced on skirt: 12 along outside edge, 12 along first felt space, and 8 on second felt space.

Cut stems off ribbon roses and glue a rose on top of each bow.

8. *To make the treetop angel,* cut a 1¾x4-inch wedge from base following shape of cone. See the Step 8 illustration.

Step 8

Cut a cone shaped piece from the bottom center of the base.

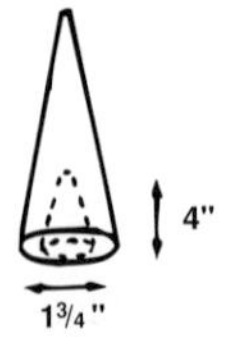

Center cone on wrong side of satin. Wrap cone, trimming fabric edges to make a straight vertical seam. Glue seam. *Note:* Apply hot glue to fabric surface, let cool a few seconds, then press to foam.

Pleat, trim, and glue raw edges to cover foam at top. At bottom, clip and glue fabric edges to inside of cone.

Slit the side of the foam cup then cut off bottom. Roll cup into a cylinder to fit inside of cone base; trim side edge so overlap is ½ inch. Glue foam cylinder inside cone so bottom edges are flush.

9. Fit doll head onto top of cone. Depress cone as needed for chest plate to fit. With satin seam at center back, glue head in place.

10. To make her skirt, glue the gathering line of a 12-inch piece of lace around base of cone with edges extended below; overlap ends at center back. Working with 11-, 10-, 9-, 7 ½-, and 7-inch pieces, glue a layer of lace every inch upward on the cone.

To make her cape, glue a 30-inch piece of ¼-inch lace around edge of right side of satin circle. Cut a 1-inch circle from center for neck and a slit from one edge to center.

Drape it over shoulders with opening at back, overlap top of closure, and glue to chest plate. Overlap and glue remainder of back opening.

11. To form arms, twist three chenille stems together then glue center beneath back of chest plate. Glue arms onto stem nds with thumbs on top. *Note:* Arms should measure 5 inches from fingertip to chest plate.

Fill in around chest plate with fiberfill, temporarily holding cape in place with pins. Tack glue cape at underarms.

Wrap an 18-inch piece of white ribbon around waist, tying ends in a bow at back. Evenly distribute folds of cape at waistline.

Glue a 4½-inch piece of 2½-inch lace around neckline for collar.

12. To form wings, cut a 25-inch piece of 2½-inch lace. Glue the lace gathering line to both sides of fourth chenille stem with ends overlapped at center. See the Step 12 illustration.

Step 12
Wrap lace around both sides of stem before bending it.

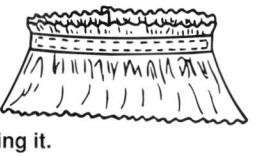

Bend wing unit into a U shape with wider lace at bottom and glue to center back.

Cut 24 inches of ribbon and tie a bow with long streamers. Glue to center of wings.

13. To finish, wrap a 12-inch piece of pink ribbon around top of hair; tie ends in a bow at center back.

Glue 12 9mm white roses, in two rows, across front of hair.

Use the Step 13 illustration as a guide to cut eight tiny leaves from silk leaves and glue them randomly behind the roses.

Step 13
Use this pattern to cut rose leaves.

Refer to the photo and randomly arrange roses with three leaf stems and typ springs behind them into a 6-inch spray; tape ends. Glue contact points between arrangement and arms, hands, and dress front.

Tie the center of an 18-inch piece of ribbon in a bow with long streamers and glue to bottom of arrangement.

Tie four bows with 8-inch pieces of ribbon. Glue one each to top of each wing and neck front; glue loops only to top of roses in hair. Cut all ends on an angle.

14. *To make the Victorian Doll,* extend arms at each side. Glue a 3½-inch piece of white lace centered across chest, wrists aligned with ends of gathering and longer ruffle hanging down. Repeat on back.

Beginning at back of heels, wrap and glue 18 inches of white lace in spiral fashion around body; overlap each layer to cover top of previous one. Wrap and glue 6 inches of pink lace around upper chest. Glue tops of sleeves together. Wrap and glue a 3-inch piece of pink lace around each wrist.

Cut chenille into five 4-inch pieces and working from front to back, glue pieces across top of head; end with an inverted U at center back. Cut four ¼-inch pieces and glue each coil on end across forehead for bangs.

Tie a bow at center of 12-inch piece of ribbon and glue to waist front. Tie a 6-inch piece in a bow and glue to top of head. Form a hanging loop from 5-inch ribbon and glue ends behind bow.

Glue center back of top layer of dress to back of head.

15. *To make the swan ornament,* spread plastic wrap on work surface and pour fabric stiffener into bowl. Submerge and saturate doily. Gently squeeze out excess stiffener.

16. Fold doily in half. Fold back about two-thirds of both layers. Slightly crimp point. Bend crimped area in an upward curve to create a neck. Shape head from one scallop on each layer and pinch to form beak. See the Step 16 illustration. Let dry flat.

Step 16
Gently squeeze end of the folded doily.

17. Gently separate layers at wide end and let wings extend slightly. Glue flowers in open end.

Tie a bow with 12 inches of ribbon and glue to back of head. Glue ends of remaining ribbon to center back for a hanging loop.

Glue a bead to each side of head for eyes.

18. *To make the parasol,* follow Step 15 to prepare doily and drape it over the pop bottle, distributing ruffles evenly. When partially dry, pinch ruffles to create ribs. Let dry.

Curve one end of a 10-inch chenille stem to form handle. Glue end of 14-inch piece of ribbon 2 inches from opposite end of stem and wrap ribbon diagonally around it toward handle. Diagonally cut ribbon end and glue to end of handle.

Remove doily from bottle. Insert unwrapped end of stem through center of doily, extending it 1½ inches. Glue stem to center of doily above and below where they meet; hold in place until dry.

Wrap 12-inch piece of ribbon around extended stem at top of parasol and tie a bow.

Glue sprigs of flowers, mums and leaves into open end of parasol.

19. *To make the hat,* cut foam ball in half and place cut side down.

Cut ¼ inch off outer edge of doily. Follow Step 15 to prepare doily then drape it centered over half ball. Wrap rubber band around base of half ball, distribute ruffles evenly, and let dry. Remove rubber band.

Wrap and glue middle of an 18-inch piece of ribbon around base of crown. Overlap ends and trim streamer ends diagonally. Bring ends of a 7-inch piece of ribbon together, pinch at center to form two loops, and glue on overlap of streamers.

Beginning at bow on one side of crown, glue on two leaves and half the flower sprigs. Repeat on other side of crown. Glue ends of remaining ribbon to top back of brim opposite bow for a hanging loop.

20. *To make the flower bouquet,* follow Step 15 to prepare doily and fold its center around cardboard roll, aligning scalloped edges. Let dry.

Insert and glue half the leaves toward center of doily. Glue mauve flowers at each side close to fold. On each side, glue remaining leaves and flowers, working with white, pink, and white again at top center.

Glue ends of an 8-inch piece of mauve ribbon to center top for a hanging loop. Make two bows, each from a 16-inch piece of pink ribbon; glue one to center top of each side.

21. *To make the satin ball,* glue lace horizontally around middle of ball; overlap and glue ends.

Using 1 yard of ribbon, form and pin seven evenly spaced vertical loops along gathering line of lace; loops will be 1½ inches apart and 4¾ inches deep.

Fold eight 6-inch pieces of ribbon into bows. See the Step 21 illustration. Glue one to top of each pin head; set one aside. Glue a bead to center of each bow around ball.

Insert an 8-inch piece of ribbon through top of ornament hanger;

89

Step 21
Bring ends to center, then cross and secure.

overlap and glue ends at top. Glue remaining bow to top of loop.

For streamers, stack three 7-inch pieces of ribbon on top of each other and fold in half. Pinch folded area firmly and glue to center bottom of ornament with streamers hanging down. Cut ends in inverted Vs.

22. *To make the heart ornament,* cut 42 inches of ribbon. Hold the middle at center top of heart frame and wrap each side with one end of the ribbon, allowing ¼ inch between wraps. Tie ends together at bottom and tack with glue. Cut ends diagonally.

Glue ends of a 6-inch piece of ribbon at back of center top for a hanging loop.

Arrange gypsophila in center of heart and glue ends at bottom of center point. Insert and glue flowers in gypsophila.

23. *To make the bow,* fold an 18-inch piece of craft ribbon into a bow as shown in the Step 21 illustration. Wrap center and with a 2-inch piece of ribbon, overlap ends and glue at back. Cut streamer ends on an angle or in a V.

Glue ends of a 9-inch piece of ribbon to center back of bow for a hanging loop.

VICTORIAN GARLAND AND ORNAMENTS

By Kathy Lamancusa

1. *To make the garland,* glue pearl string over elastic thread on the gathered lace.

Cut ribbon into ½-yard pieces. Form each one into a five-loop bow as shown in the Step 1 illustration. Wire center.

Glue bows 6 to 8 inches apart over top of pearls.

Step 1 Side View

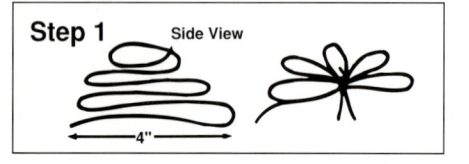

2. Follow the Ribbon Rose Instructions on page 93 to make ribbon roses for the ornaments.

MATERIALS: VICTORIAN GARLAND AND ORNAMENTS

For Each Project
Cloth-covered wire
Hot glue or tacky glue

For the Garland
1 ½-inch peach gathered elastic lace, 10 yards
⅝-inch celadon metallic ribbon with woven edge, 17 ½ yards
4mm white fused pearl string, 10 yards

For Each Lace Pocket
Ribbon: 2 ½-inch eggshell lace, ⅓ yard; ⅛-inch peach moire, ½ yard; ⅛-inch celadon satin, 2 yards
Pearl stems with double-end branches, two
White floral tape

For Each Ring of Roses Ornament
Ribbon: ⅛-inch peach moire, 3 yards; ⅜-inch celadon feather-edge satin, 1 ⅔ yards; ⅛-inch celadon woven-edge satin, 2 yards
Preserved baby's breath
Green floral tape

3. *To make each lace pocket ornament,* form a 3-inch loop of lace with 2-inch loop on top. See the Step 3 illustration.

Step 3
Fold a 2-inch loop in front of a 3-inch loop.

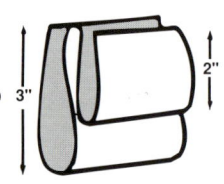

Pinch top edges together and wire, leaving 1-inch ends.

Bring ends of a 9-inch piece of ⅛-inch ribbon together and wire to top of lace for a hanging loop.

Form a multi-loop bow with remaining ribbon and wire to top of ornament.

Follow Ribbon Rose Instructions to make a rose with peach ribbon. Bend pearl stems in half and tape to base of rose; trim rose stem to ¼ inch.

Glue rose arrangement to center of bow.

4. *To make each ring of roses,* cut peach ribbon into six ½-yard pieces and follow the Ribbon Rose instructions on page 93.

For Each Dove
5-inch white dove
Ribbon: ⅛-inch peach moire, 1 ½ yards; ⅛-inch celadon satin, 2 yards
Pearls: wired stems, six; shooting pearls, 6-inch containing 10 strands
White floral tape

For Each Pearl Wreath
1 ½-inch peach gathered elastic lace, ⅓ yard
Ribbon: ⅜-inch celadon woven metallic, ½ yard; ⅛-inch celadon satin, ½ yard
2mm white fused pearl string, 1 ½ yards
White chenille stem, three
Masking tape

For Each Ball
Ribbon: ⅛-inch celadon woven-edge, ⅔ yard; ⅝-inch lace-edge, peach, eggshell or celadon (optional), 1 yard each
White fused pearls: 4mm, ⅔ yard; 2mm, 1 ⅓ yard (optional)
2 ½-inch Styrofoam ball
Straight pins

Tape together a bundle of three 9-inch pieces of wire.

Along one side of bundle and beginning at one end, tape a small bunch of baby's breath then a rose. Add three 4-inch pieces of featheredge ribbon, each of which has been formed into a loop.

Continue by taping the sequence of baby's breath, a rose, and set of loops five more times to fill the wire.

90

Form into a circle and tape ends together.

Make a hanging loop with 6 inches of ⅛-inch ribbon and tie to taped ends. Make a multi-loop bow from remaining ribbon and tie to center top.

5. *To make each Victorian dove,* cut the peach ribbon into three ½-yard pieces and follow Ribbon Rose Instructions to make a rose from each.

Tape two wired pearl stems to each rose. Tape the three roses into a bunch.

Make a multi-loop bow with celadon ribbon and wire to center of roses.

Glue arrangement to top of dove and the pearl stem cascading over back of dove.

6. *To make each pearl wreath,* tape chenille stems into a bundle. Curve into a circle and tape ends together. Glue elastic lace around back of circle.

Cut four 12-inch strands of pearls and use a 3-inch piece of wire to secure ends together with one end of ⅛-inch ribbon. Tape end to a secure surface. Using each pair of pearl stems as one, braid pearls with the ribbon. Wire and trim opposite end.

Glue pearl braid on top of wire ring. Form a loop with a 6-inch piece of pearl strand and glue ends to top of wreath.

Follow Step 1 to make a five-loop bow and glue to top of ornament.

7. *To make each Victorian ball,* cut lace-edge ribbons into 8-inch pieces. Wrap one peach piece around center of ball and pin ends at center bottom. Repeat with another peach piece, dividing ball into quarters. Wrap two more times with remaining peach pieces, dividing ball into eighths.

Repeat, using eggshell or celadon ribbon, filling the spaces between peach ribbon. Cover ball completely.

Knot ends of a 6-inch piece of ⅛-inch ribbon together; pin and glue to top of ball for a hanging loop. Cut off 6 4mm pearls and glue around knot at top of ball.

Cut three 6-inch lengths each of 2mm pearls and ⅛-inch ribbon. Wire them together at one end, then pin and glue to bottom of ball as a tassel.

Cut two 4mm pearl strands, each having seven pearls. Glue one around top of tassel and second one to first.

Glue a 3½-inch strand of 2mm pearls from top to bottom over the center of each eggshell ribbon strip between rings of pearls.

SATIN AND LACE TREE

By Sallie Anderson

MATERIALS: SATIN AND LACE TREE

For All Ornaments

Gold metallic thread

Lightweight wire

White craft glue *

For Each Starflake

⅜ -inch ecru flat lace, 1 yard

⅛-inch satin ribbon, 6 inches

White beads: 15mm iridescent berrybead, two; 4mm pearls, 16

For Each Ribbon Rose

1⅜-inch satin ribbon, 1 yard

Rose leaves, two

Green floral tape

For Each Lace Bow

1⅜-inch ecru flat lace, ½ yard

⅛-inch satin ribbon, 12 inches

For Each Satin Cone

Ribbon: 2⅝-inch satin, 6 inches; 1⅜-inch lace edge velvet, 6 inches; ⅛- or 1/16-inch satin, 12 inches

⅝-inch ecru flat lace, 6 inches

Baby's breath

Short cinnamon sticks, three

For Each Ribbon Fan

Ribbon: 2⅝-inch satin, 9 inches; ¾-inch lace edge, 9 inches; lace edge velvet, 9 inches; ⅛- or 1/16-inch satin, two contrasting colors, 8 inches each

For Each Potpourri Heart

3-inch felt squares, two

½- to ¾-inch lace applique

1/16-inch satin ribbon, 6 inches

Potpourri, small amount

For Each Pine Cone

Small pine cone

Cranberry spray paint, matte finish

⅛-inch satin ribbon, 6 inches

Small silk flower

For Each Felt Dove

Felt, two 3x4-inch pieces

1/16-inch satin ribbon, 6 inches

Gold sequins: 3mm, one; 8mm, three

Pearls: 2mm, four; 6mm, two

Fiberfill, small amount

For Each Satin Ball

2½-inch satin ball

Contrasting colors of satin ribbon: ⅛-inch, 20 inches; 1/16-inch, two colors, 5 inches each

1- to 1½-inch lace applique, two

Note: Full-size patterns are given on page 94.

* Aleene's Tacky glue was used in the sample projects.

1. *To make each starflake,* cut lace into eight 4½-inch-long pieces. Fold each piece in half and trim ends together at an angle. Open, then fold ends back and together to make a cone. See the Step 1 illustration. Glue overlapped ends, using a clothespin to hold until glue dries. Repeat for all eight pieces.

Step 1

Glue ends together in back; the center of the ribbon forms front of cone.

2. Glue two cones together along sides until all eight cones are glued together, forming a starflake. Glue a berrybead in center on each side.

3. Tie ribbon in a bow and glue to center of bead on front side. Glue two 4mm pearls to each cone point. Add gold loop for hanging.

4. *To make each ribbon rose,* follow the Ribbon Rose Instructions on page 93. Tape rose leaves to stem. Add gold loop for hanging.

5. *To make each lace bow,* fold left end of lace to center, then right to center, forming one loop on each side. Wrap wire around center, leaving excess for tying to tree. Tie ribbon in a bow and glue to center of lace bow.

6. *To make each satin cone,* glue lace along top edge of satin ribbon. Glue lace-edged ribbon along 2⅝-inch ribbon, just off center toward the bottom. Let dry. Fold in half and trim ends together at an angle. Follow Step 1 to fold into a cone.

7. Cut narrow ribbon in half and tie the two pieces in a double bow. Glue bow to top point of cone. Fill cone with baby's breath and cinnamon sticks. Add a gold loop for hanging.

8. *To make each ribbon fan,* glue ¾-inch lace-edged ribbon across top of 2⅝-inch ribbon. Glue lace-edged velvet ribbon along the 2⅝-inch ribbon, a little off center toward the bottom. Let dry. Fold ribbon into ½-inch-wide accordion pleats. Tightly wrap bottom with wire, leaving excess for tying fan to tree. Tie narrow ribbon in a double bow and glue to bottom center to cover wire.

9. *To make each potpourri heart,* trace the heart pattern on page 94 onto tracing paper and cut two from felt. Glue together around outer edge, leaving a small opening. Let dry. Loosely fill with potpourri and glue opening closed. Glue applique to center front. Tie ribbon in a bow and glue to center of applique. Add gold loop for hanging.

10. *To make each pine cone,* spray pine cone with paint and let dry. Tie ribbon in a bow and glue to top. Glue small silk flower to center of bow. Add gold loop for hanging.

11. *To make each felt dove,* trace the pattern on page 94 onto tracing paper and cut two from felt. Overcast outer edges together, leaving an opening. Stuff lightly and glue opening closed. Tie ribbon in a bow and glue to wing bottom. Following the placement on pattern, glue sequins to body and pearls on top of sequins. Add gold loop to wing top for hanging.

12. *To make each satin ball,* thread 8 inches of contrasting ribbon through lace. Glue lace lengthwise around ball, overlapping ends at top. Knot two 5-inch lengths of ribbon together at the center. Glue knot to top center of ball. Glue three silk flowers around top.

13. Glue an applique to each half of ball. Cut 12 inches of ribbon in half and tie two bows. Glue bows to center of appliques.

COUNTRY CALICO TREE

By Lela Gunning

MATERIALS: COUNTRY CALICO TREE

Assorted calico fabrics

Styrofoam shapes: balls: 1-inch, 4-inch, 3-inch, 1½-inch; cones; eggs; 3½-inch rings with center discs

Cornhusk dolls: 3-inch, 2½-inch, 5-inch for tree topper (optional)

¼-inch satin picot ribbon: red, royal, medium blue, brown

Baby rickrack

6½-inch straw broom

Gift wrap cord: gold, red, green, blue

Potpourri

Christmas decorations and trims

Glitter, one jar each: clear crystal; multi-color

White craft glue

Wheat heads (optional)

Miscellaneous items: scissors; ice pick; straight and sequin pins; craft knife; tracing paper; pencil; ruler; 24-gauge wire

Note: Full-size patterns are given on page 94.

1. *To make the tree skirt,* cut 4-inch squares of calico and sew with right sides together in a strip of 24 or to fit around tree. Sew 12 strips together to make a 12x24-square strip and hem all edges.

2. Trace the patterns on page 94 onto tracing paper. Set aside apron pattern and cut several triangles from assorted calicoes.

3. *To make patchwork balls,* mark top of ball with straight pin. Spread a thick layer of glue on ball. Starting with a triangle point against straight pin, cover ball with patchwork pattern. Let dry. Coat with paper glue and clear crystal glitter; let dry.

4. Pin ends of 5-inch piece of ribbon to top of ball for hanger. Tie a multi-looped ribbon bow and pin over hanger ends.

5. Fold four or five 10-inch pieces of ribbon in half and knot together near fold to make a tassel. Pin tassel to bottom of ball.

6. *To make patchwork ball* garland, repeat Step 3 using 1½-inch balls. Punch a hole through each ball with an ice pick. Thread balls ½ inch apart on gold cord.

7. *To make potpourri ball garland,* step on 1½-inch balls to flatten them. Punch a hole through each one, coat with glue, then roll in potpourri. Let dry. Thread balls ½ inch apart on red cord.

8. *To make glitter balls,* coat with glue then roll in colored glitter. Repeat Steps 4 and 5 to finish.

9. *To make cones,* follow Step 3 to cover cone, leaving top plain. Let dry. Cut 10 inches of cord or ribbon and glue an end to each side for hanger. Glue a small bow over each end. Cut a hole in top center and fill with Christmas decorations. Repeat Step 5 to make a tassel.

10. *To make an egg,* cut out a hole in one side. Repeat Step 3 to cover egg. Glue gold cord lengthwise around egg and gold trim around opening. Glue Christmas decorations in opening.

Repeat Steps 4 and 5 with gold cord to finish.

11. *To make cornhusk doll rings,* repeat Step 3 to cover ring. Let dry. Glue cornhusk doll in center and repeat Steps 4 and 5 to finish.

12. *To make potpourri rings,* cover ring with glue and roll in potpourri. Let dry. Glue cornhusk doll in center and repeat Step 4 to finish.

13. *To make patchwork disc,* cut two circles ¼ inch larger than disc or 16 triangles from calico. Glue to disc and let dry. If using triangles, points should meet at center. Coat with glue and clear crystal glitter and let dry.

Glue trim around sides and center, and finish as in Steps 4 and 5. Or, evenly space and glue four wheat heads around sides.

14. *To make the mini-broom,* dab glue at top back of handle. Place center of 12 inches of ribbon on glue, wrap around handle once at top, then wrap entire handle to bottom. Glue ends to back and let dry.

15. Cut apron from calico. Glue rickrack around side and bottom edges. Gather top of apron and place it right side against front of handle. See the Step 15 illustration. Wire apron to

Step 15

With right side facing handle, wire the apron upside down to the broom.

broom, then fold it down. Wrap ribbon around top of apron and tie in a bow in back.

RIBBON ROSE INSTRUCTIONS

MATERIALS: RIBBON ROSE
For Each Rose
⅛- to 1 ½-inch satin ribbon, 1 yard
Rose leaves, two (optional)
Green floral tape
Floral wire
Miscellaneous items: scissors; wirecutters

1. Follow the Step 1a illustration and fold left end of ribbon forward at a right angle.

Step 1a

Fold left end of ribbon forward at a right angle.

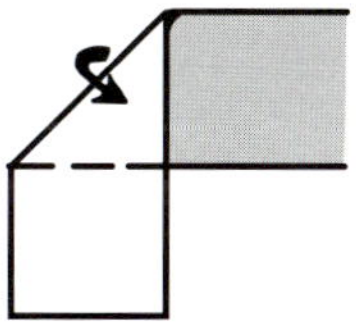

Fold long end of ribbon back, then down at a right angle to form a point. See the Step 1b illustration.

Step 1b

Fold ribbon back then down at a right angle to form a point.

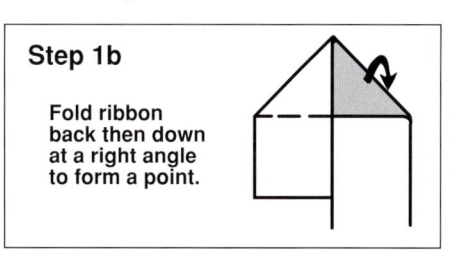

2. Continue folding ribbon back at right angles to desired size. See the Step 2 illustration.

Step 2

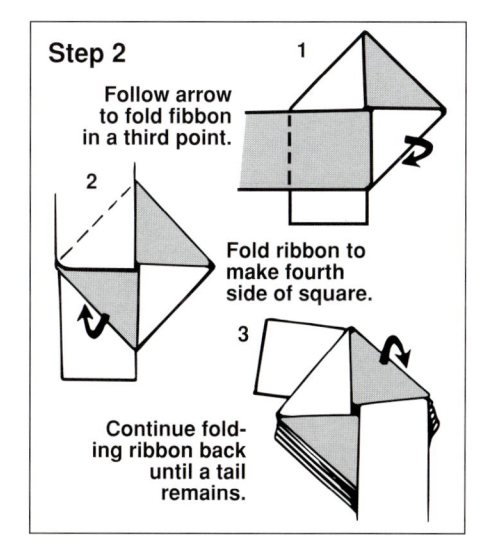

1. Follow arrow to fold ribbon in a third point.
2. Fold ribbon to make fourth side of square.
3. Continue folding ribbon back until a tail remains.

3. Cut a 9-inch piece of floral wire and fold in half. Push the folded end up through the center hole of folded ribbon. Insert top end of ribbon through wire fold. See the Step 3 illustration.

Step 3

Insert folded wire through the center: slide the top tail through pin.

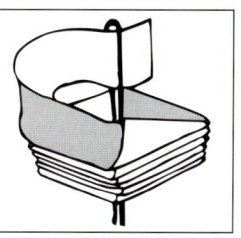

Twist wire a few turns, then push ribbon down through center hole.

4. Holding ribbon tail, twist clockwise, releasing ribbon folds to form petals. See the Step 4 illustration. Remove wire.

Step 4

Pull top tail to bottom and twist it to seperate the petals.

5. Wrap wire tightly around ribbon ends. Wrap green floral tape around ends and wire to make a short stem.

Tape rose leaves to stem if desired.

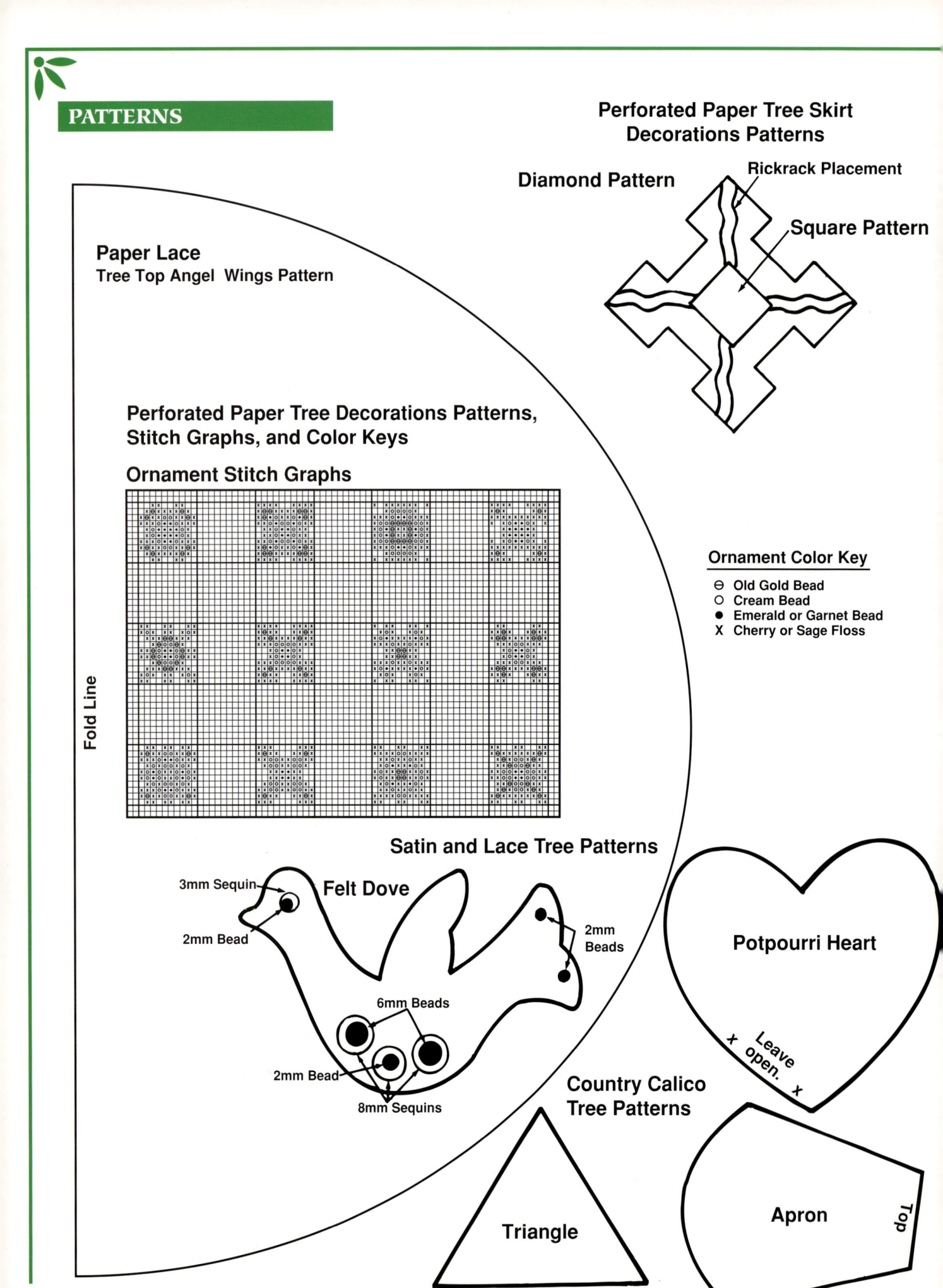

PATTERNS

Perforated Paper Tree Skirt Decorations Patterns

Diamond Pattern

Rickrack Placement

Square Pattern

Paper Lace
Tree Top Angel Wings Pattern

Perforated Paper Tree Decorations Patterns, Stitch Graphs, and Color Keys

Ornament Stitch Graphs

Ornament Color Key

⊖ Old Gold Bead
○ Cream Bead
● Emerald or Garnet Bead
X Cherry or Sage Floss

Fold Line

Satin and Lace Tree Patterns

Felt Dove
- 3mm Sequin
- 2mm Bead
- 2mm Beads
- 6mm Beads
- 2mm Bead
- 8mm Sequins

Potpourri Heart

Leave x open. x

Country Calico Tree Patterns

Triangle

Apron

Top

94

General Cross Stitch Instructions

1. To stitch on evenweave fabric, overcast edges to prevent raveling. Fold fabric in half vertically and horizontally to find center and mark with a temporary stitch.

To stitch on perforated paper, count to find center and mark with a temporary stitch.

Find design center by following the arrows on the Stitch Graph. Count up and over to the top left stitch or specified point to begin.

2. Each square on the Stitch Graph represents one square of evenweave fabric or perforated paper. The symbols correspond to the colors given in the Color Key.

3. Cut floss into 18-inch lengths. Separate strands and use number specified. To begin, do not knot floss, but hold a tail on back of the work and anchor with first few stitches.

To carry a color, weave floss under previously worked stitches on the back.

Do not carry floss more than three or four stitches.

To end floss, run it under several stitches on the back, then cut.

4. Work all cross stitches first, working horizontal rows wherever possible. Backstitch design after all cross stitching is completed.

5. When all stitchery is completed, wash fabric in warm sudsy water if needed. Roll in a terrycloth towel to remove excess moisture. Press face down on another towel to dry.

Cross Stitch Chart

Evenweave Fabric

Cross Stitch

Stitch from left to right then cross back.

Backstitch

Stitch back to meet prior stitch.

Beaded Half Cross
Up at lower left, slide on bead, down at upper right.

3/4 Cross Stitch
Stitch from any corner to center, then corner to corner.

1/4 Cross Stitch
Stitch from corner to center of thread intersection.

Perforated Paper

Cross Stitch
Stitch from lower left to upper right hole; cross back.

Battenberg Lace Stitch Chart

Spider Web

Following numbers, stitch from side to side to make eight spokes. Wrap thread around last spoke to center. Weave thread under and over spokes. Continue rounds, skipping one spoke at beginning of each round so thread alternates under and over each round.

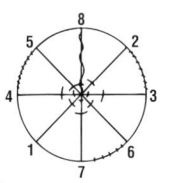

Wheel

Following numbers, make four spokes. Come up at 1 and go down at 6, crossing thread intersection. Weave in rounds over and under spokes.

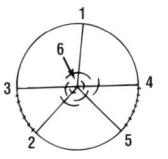

Russian Foundation

Start at bottom center of lace and work from side to side, stitching from front to back each time.

Buttonhole
Wrap thread around from A to B; come up at C, pull taut and wrap around at D.

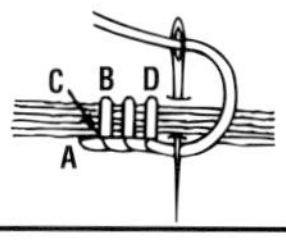

Single Net
Work evenly spaced loops, making each loop as deep as it is wide. Work next row of loops between loops of previous row.

Double Net
Work one large loop then two small loops close together across top. For next rows, work two small loops in each large loop of previous row.

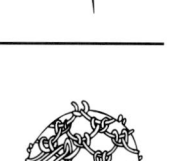

Branched Bar
Up at A, down at B; repeat twice. Begin at B and work buttonhole stitches over all three threads to C. Stitch down at D, come up at C and return to D. Repeat and work buttonhole stitches to E. Continue until space is filled.

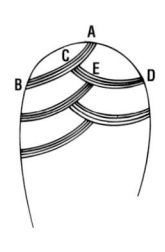

Woven Leaf
Stitch from A to B, come up at B, down at C, and up at D to make first leaf. Go down directly across at E and up to F. Wrap thread behind intersecting threads, make a loop and pull taut to secure leaves. Repeat to make pairs of leaves to A.

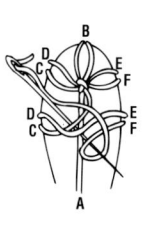

General Plastic Canvas Instructions

1. Each line on the Plastic Canvas Stitch Graph represents one bar of plastic canvas.

2. To cut plastic canvas, count the lines on the graph and cut the canvas accordingly, cutting up to, but not into, the bordering bars.

3. To stitch, do not knot the yarn, but hold a tail in back and anchor with the first few stitches. To end yarn, weave it under stitches on back, then cut it. *Note:* Do not stitch over edge bars.

4. When finished stitching individual pieces, finish edges and join pieces with an overcast stitch.

Plastic Canvas Stitch Chart

Gobelin Stitch
Up at odd, down at even numbers, covering bars in specified direction.

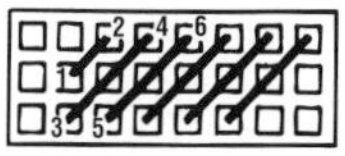

Continental Stitch
Up at odd, down at even numbers; work toward left, then toward right. 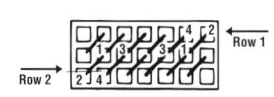

Overcast
Use a whipping motion over the outer bars to cover or join canvas edges.

Backstitch
Up at 1, down at 2, up at 3, down at 1, stitching back to meet prior stitch.

Straight Stitch
Up at 1 and down at 2, covering specified number of bars.

Crochet Stitch Chart

Abbreviations

ch	Chain
dc	Double Crochet
dec	Decrease
hdc	Half Double Crochet
lp(s)	Loop(s)
rem	Remaining
rep	Repeat
rnd	Round
sc	Single Crochet
sk	Skip
sl st	Slip Stitch
sp	Space
st(s)	Stitch(es)
t	Triple Crochet
yo	Yarn Over
*	Repeat following instructions a given number of times.

Beginning Slip Knot

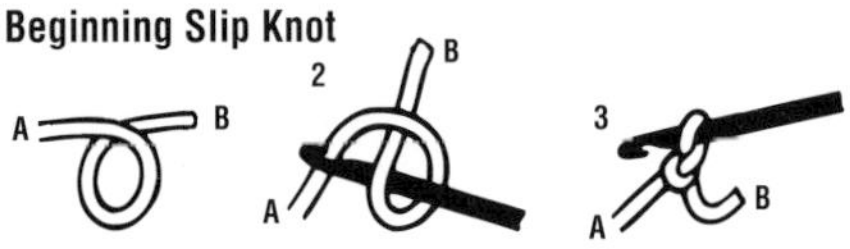

Insert hook from the front of lp and pull yarn A, the working yarn, through lp.

Triple Crochet (tr)
1. Yo hook twice.
2. Insert hook into 5th ch from hook and pull lp through. (4 lps)
3. Yo once; pull another lp through 2 lps in direction of arrow. (3 lps)
4. Yo; pull another lp through next 2 lps on hook in direction of arrow. (2 lps)
5. Yo; pull lp through last 2 lps on hook in direction of arrow.
6. One tr completed.

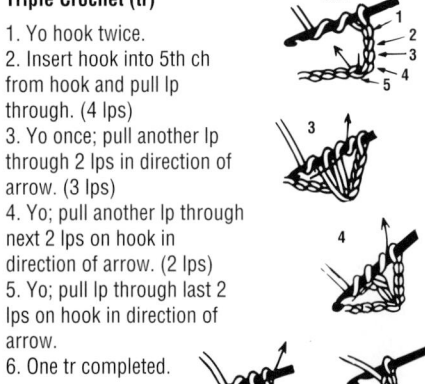

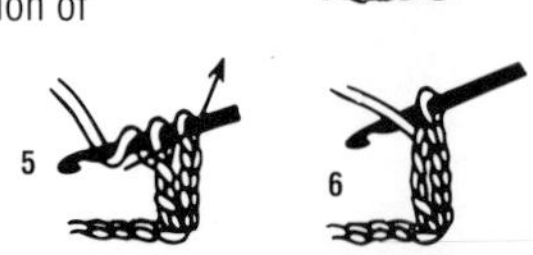

Slip Stitch (sl st)
Insert hook in lp of st, yo, and draw through 2 lps in direction of arrow.

Single Crochet (sc)
1. Insert hook into 2nd ch from hook.
2. Yo; pull yarn through lp of ch in direction of arrow.
3. 2 lps on hook.
4. Yo; pull yarn through 2 lps on hook. 1 lp left on hook.

Double Crochet (dc)
1. Ch 3, yo. Insert hook under next st.
2. Yo; pull yarn through in direction of arrow.
3. 3 lps on hook. Yo; pull yarn through 2 lps.
4. 2 lps on hook. Yo; pull yarn through 2 lps in direction of arrow.

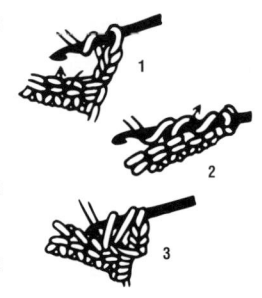

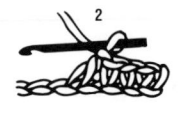

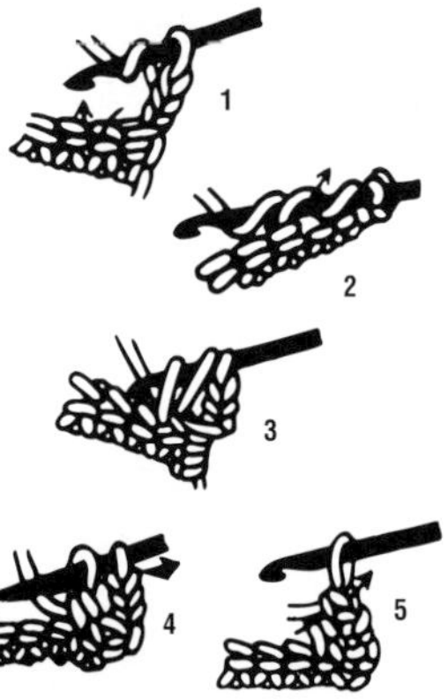

Decreasing in Single Crochet
1. Draw up a lp in each of next 2 sts; yo and draw yarn through all 3 lps on hook in direction of arrow.
2. 1 lp on hook.

Decreasing in Double Crochet
1. Yo; insert hook into 1st st; yo and pull up a lp; yo and pull lp through 2 lps on hook. (2 lps)
2. Yo; insert hook into 2nd st; yo and pull up a lp; yo and pull a lp through 2 lps. (3 lps)
3. Yo and pull lp through all 3 lps on hook.
4. 1 lp on hook.

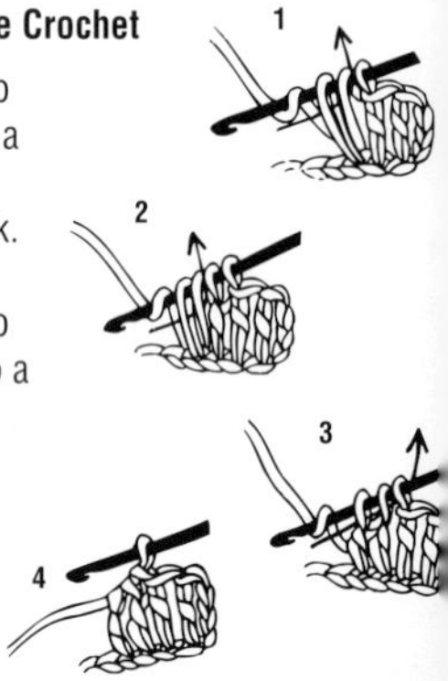

Half Double Crochet (hdc)
1. Yo; insert hook into 3rd ch from hook and pull a lp through in direction of arrow.
2. 3 lps on hook.
3. Yo; pull lp through all 3 lps on hook in direction of arrow.
4. Hdc completed.

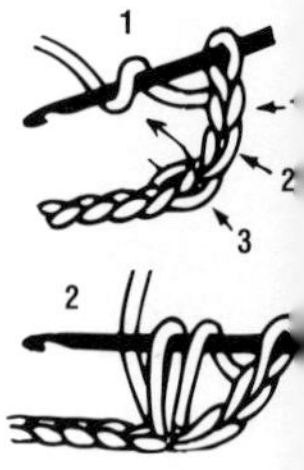

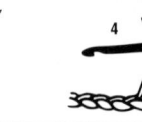

Chain Stitch (ch)

Yo from back to front; pull through lp on hook.

Forming a Ring With a Slip Stitch

Insert hook into first ch, yo, and pull through both lps on hook.